Easy PC peripherals troubleshooting

Other Computer Titles

by

Robert Penfold

Easy PC peripherals troubleshooting

Robert Penfold

Bernard Babani (publishing) Ltd
The Grampians
Shepherds Bush Road
London W6 7NF
England
www.babanibooks.com

Please note

Although every care has been taken with the production of this book to ensure that any projects, designs, modifications, and/or programs, etc., contained herewith, operate in a correct and safe manner and also that any components specified are normally available in Great Britain, the Publisher and Author do not accept responsibility in any way for the failure (including fault in design) of any projects, design, modification, or program to work correctly or to cause damage to any equipment that it may be connected to or used in conjunction with, or in respect of any other damage or injury that may be caused, nor do the Publishers accept responsibility in any way for the failure to obtain specified components.

Notice is also given that if any equipment that is still under warranty is modified in any way or used or connected with home-built equipment then that warranty may be void.

© 2002 BERNARD BABANI (publishing) LTD

First Published - February 2002

British Library Cataloguing in Publication Data
A catalogue record for this book is available from the British Library

ISBN   0 85934 518 1

Cover Design by Gregor Arthur
Printed and bound in Great Britain by Cox & Wyman

Preface

One of the reasons for the initial success of the IBM PCs was almost certainly the range of ports that were fitted either as standard or available as optional extras. The original ports are still included on the vast majority of PCs, and new ones such as USB and Firewire are now in common use. The range of peripherals has blossomed over the years and a wide range of general and specialist peripherals are now available. This gives PCs great versatility, but it also gives enormous scope for things to go awry when you start expanding a basic PC into a powerful computer system. Most of the solutions are quite simple, once you know how to sort things out. This book provides solutions to many of the problems that can occur when using external PC add-ons.

The older PC interfaces are generally more troublesome than the newer ones. The RS232C serial interface is responsible for a substantial percentage of the interfacing problems that occur when adding PC peripherals, and chapter 1 therefore provides detailed coverage of using this interface. Chapter 2 covers the other types of port that are used with PCs, such as parallel and USB types. It also covers the audio and game ports, together with the peripherals that are used with them. Many of the problems encountered with PC add-ons are actually due to the ports and connecting leads rather than the devices themselves, so answers to problems with many peripherals will be found in these two chapters.

The other three chapters cover common problems with the three most popular types of PC gadget, which are modems, imaging devices (scanners and digital cameras), and printers. The subjects covered here include general things such as device drivers and installation problems. Topics that are more specific are also covered, such as using a modem to send faxes, clearing and avoiding paper jams in printers, and correcting colour casts in digital images. Getting peripherals connected to and communicating with the PC does not always guarantee perfect results every time, and these three chapters help you to "fine tune" the system so that optimum results are obtained.

You do not have to be a computer expert in order to follow the procedures detailed in this book, but you do have to be familiar with the basics of using the Windows user interface. None of the suggestions should be beyond someone having at least a few months experience with Windows. You need to be someone who is reasonably practical in order to deal with the few procedures that involve the computer's hardware, but again, you by no means need to be an expert.

Robert Penfold

Trademarks

Microsoft, Windows, Windows Me, Windows 98 and Windows 95 are either registered trademarks or trademarks of Microsoft Corporation.

All other brand and product names used in this book are recognised trademarks, or registered trademarks of their respective companies. There is no intent to use any trademarks generically and readers should investigate ownership of a trademark before using it for any purpose.

Contents

1

Serial port troubleshooting 1

2

Parallel ports, USB, etc. 81

3

Modem troubleshooting 185

4

Imaging 229

5

Printers 267

Serial port troubleshooting

Standardisation?

You do not need to understand how computer interfaces function in order to use them, but in some cases it certainly helps if you have at least a basic understanding of how things operate. The humble RS232C serial interface is certainly one that is easier to use if you have at least a basic understanding of what is going on. I think it is fair to say that the newer interfaces such as USB are less troublesome than the older types such as RS232C. Although the newer interfaces are generally much more complex they are also much better standardised. Any problems are more likely to be due to faulty or incorrectly installed software than hardware or cabling issues. If a device connected to a USB port fails to work because of a hardware problem, it is unlikely that "playing" with the cables will sort out the problem. A repair to the PC or peripheral will be required.

The situation is different with some of the older interfaces, where there is a definite problem with different designers interpreting standards in different ways. In addition, some of these interfaces have evolved over the years, which has inevitably led to some inconsistencies. Either of these factors can give problems with incompatibility between what should be two perfectly matched items of equipment. A fair amount of experimentation with various cables can be needed to get some of the more awkward devices to operate properly.

I do not think that there is any doubt about the most problematic of the common computer interfaces. The RS232C serial variety probably causes far more problems than all the other types put together. It is actually a general-purpose interface that has been around far longer than PCs, and it was used with many of the old Teletype machines amongst other things. Fortunately, it is gradually being phased out in favour of more modern interfaces. In particular, the USB interface is now being used for

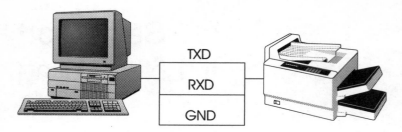

Fig.1.1 A basic three line serial connection

many peripherals that would previously have used a serial port, and this avoids a lot of problems of the past. However, serial ports are still a feature of new PCs and it will be some time yet before the RS232C serial interface finally reaches its "use by" date.

One of the main causes of problems with RS232C serial ports is undoubtedly a lack of rigid standardisation. The original specification is actually quite rigid, but designers have tended to "do their own thing" in an attempt to broaden the use of serial ports. A full RS232C serial port is fairly complex and uses numerous lines to provide communications between the two items of equipment. However, at its most basic level as few as two connecting lines will suffice, which has resulted in a lot of equipment having cut-down versions of RS232C ports. Some RS232C interfacing difficulties arise when a basic port is connected to a "bells and whistles" type, and some of the signals that the full port expects to receive are not present. Unfortunately, there are several other common causes of serial interfacing problems.

Basic connections

A basic full duplex serial link uses the method of connection shown in Figure 1.1. Full duplex simply means that the system is capable of two-way communications, and this is achieved by having separate lines for sending and receiving. The only other connecting wire carries the ground (earth) connection. If communications is only provided in one direction it is called half-duplex operation, and one of the data lines can then be omitted, giving just two connecting wires.

Although this basic method of interconnection may seem to be foolproof, even at this level there can be problems. A normal RS232C port sends data on the TXD (transmit data) line and receives it on the RXD (receive

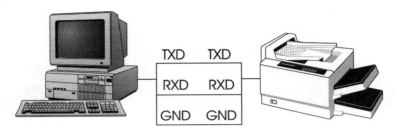

Fig.1.2 The "straight" method of connection

data) terminal. Therefore, simply connecting each terminal of one port to its corresponding terminal on the other port, as in Figure 1.2, should not work. Two inputs are connected together, as are two outputs, and no exchange of information can occur. Fortunately, all RS232C outputs should include current limiting circuits that prevent an excessive current from flowing if two outputs are accidentally connected together. On the other hand, it is not a good idea to test this type of thing in practice just in case it does not provide full protection, so always endeavour to get the connections right first time.

DCE and DTE

On the face of it, the method of connection shown in Figure 1.3 is needed in order to provide a two-way link. Each TXD terminal connects to an RXD type, so that each output drives an input at the opposite end of the system. This method of connection will sometimes work in practice, but in some cases it is actually the connection method of Figure 1.2 that is needed. Having two categories of RS232C equipment causes this anomaly. The general idea is to have a main item of equipment such as a computer that sends data on the TXD terminal and receives it on the RXD one. In RS232C terminology, a unit of this type is a DTE (data terminal equipment) unit.

A minor item of equipment such as a printer or modem is normally a DCE (data communications equipment) unit. Equipment of this type sends on its RXD terminal and receives on the TXD one. The point of having the two types of equipment is that it avoids the complication of having a cable that cross-couples the TXD and RXD terminals. Each pin on one connector is wired to the same pin on the other connector.

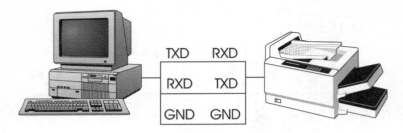

Fig.1.3 Apart from modems, most peripherals require cross coupling

Life for users of serial interfaces would be much easier if real world equipment adhered to the rules. Connecting practically any serial device to a PC would then just be a matter of using a "straight" cable of this type, with no cross coupling needed. Needless to say, some items of equipment that one would expect to be in the DCE category are actually wired as DTE units, and vice versa. Over the years I have used several printers and plotters that have serial interfaces, but I have yet to encounter one that has its serial port wired for DCE operation. In fact the vast majority of computer peripherals that have an RS232C port have it configured for DTE operation.

The fact that both items of equipment are of the same type does not mean that they are totally incompatible. Both types of interface have terminals for sending and receiving data, and a two-way link is still possible, but it does mean that a different connecting cable is needed. There are two completely incompatible types of serial cable, and it is clearly essential to choose the right one in order to have any chance of success. Where the two items of equipment have the same type of interface it is necessary to use a cable that has the terminals cross-coupled, and this is normally called a null modem cable.

Connectors

In theory it should be possible to tell at a glance whether a unit has a DCE interface or a DTE type, since DTE units have male connectors and DCE units have the female variety. In both cases the standard type of connector is a 25-way D type. However, not all equipment has a connector of the appropriate gender, and some equipment does not use a 25-way D connector at all. The exceptions include practically all modern PCs, which use a 9-way D connector. Pin functions for the standard 25-way

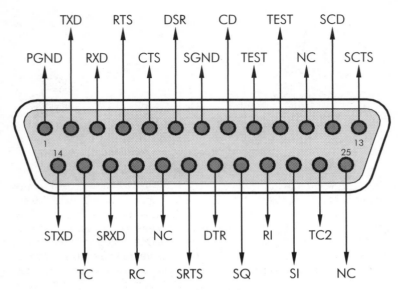

Fig.1.4 Pin functions for a 25-pin PC serial port

and cut down PC 9-way serial ports are provided in Figures 1.4 and 1.5 respectively.

The early PCs did actually have serial ports that used 25-way D connectors, and there are still some serial port expansion cards around that have 25-way connectors. The 9-way connectors were introduced with the original IBM AT computers, and an RS232C port of this type is still sometimes referred to as an AT serial port. This lack of standardisation has resulted in the production of two types of adapter that cure potential incompatibility problems with PC serial ports. In the past it was common for serial port devices such as mice to be supplied complete with an adapter

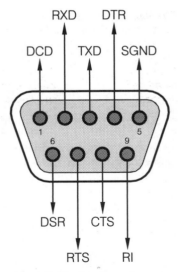

Fig.1.5 Pin functions for a 9-pin PC serial port

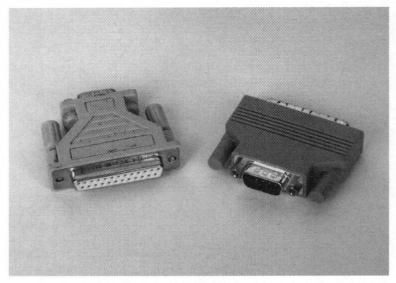

Fig.1.6 Two 9 to 25-pin serial port adapters

that permitted the 25-way connector of the unit's cable to be used with a port having a 9-way connector.

Later on as the 9-way ports became the norm, serial devices specifically for use with PCs were normally supplied with a 9-way connector and an adapter to permit operation with a port having a standard 25-way connector. Figure 1.6 shows two adapters of this type. These days it is rare for equipment to be supplied with either type of adapter, but they are still available from some computer accessory suppliers. These 9- to 25-way and 25- to 9-way adapters are produced in an alternative form known as "pig tail" leads. This is just a short lead having a 25-way connector at one end and a 9-way type at the other (Figure 1.7).

There is a slight problem with the other type of adapter in that adding it to the connector on the end of the serial lead effectively produces a connector 80 to 90 millimetres long. Having a connector that long sticking out the back of a PC can produce problems, especially in cases where the PC is backed against a wall. Although in some ways less neat, the "pig tail" leads are the more practical type of adapter. It is now quite common for modems to be supplied with a serial lead like the one shown in Figure 1.8. This has a 25-way connector at the end that connects to

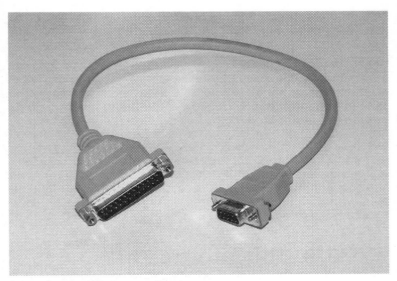

Fig.1.7 A serial port "pig tail" adapter

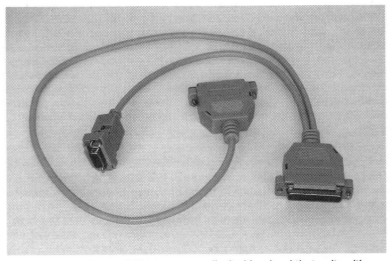

Fig.1.8 Many serial modems are supplied with a lead that suits either type of PC serial port

the modem, plus 25 and 9-way connectors at the computer end of the lead. This enables the modem to be used with either type of PC serial port.

On the face of it, using one of these adapters does not provide a complete solution because there are clearly many functions available on the 25-way ports that are not present on the 9-way type. In fact there is no problem here, because only nine pins of a PC serial port are actually implemented regardless of the type of connector used. When dealing with serial ports you have to bear in mind that real world ports rarely (if ever) have a full implementation of the RS232C standard. This gives the potential incompatibility problem between complex and basic port implementations. An input terminal of one port might be connected to an output on the other port that is not actually implemented. Although this is not normally a problem with the sending and receiving data lines, it is a common cause of problems with the other lines.

Unused terminals

A full RS232C port has 25 terminals, but a basic two-way link requires just three. What are the other 22 terminals used for? A few are not used at all, and the ones labelled NC (no connection) in Figure 1.4 are totally unused. Many of the terminals are used as secondary lines, and in a full implementation there are secondary versions of all the main lines. These are presumably intended to provide a backup system if the primary interface fails. However, in practice, the secondary lines are rarely implemented, and they are not included in PC serial ports. The terminals marked TEST do not serve any useful purpose in normal use, and most serial ports have no connections to these pins. They are sometimes connected to a +12 volt supply, which can be useful when trying to sort out cabling problems, but you can not rely on this supply being present.

It is perhaps worth mentioning that RS232C serial ports operate at nominal voltages of plus and minus 12 volts, and not at the 0-volt and 5-volt levels normally associated with digital circuitry. The actual signal voltages can be anything from about plus and minus 3 volts to plus and minus 24 volts. This is largely of academic importance, but it does make it important not to connect an RS232C port direct to a parallel type or any other port that operates at normal 5-volt logic levels. Apart from the fact that basic incompatibilities would prevent anything useful from being achieved, the higher voltages used by the serial port could damage the other port.

Handshaking

Some of the other terminals are used to implement handshaking, which is a means of ensuring that the flow of data is properly regulated. Matters are complicated by the fact that there are two types of handshaking, and these are the hardware and software varieties. There is a further complication in that handshaking is not always needed or used. Handshaking is not really necessary with something like a link from one PC to another. A serial interface is quite slow by normal computing standards, and there is little risk of data being sent at such a high rate that the receiving PC will not be able to keep up. It is more likely that the PC will spend much of the time waiting for data to be received so that it can get on with things.

Handshaking is needed when the receiving device is quite slow and it is in danger of being overloaded with data. It is normally used with printers and modems, both of which are usually quite slow in comparison to a serial interface. Most receiving devices have some memory called a buffer, and this is used to store data prior to it being processed. However, even with a large buffer there is still a danger of the data being sent too fast and the buffer being overloaded. With the buffer full and more data being received, either newly received data has to be discarded or some of the data already in the buffer has to be overwritten by the new data. Either way there is a loss of data and results are unsatisfactory.

Handshaking works by having some means for the receiving device to indicate to the sending unit that its buffer is full and that no more data can be processed for the time being. The sending unit then ceases transmission until it receives a message from the receiving unit indicating that it is ready to accept more data. With hardware handshaking, an additional line is used to carry the start and stop messages. A +12-volt level is used to indicate that the receiving device is ready to receive data and a −12-volt level signals that a hold-off is required. A full duplex system requires two handshake lines, with a separate line being used to regulate the flow of data in each direction.

XON/XOFF

Software handshaking sends start and stop messages via the data lines. You may encounter references to XON/OFF handshaking, and this is just another term for software handshaking. The ASCII codes 17 and 19 are normally used to respectively switch on (XON) and switch off (XOFF) the flow of data. The first point to note about this system is that it requires

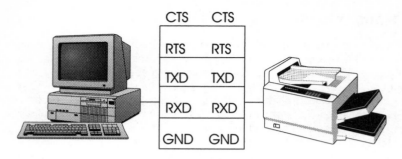

Fig.1.9 Hardware handshaking via a "straight" cable

a full duplex link even if data is only being carried in one direction. One link is needed to carry the data, and the data link in the opposite direction is needed to carry the handshake messages. A second point to note is that even where software handshaking is used, the equipment may not totally ignore the handshake lines. Unless the appropriate handshake input is at +12 volts the sending device may simply "freeze" and refuse to send any data. A third point to note is that this method of handshaking can only work if both ends of the system are set up to utilise it.

Hardware handshaking uses the CTS (clear to send) and RTS (request to send) terminals of the RS232C ports. CTS is an output line that the receiving device sets at +12 volts when it is able to process data, and at −12 volts when it needs to halt the flow of data. RTS is the input on the sending device that CTS controls. A serial connection using handshaking therefore uses the arrangement of Figure 1.9 when using a "straight" connecting cable, or the one of Figure 1.10 when using a null modem cable.

In an ideal world there would be no more to serial port handshaking than coupling or cross coupling the CTS and RTS lines. Unfortunately, in practice it is often somewhat more involved than this. There are other inputs and outputs on a serial port that are not really intended for what could really be described as handshaking, but are sometimes used in this role anyway. The CD (carrier detect) terminal at pin 8 can be used by a modem to indicate that it is receiving a carrier wave. In other words, that it is receiving the usual warbles and noises from the modem at the other end of the system.

This terminal obviously has no validity when an RS232C interface is used with something like a printer, but that will not necessarily stop the printer

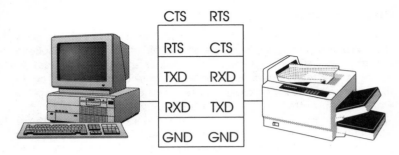

Fig.1.10 Hardware handshaking using a null-modem cable

manufacturer from using it to indicate whether or not the printer is loaded with paper. If there is no paper in the printer, a hold-off must be provided until the printer has been refilled with paper. This terminal is then being used to implement a form of handshake line. The practical implication of this is that simply coupling the CTS and RTS lines of the two ports may not be sufficient, and other lines may be needed to complete the handshaking and (or) provide status information. In the case of a modem, it is very likely that some additional lines will be needed in order to provide status information to the PC. With other equipment, some additional lines may be needed in order to obtain satisfactory results.

Functions

This is list of the RS232C pin functions, together with some notes on each one which should be useful for reference purposes. Note that this description is for a DTE interface, which is the type found on PCs and most computer peripherals.

Pin 1 (protective ground)

This normally connects to the chassis of the equipment and the metal frame of the connector. In most cases it is also connected to the signal ground terminal at pin 7. RS232C serial cables normally have a metal screen surrounding the connecting wires, and this screen is earthed to prevent the wires from radiating radio interference. The screen is normally earthed to the chassis of the connector, and it should therefore be earthed to the chassis of the equipment even if the protective ground terminal is not implemented.

Pin 2 (transmitted data)

Serial data is transmitted on this pin. This line is always active, even when no data is being sent. Since there is no "off" state it is not acceptable to connect two transmitted data lines together and then send data on whichever one takes your fancy. There is little risk of the two ports being damaged, but there is little prospect of success either, with the two ports wrestling each other for control of the transmission line. A proper switching unit (see chapter 2) is needed in order to share a peripheral between two PCs. Incidentally, it should be possible to drive two inputs from one transmitted data output provided only short connecting cables are used. However, this would only be practical in cases where no handshaking was required.

Pin 3 (received data)

Data from the other serial port is received on this input terminal.

Pin 4 (request to send)

The request to send terminal is the main handshake output. It is set at +12 volts to indicate to the sending unit that it is ready to receive data. With a null modem cable it connects to the clear to send handshake input.

Pin 5 (clear to send)

The clear to send terminal is the main handshake input. No data is sent unless this is taken to +12 volts. This pin connects to the request to send output on the other serial port when a null modem cable is used.

Pin 6 (data set ready)

This is an input, and it is taken to +12 volts when the device at the other end of the system is switched on and fully operational. Data set is simply an old and obsolete term for a modem, so these days it would be more appropriate to call it modem ready. Obviously it can be used with other items of equipment to indicate that the unit is powered up and ready for use. With a null modem cable this input is often linked to the data terminal ready (DTR) output at pin 20.

Pin 7 (signal ground)

The ground (earth) connections of the two items of equipment must be linked, and this is the purpose of the signal ground pin. It is always connected to the same pin at the other end of the system, even if a null modem cable is used. The earth connection may be provided by the screen of the connecting cable, but the link via this pin should always be included to make absolutely certain that a reliable signal earth connection is provided.

Pin 8 (carrier detect)

This input terminal is also known as data carrier detect (DCD). It is taken to +12 volts by the modem when it has detected a signal from the modem at the other end of the system.

Pin 9 (test)

A pin reserved for testing purposes, but in practice it is usually left unconnected. A +12-volt supply is sometimes available from this pin, which can be useful for holding unused handshake inputs in the "on" state.

Pin 10 (test)

A pin reserved for testing purposes, but in practice it is usually left unconnected. A +12-volt supply is sometimes available from this pin, which can be useful for holding unused handshake inputs in the "on" state.

Pin 11 (no connection)

No internal connections are made to this pin, which is totally unused.

Pin 12 (secondary carrier detect)

The backup version of the carrier detect line. Like the other secondary lines, it is not usually implemented, and is never included in the serial port of a PC.

Pin 13 (secondary clear to send)

This is the backup version of the clear to send line. It is not implemented in PC serial ports and most other serial ports.

Pin 14 (secondary transmitted data)

The backup version of the transmitted data line, and little implemented in practice.

Pin 15 (transmit clock)

RS232C ports support two types of serial interface. The synchronous type uses a clock signal that indicates when the data line should be sampled to detect the logic state of each bit of data. The asynchronous type relies on standard transmission rates so that timing circuits in the receiving circuit can determine the correct times to sample the data line. This pin is used to send the clock signal when synchronous communications is used. In practice, the clock signal is hardly ever used, and synchronous serial links are not used with PC serial ports. Consequently, this pin is usually left unconnected.

Pin 16 (secondary received data)

The backup version of the received data line. This pin is left unconnected on most serial ports including normal PC types.

Pin 17 (receive clock)

This pin receives the clock signal from the sending device when a synchronous link is used. With most RS232C ports this pin is simply left unconnected because synchronous communications is hardly ever implemented.

Pin 18 (no connection)

Has no assignment and is left unconnected.

Pin 19 (secondary request to send)

The backup version of the request to send line, and almost never implemented in practice.

Pin 20 (data terminal ready)

An output that is used to indicate to the modem that the sending device is operational. Taking this line to the "off" state (–12 volts) will usually cause the modem to hang up the telephone connection and stop sending data. It can therefore be used as a means of switching the modem on and off.

Pin 21 (signal quality)

The modem sets this at the "on" state if the quality of the received signal is deemed to be of adequate quality. It is set to the "off" state if the incoming signal is of poor quality and there is a likelihood of decoding errors. This line is little implemented in practice and is not present on a standard PC serial port.

Pin 22 (ring indicator)

This input monitors an output on the modem. The output goes high when the telephone rings. The data terminal ready line can then be used to activate the modem so that it will answer the call.

Pin 23 (speed indicator)

This output is used to tell the modem to switch to a higher speed. It does not have much relevance with modern modems and it is not usually implemented. It is never included on a standard PC serial port.

Pin 24 (transmit clock)

Similar to pin 15, but this pin is used where the data terminal device rather than the data communications device is providing the clock signal for an asynchronous link. In the rare instances of synchronous communications being used, it is normally the modem (DCE) device that provides the clock signal. Consequently, this line is almost never implemented. It is not included on a standard PC serial port.

Pin 25 (no connection)

This pin is unassigned and no internal connections are made to it.

Connections

It is only fair to point out at this stage that there is more to getting a serial link to work than getting the right connections between the two units. Things such as the baud rate and word format also have to be correct, and this type of thing should certainly be checked before spending masses of time experimenting with various connection methods. The original method of connection could be perfectly all right, with the problem residing elsewhere. Setting the baud rate, checking the word format, and similar matters are covered later in this chapter.

Where the peripheral device is a modem, you should be in luck and it will almost certainly be a DCE unit. A DTE device such as a PC normally has a male D connector (Figure 1.11) whereas a DCE unit normally has a female connector (Figure 1.12). It is therefore easy to determine whether the peripheral device is a DCE or DTE unit, provided the peripheral manufacturer has not opted for a non-standard approach of course. With

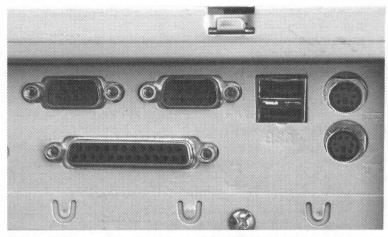

Fig.1.11 The two 9-pin serial ports have male connectors, and are therefore DTE types

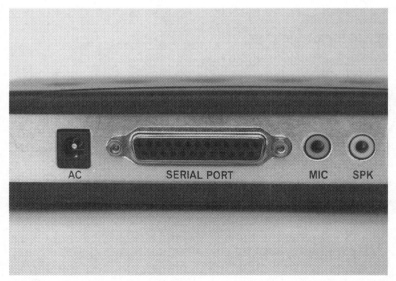

Fig.1.12 This modem has a female serial port connector, and it is therefore a DCE device

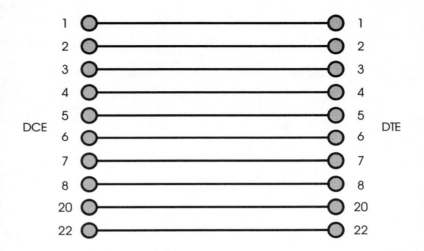

Fig.1.13 The interconnections for a "straight" serial cable

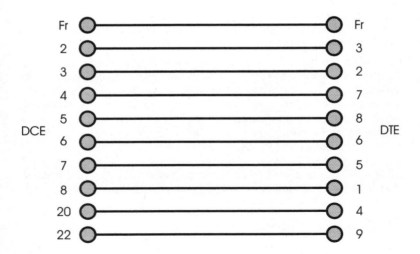

*Fig.1.14 The interconnections for a "straight" serial cable that has a
9-pin connector for a PC serial port*

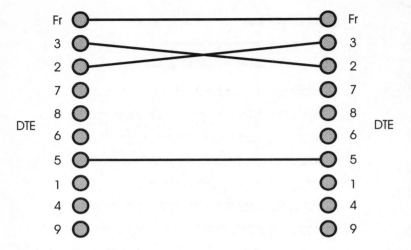

Fig.1.15 Connections for a null-modem lead for use with two PCs

a DCE peripheral it is a "straight" serial cable that is required. New serial port modems are normally supplied with a lead that is suitable for use with 9- or 25-pin PC serial ports. There should only be a problem if the cable becomes damaged or you are using a second-hand modem that has become separated from its original cable.

A "straight" cable can have all 25 terminals on one connector connected to the 25 terminals on the other connector, and some ready-made cables do so. This has to be regarded as doing things the hard way though, since only nine pins are used by a PC serial port and 16 of the connecting wires would not actually connect to anything. A lead having the connections shown in Figure 1.13 will suffice, or the connections of Figure 1.14 can be used if the PC serial port has a 9-pin connector. It should not be necessary to resort to making your own cable since "straight" serial cables for use with PCs are a standard item that should be available from any computer store or at your local computer fair.

Null modem leads

Null modem cables are inevitably more awkward than the "straight" variety because a serial interface is not designed for this method of operation. It is designed for use with one DTE unit and one DCE type, and not two DCE or two DTE units. In practice, most serial port peripherals, apart

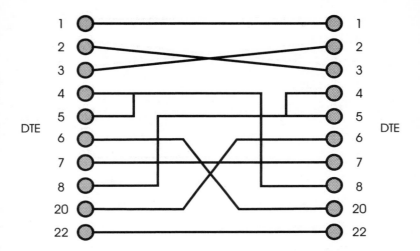

Fig.1.16 This type of null modem cable was often used in the past

from modems, are of the DTE variety. This means that it is often necessary to link two DTE units, with the cable being wired so that each unit "thinks" it is connected to a DCE device. The problem with a set-up of this type is that it has no single solution. There is more than one way of utilising the handshake lines, if they are needed at all. An "off the shelf" null modem cable from your local computer store might work perfectly, but with some peripherals it will not work at all.

With software that enables two computers to be linked via their serial ports it is unusual for the handshake lines to be used, or for software handshaking to be implemented. The PCs can process data far faster than the serial ports can supply it, making handshaking unnecessary. A very simple cable that couples the signal ground lines and cross couples the data lines is all that is required. Figure 1.15 shows the connections for a cable of this type that has two 9-pin connectors for use with PC serial ports. Using a cable that couples some of the handshake lines should not give any difficulties because it is normal for this type of software to totally ignore the signals on the handshake inputs. Any null modem cable should work properly in this application. There are ready-made serial cables that are specifically designed for linking two PCs, and these are sometimes referred to as "Laplink" cables. Although designed for use with the popular file transfer utility of that name, they are suitable for use with most other programs of the same general type.

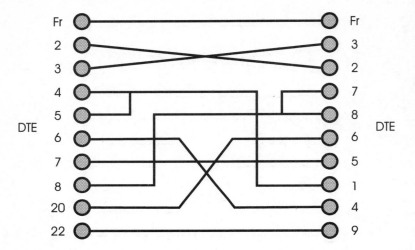

Fig.1.17 The version of Fig.1.16 for a 9-pin PC serial port

There may be other instances where no handshake lines are required, but in most cases some form of hardware handshaking will be used. A "Laplink" cable is then unsuitable, as it is essential for the appropriate handshake couplings to be provided by the serial lead. The arrangement shown in Figure 1.16 was often used in the past. This shows the connections for two 25-pin ports, but in most cases there will be a 25-pin connector at the peripheral end of the cable and a 9-pin type at the PC end. A cable having the connections shown in Figure 1.17 is then needed. As one would expect, the transmit and receive data lines are cross-coupled.

The cross coupling of the handshake lines is less straightforward, and is perhaps something less than totally logical. Each request to send output controls its own clear to send input and the carrier detect input at the other end of the system. Presumably the point of connecting each clear to send input to its own request to send output is to ensure that it is initially taken to the "on" state. Some serial ports, including PC types, can have a definite reluctance to start sending data, and this can usually be cured by connecting the clear to send input to the "on" (+12-volt) level.

The other handshake coupling is from the data set ready output at one end of the system to the data terminal ready input at the other end. This coupling is often used as a means for the peripheral to indicate to the PC

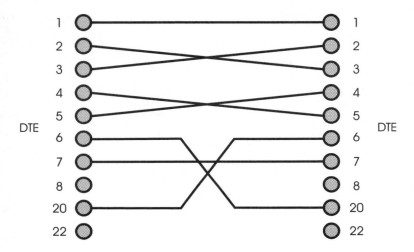

Fig.1.18 This method of connection is more is often successful with modern equipment

that it is switched on and operational. Its exact purpose varies somewhat from one peripheral to another. With a printer for example, this coupling could be used to indicate an error condition, such as the printer being out of paper or a paper jam having occurred. The flow of data is then controlled by other lines, which provide the true handshaking. With this type of cable the handshaking is provided by the coupling from the clear to send output to the carrier detect input.

I am not sure what purpose the connection between the two ring indicator inputs serves, and it is not always included. On the face of it, connecting two inputs together will have no effect. Presumably, it will not stop the system from working either, so there is no harm in including it. Note that the version of the cable that has two 25-pin connectors is symmetrical, and that it can therefore be connected either way around.

This type of serial cable will work with many items of equipment, and it is perhaps the best bet when trying to connect older serial devices to a PC. In my experience, the method of connection shown in Figure 1.18 is more likely to be successful with modern equipment. The connections for a 25-pin to 9-pin version are shown in Figure 1.19. As before, the data lines are cross-coupled, as are the data set ready and data terminal ready lines. Also as before, these handshake lines are normally used to indicate an error condition rather than providing true handshaking. The

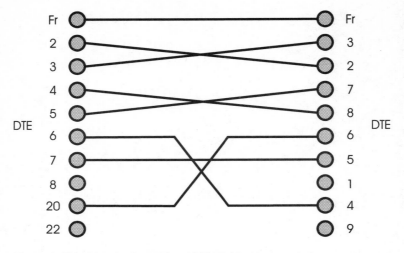

Fig.1.19 The 25 to 9-pin version of Fig.1.18

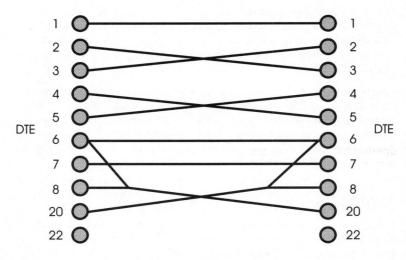

Fig.1.20 Interconnections for the "belt and braces" serial lead

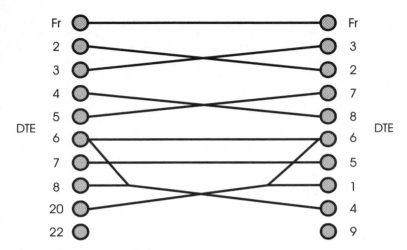

Fig.1.21 The version of Fig.1.20 for use with a 9-pin PC serial port

handshaking is provided by the cross coupling of the request to send and clear to send lines.

Figure 1.20 shows another yet another form of null modem lead. Connections for the 25-pin to 9-pin version are provided in Figure 1.21. This takes the "belt and braces" approach, and I suppose it is the one that is most likely to give correct operation with awkward items of equipment. Again, the data lines are cross-coupled, as are the clear to send and request to send handshake lines. Each data terminal ready output drives both the data set ready and carrier detect inputs at the other end of the system. The clear to send and request to send lines provide the handshaking. It does not matter whether the data set ready or carrier detect input is used to check that the other end of the system is operational, since they are both driven from the data terminal ready output.

Avoidance

Before getting involved in making up serial cables it is worth considering whether it is really necessary. There is not really any point in making up your own cable if the peripheral device is a DCE unit. A ready-made "straight" cable should do the job perfectly well and is likely to cost less than buying the parts to make your own cable. Where the peripheral is a DTE unit, does the manufacturer offer a matching serial cable for use with a PC? Where such a cable is available, it is definitely a good idea to use it. Even if you are used to dealing with cables it can still be quite time consuming to make up your own. It can be even more time consuming if the peripheral is one that requires some juggling with the interconnections before it will work.

With a major peripheral such as a printer, is there another port that can be used? Printers that have serial ports often have a parallel (Centronics) port as well. A Centronics style port can be connected to the parallel port of a PC using an "off the shelf" cable that costs very little and is virtually certain to work first time. The serial option may or may not work properly with a ready-made serial lead. At one time it was virtually impossible to obtain ready-made null modem cables, but they are now available from the larger computer stores and are often available at computer fairs. However, as pointed out previously, many of these cables cross couple the data lines but leave the handshake lines unconnected. Even if an adapter or "pigtail" lead is used to make the connection to the peripheral, a lead of this type will not work with most peripherals.

You need to make some enquiries when buying serial leads, so that you know exactly what you are buying. You may be able to find a lead having the correct connectors and a likely looking set of connections, but there is no guarantee that it will work. You could end up having to junk the ready-made cable and make your own. Incidentally, it is worth studying the packaging of serial cables because these sometimes show the interconnections provided by the cable. This can help you to avoid buying a simple data cable when you need one that implements the handshake lines.

Slow, slow...

Another point to bear in mind when using the serial interface of a printer is that it can provide painfully slow results. A standard PC printer port tends to be maligned for its lack of speed, but it is actually capable of outputting up to 200,000 bytes of data per second. Modern parallel PC ports can input or output up to two million bytes per second. This is far faster than a serial port or even a standard (version 1.1) USB port come to that. The highest normal transfer speed for a serial port is 19200 bits per second, or 19200 baud as it would normally be termed. A PC serial port will actually work at higher rates, but about 115,000 baud is the normal maximum. This equates to only about 11,500 bytes per second.

A serial port is fine where the data being output to the printer is just a string of ASCII codes, but these days most printing involves complex bitmaps and not just a series of ASCII characters. A laser printer can require over a megabyte of data per page, or with higher resolutions, several megabytes of data per page may be required. Even if a baud rate of 115,000 baud were supported by the printer, it would take over a minute to transfer the data for each page, and could take several minutes. I once used a laser printer that produced six pages per minute when driven via its parallel port, but needed about 20 minutes per page when driven by way of its serial port! This was with the serial port of the printer operating at its maximum supported baud rate of 9600 baud incidentally, and therefore represented the shortest time per page that the printer could achieve using its serial port.

Where there is a choice of using a parallel or a serial interface, the parallel option is almost invariably the right one. A standard cable provides fast communication with the printer or other peripheral device, and should give hassle-free connection. A parallel interface also has lines that are specifically designed to handle functions such as a general error signal and the printer being out of paper. The only drawback of a parallel printer interface is that it is only designed for use with relatively short cables of about two or three metres in length. This is more than adequate for most purposes, and low capacitance cables for operation over 10 metres or more are produced. The maximum operating range for a serial interface depends on the baud rate used, but even at high baud rates, it is likely to be at least 20 metres.

Custom cables

What are the options if the worst comes to the worst and you are faced with the task of connecting a PC to an uncooperative piece of equipment that does not work with ready-made cables? Some would say that the best option is to give up. There is no guarantee that the peripheral will ever be linked successfully to the PC, even if a fair amount of time and effort are devoted to the problem. It might not be worth spending time and money on the problem unless it really is important to link the unit to the PC. Another possibility is to seek professional help with the problem, but this is likely to be prohibitively expensive. Buying a new peripheral having a USB interface would probably be cheaper!

If you are determined to press on there is only one option available, and that is to build your own custom cable. In days gone by the standard approach was to try a ready-made cable first, and then modify this cable

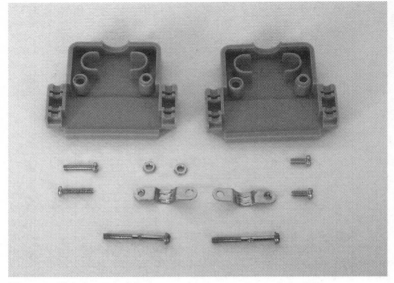

*Fig.1.22 This is probably the most common type of shell for a
         D connector*

if it did not give the desired result. These days virtually all computer
cables have moulded connectors that can not be opened up to give
access to the connections inside. With some, it is actually possible to
break them open without too much difficulty, but the shells of the
connectors are likely to be damaged beyond use in the process.
However, it should be possible to obtain new shells, so this approach
may be possible. In most cases though, there will be no option but to
start from scratch.

The components needed to make up computer leads are unlikely to be
available from your local computer store, and it is necessary to obtain
them from an electronic component supplier. The connectors are
normally sold as two separate parts, which are the bit that actually makes
the connections and the shell that provides it with a neat outer casing.
The shells come in various styles, but they are broadly similar. Figures
1.22 and 1.23 show two shells prior to assembly.

The casing is normally in two sections that are held together by a couple
of nuts and bolts. A metal clip is fixed tightly onto the cable and is then
fitted into a receptacle inside the shell. This provides what is quaintly

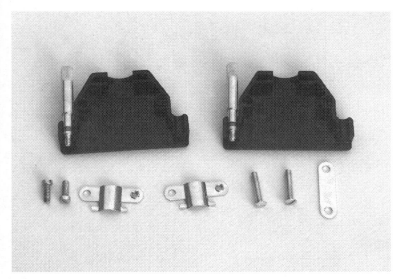

Fig.1.23 *An alternative form of shell for a D connector. Both types of shell include metal brackets to provide strain relief*

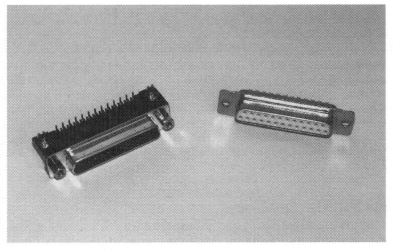

Fig.1.24 *The connector on the right is the correct type for serial cables. The one on the left is for printed circuit mounting*

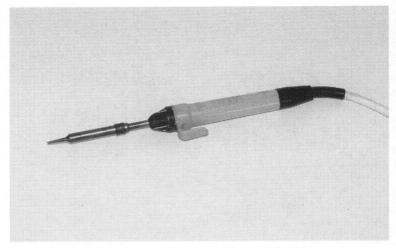

Fig.1.25 This 18-watt iron is ideal for making serial cables

termed strain relief. In other words, if someone trips over the cable the strain is taken by the outer sleeving of the cable and the shell of the connector. This does not guarantee the survival of the cable, but it greatly reduces the risk of the wires in the cable being ripped away from the connector. Always include the strain relief clip and make sure that it is installed correctly. Without it, the cable has a very short life expectancy. It should not take long to work out how the pieces fit together.

You have to be careful to obtain the right type of connector, since D connectors are produced in various types and sizes. Assuming you are trying to link two DTE units, it is 25-way female D connectors that are required. It is the standard type having terminals for soldered connections that is needed, and not one of the connectors for printed circuit mounting. In Figure 1.24 it is the connector on the right that is the correct type. The one on the left is a right-angled printed circuit type that will not fit into a shell.

Soldering iron

A good quality screened cable is needed for a serial link, and at least seven-way cable is needed to cross couple the data lines, two sets of handshake lines, and to link the signal ground terminals as well. If you are new to electrical soldering you will need to buy a small electric

Fig.1.26 A proper soldering iron stand is an essential accessory

soldering iron having a rating of between about 15 and 20 watts (Figure 1.25), although one having a rating as high as 25 watts will do. A bit having a diameter of only about two or three millimetres is required for small-scale work such as this. These days most small electric irons are supplied with a bit of about this size, so it is unlikely that a change of bit will be required. In order to use an iron safely a proper stand is required (Figure 1.26). Apart from providing a safe place to park the hot iron, the metal part of the stand also removes heat from the bit. This helps to avoid overheating if the iron is left switched on but unused for a while.

Solder

Special solders are available for electrical work, and a "bog standard" solder is all that is needed for making up cables. These are usually made from an alloy that contains 60 percent tin and 40 percent lead. Avoid solders that contain 40 percent tin and 60 percent lead, as they are difficult to use, and tend to produce physically weak joints when used for manual soldering. Only use solder that contains cores of flux, which means the vast majority of electrical solders these days. The flux helps the solder to flow over the surfaces to be joined, and in most cases it also helps to clean the surfaces. This does not guarantee perfect results every time, but it certainly makes it much easier to produce good quality joints.

Electrical solder is generally available in two widths. The thicker 18 SWG (1.22 millimetre diameter) solder is intended for general electric and electronic work, and I suppose that this includes soldering cables to connectors. The thinner 22 SWG (0.71 millimetre diameter) solder is primarily intended for precision work on printed circuit boards. D connectors have quite small terminals though, and only minute amounts of solder are required to connect the wires to them. Consequently, I definitely recommend using the thinner gauge when making serial cables. When using the thicker gauge for this type of thing it becomes difficult to avoid short-circuits between the terminals due to excess solder.

Making connections

Making good soldered connections is not particularly difficult, but like any manual skill it takes a while to become proficient at it. A useful exercise when you first start soldering is to bang some small nails or panel pins into a scrap of timber or MDF and then try soldering some bits of wire to them. The metal surfaces need to be reasonably clean in order to produce strong soldered joints, so it may be necessary to use some fine sandpaper to clean the nails or pins prior to starting work. This should not be necessary with the terminals on the connectors incidentally. Cleaning them should only be necessary if they have been in storage for some time and are showing clear signs of dirt or corrosion on the terminals.

The easiest way to make good quality joints with this type of soldering is to tin both surfaces with solder prior to making the connection. Place the hot bit onto the top of the pin or nail and hold it there for about half a second to a second before applying the solder. Heating the pin helps the solder to flow over it properly. Do not leave the bit in place for more than a second or so as this could cause the surface to oxidise, making the solder flow less well rather than better. Sometimes the solder may refuse to flow properly, instead going into a blob on top of the surface you are trying to tin. It may even drop off the surface and refuse to adhere to it at all. This occurs where there is excessive dirt or corrosion on the surface. Scraping the surface with the small blade of a penknife should clear away the contamination and enable the solder to flow properly.

The end of the wire is tinned with solder in the same way. Again, if the solder does not flow over the surface properly, scrape it clean and try again. Ideally, the connection is made by placing the end of the wire and the pin together, applying the bit of the iron, and then feeding in some solder. In practice, this can be difficult because you need three hands! One to hold the solder, a second to hold the soldering iron, and a third to hold the wire. You will probably find your own way around this problem.

The method I use is to place some solder on the bit of the iron prior to applying it to the two surfaces to be joined. This method is not normally to be recommended because the flux in the solder that is placed on the bit tends to burn away before it is applied to the joint. However, provided both surfaces are liberally tinned with solder before making the joint, this is of no consequence. The solder has already flowed properly over both surfaces, and they will readily join without the benefit of any more flux. Strong joints should be produced provided the solder on the bit is fresh and has not been there for a minute or two.

Preparation

Both ends of the cable must be properly prepared before the lead can be wired to the connectors. There are two main types of screened cable, which are the overall and individually screened varieties. In other words, each lead can be individually screened, or there can be one screen covering all the inner conductors. For any type of cable there is an advantage in having individually screened leads. An overall screen prevents the cable from radiating significant amounts of radio frequency interference, and it prevents electrical noise from being picked up in the cable.

However, it does not reduce any stray coupling from one wire to another. This coupling is primarily caused by capacitance in the cable. The longer the cable the greater the capacitance and the degree of stray coupling. High baud rates also exacerbate problems with this "cross talk". If you are making a long cable and (or) it will be used at high baud rates it is probably best to opt for a high quality cable, which will almost certainly be an individually screened type. This type of cable is significantly more expensive than the overall screened variety, and it is more difficult to use. However, it is clearly worth the added trouble and expense if it produces a cable that works properly rather than one that gives constant problems with corrupted data. A flat ribbon-like cable (Figure 1.27), not surprisingly called ribbon cable, is sometimes used for parallel data leads.

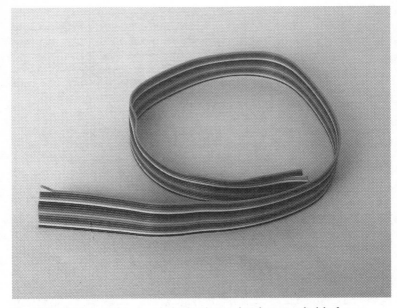

*Fig.1.27 Ribbon cable is relatively cheap, but is not suitable for
          serial cables*

It is not well suited to serial cables though, and it is better to use a good
quality screened cable.

The first task is to remove about 20 to 25 millimetres of sleeving from
one end of the cable. Provided the cable is only about four or five
millimetres in diameter this can be achieved using a pair of ordinary wire
strippers. There is no need to buy expensive wire strippers for this type
of thing, and inexpensive wire cutters and strippers (Figure 1.28) are
perfectly adequate for making do-it-yourself serial cables. Most wire
strippers can not handle cables of much more than about five millimetres
in diameter, leaving the choice of buying an expensive type that can
accommodate thicker cables, or improvising.

Unless you have just won the lottery, it will probably be a matter of
improvising. It is not too difficult to cut away the sleeving using a sharp
modelling knife and a cutting board, but you should obviously take due
care to avoid cutting yourself. It is also necessary to take due care to
avoid cutting too deeply and damaging the inner part of the cable. Try to
cut slightly less than all the way through the sleeving and then tear it

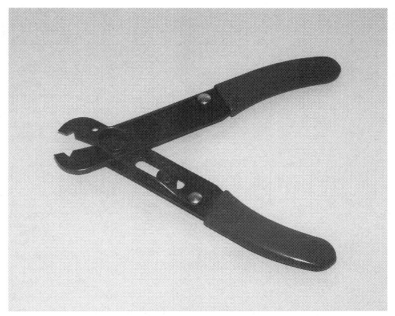

Fig.1.28 Combination wire cutters and strippers are adequate for making serial cables

away from the rest of the cable. This is the way in which wire strippers remove the sleeving without damaging the inner part of the cable.

Next the wires and the shield should be splayed apart so that you can see what exactly you have to work with. The shield or screen will usually be in the form of numerous fine copper wires that may be woven together or just laid side by side. These should be gathered together and tinned with plenty of solder. They will then effectively form a thick wire that can be soldered to pin 1 of a 25-way connector, or to the metal frame of a 9-way type. The end of each wire should have the insulation removed using the wire strippers, and it is only necessary to remove two or three millimetres of the sleeving.

It is not a good idea to improvise with scissors and knives when stripping the sleeving from fine wires. The wires are quite likely to be nicked in the process, which would render them prone to snapping. While the last two or three connections were being made, there would be a strong likelihood of the first two or three wires snapping away from the connector.

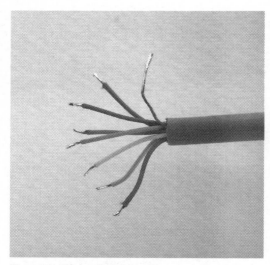

It is easy to end up going round in circles, never quite finishing all the connections. Even if the cable is eventually completed, it will be hopelessly unreliable if the wires have been damaged.

Tinning

When the pieces of sleeving have been removed, the bare ends of the wires are tinned with solder. If the cable has more wires than you

Fig.1.29 The prepared cable, ready for connection

actually need, trim off those that will not be used so that they can not cause confusion when you are wiring up the connector. You should then have something like Figure 1.29, and the cable is ready to be wired to the connector. The only preparation the connector needs is to have the terminals tinned with solder so that it is easy to make reliable connections to them. In most cases there will be some terminals left unused. There is no point in tinning any of these unused pins, and it is advisable not to do so. Apart from wasting solder, it will tend to confuse matters when you start connecting the wires.

Wiring up the connector is reasonably easy provided it is fixed to the workbench. One option is to fix it into a small vice, but my preferred method is to fix it to the workbench using some Bostik Blu-Tack or Plasticine (Figure 1.30). Tin the appropriate terminals with solder and then connect the wires. Work methodically along the top row of pins first, and then fix the connector the other way up and add any necessary connections to the bottom row.

Any links between terminals are added once the cable has been connected, being careful not to disconnect any of the joints already made. A thin multi-strand connecting wire is suitable for making the links. Do not use any form of non-insulated wire because it would be quite likely

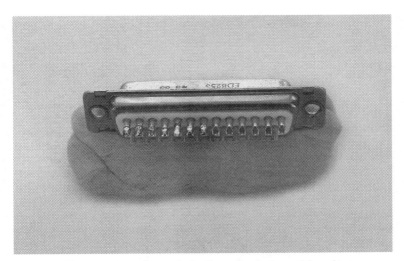

Fig.1.30 The connector is ready for the wires to be soldered to the terminals

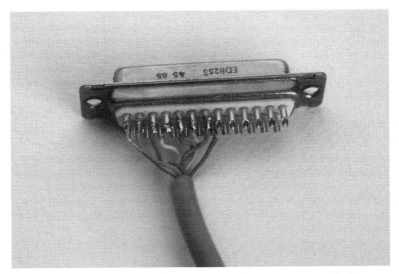

Fig.1.31 All the connections have been completed and the shell can now be fitted

25-way female D connector

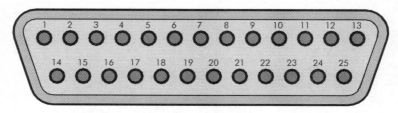

Fig.1.32 Pin numbering for a 25-way female D connector

to produce short circuits. Even if the wire is kept well clear of any terminals, it could easily be pressed against one or two terminals when the shell of the connector is bolted in place. Having completed all the connections, you should have something like Figure 1.31.

When making the connections you need to take care with the pin numbers. Bear in mind that the pin numbering on a male D connector (Figure 1.32) runs the opposite way to that on a female connector (Figure 1.33). This correctly gives pin 1 connected to pin 1, pin 2 connected to pin 2, etc., when two connectors are fitted together. Make sure that you wire each connector correctly and not as a "mirror image" of the correct connections. If in doubt, the pin numbers are actually marked on most computer connectors, although you may need a magnifier in order to see them. In fact you will almost certainly need quite a powerful magnifier even if you have quite good eyesight. In the case of a D connector, the numbers are moulded into the section that carries the terminals.

Colour coding

Having wired up one connector, you have to make sure that the other connector is wired in the appropriate fashion, with no crossed wires. This is made easier by multi-way screened cables having a different colour for the sleeving on each wire. If there are more than about 10 wires, some of the wires will probably have two-colour sleeving. In order to avoid wiring errors it is a good idea to make a sketch of the correct method of connection for the lead, or make a list of the connections like this one:

25-way male D connector

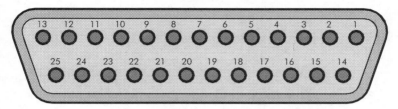

Fig.1.33 Pin numbering for a 25-way male D connector

Connector 1	Lead colour	Connector 2
Pin 1	Black	Frame
Pin 2	Brown	Pin 2
Pin 3	Red	Pin 3
Pin 4	Orange	Pin 8
Pin 5	Yellow	Pin 7
Pin 6	Green	Pin 4
Pin 7	Blue	Pin 5
Pin 20	Violet	Pin 1 and pin 6

Finishing off

To complete the cable, fit the strain relief clamp and fit the connector into one half of the shell (Figure 1.34). The strain relief clamp sometimes has two curved sections and one flat plate. It is normally the two curved pieces that are used, and the flat plate is only needed when the cable is very thin. Using two curved pieces will not grip very thin cable properly, so the flat section is used instead of one curved piece. With the strain relief grip in position, complete the assembly by manoeuvring the second half of the shell into position and adding the fixing bolts (Figure 1.35). Repeat this process for the other connector, and the new cable is then ready for testing.

Note that the D connectors sold for do-it-yourself cables do not always fully fit together with the connectors on the PC, printer, etc. The part of the shell that grips the connector also tends to restrict the extent to which

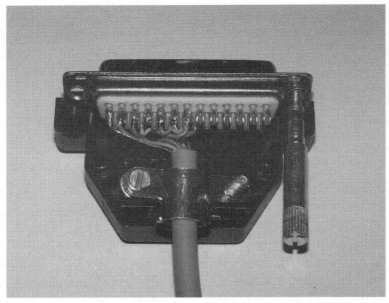

Fig.1.34 The strain relief clamp and half the shell fitted to the cable

it fits into the other connector. This should not prevent proper electrical connections from being made, but make sure that this type of connector is fitted into place as fully as possible. In rare cases where connector is clearly not fitting into place properly, it is necessary to file down the front section of the shell in order to rectify matters. Omitting the shell is a simpler alternative, but leaves the cable vulnerable to physical damage. It is only worth doing this as a desperation measure if all else fails.

Trial and error

Finding the right interconnections with uncooperative equipment often ends up as a matter or trial and error, with every method of cross coupling being tried. However, it is worth adopting a more logical approach before resorting to the try everything in desperation method. Serial interfacing problems fall into three main categories, and all three will be considered in detail here.

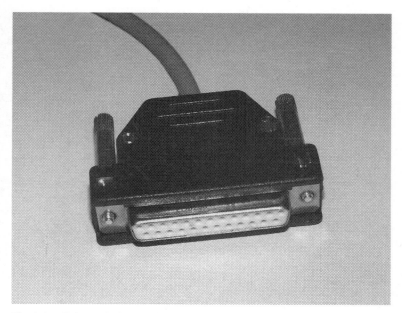

Fig.1.35 One end of the cable completed

1. No data

If a serial interface fails to output any data, it is due to the absence of an "on" state (+12 volts) on one of the handshake or status inputs. With luck, the instruction manual for the equipment will give a description of the serial interface, and this will includes details of the handshake lines that are implemented. Alternatively, there might be a diagram for the serial port that shows which terminals of the connector actually do something. The handshake and status inputs are clear to send, data set ready, carrier detect, and ring indicator. Unconnected inputs might go to the "on" state, but with many serial ports they drift to the "off" state. If the sending device is looking for an "on" condition on an input that is left unconnected, it is quite likely that no data will be output.

The standard solution is to find an output that is at +12 volts and then connect any unused handshake or status inputs to it. With the handshake and status inputs at the "on" state, the sending device must transmit something. If it does not, either the equipment has a serious fault or it is

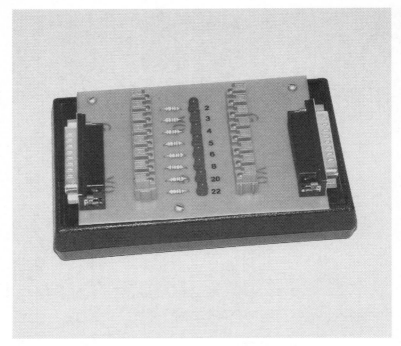

Fig.1.36 A simple but effective home-made breakout box

set up for software rather than hardware handshaking. The obvious problem with this approach is that you need some means of finding the states of the various terminals on the ports so that you can find one that is at +12 volts.

Breakout

The professional way of tackling RS232C interfacing problems is to use a device called a breakout box. In essence, this consists of two banks of solderless connectors, each of which connects to a standard RS232C lead and connector. The two leads connect to the ports of the two devices that you are trying to interface, and the solderless connector blocks enable various methods of connection to be tried without resorting to a soldering iron. Some connector blocks have spring terminals while others have the screw variety, but either way it does not take long to make changes

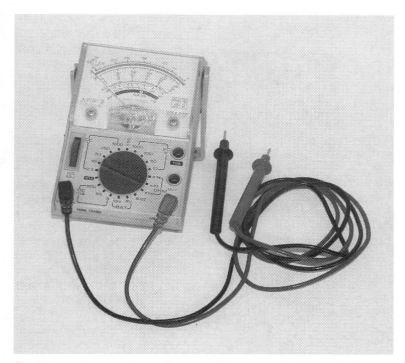

Fig.1.37 An inexpensive analogue multimeter is suitable for basic checks on cables and RS232C ports

to the connections. RS232C breakout boxes also have light emitting diodes that indicate the state of each line. You can therefore see at a glance which terminal or terminals are at the "on" state, and are suitable as candidates to drive any spare inputs.

It is not too difficult to devise your own breakout box if you are used to building or repairing electronic gadgets. Figure 1.36 shows a home-made breakout box that I constructed many years ago. There are plenty of ready-made units available if you do not fancy the do-it-yourself approach, but these tend to be quite expensive. A ready-made unit is probably not a practical proposition if you only have infrequent serial interfacing problems to sort out.

Another option is to use a test meter to check the voltages. It is not necessary to have an expensive test meter for simple voltage checks of the type involved here. The most basic of analogue or digital instruments

will tell you what you need to know. A digital meter (Figure 1.38) is the easier to use in the present context, where positive and negative voltages are involved. It will measure voltages of either polarity, with the polarity being shown on the display. An analogue meter (Figure 1.37) probably represents the cheaper choice, although the cost of digital test meters has been steadily reducing in recent years.

Fig.1.38 A digital test meter is ideal for testing cables and serial ports

An analogue meter will only measure voltages of the correct polarity, which makes it a bit awkward to use in the current context. The usual ploy is to set it to a high voltage range when making tests on serial ports. A high voltage range does not give good accuracy when measuring low potentials of around 12 volts, but accuracy is not really of any interest in the current application. You simply need to know if each output is at around +12 volts, –12 volts, or at ground potential (0 volts).

If the meter's pointer moves slightly forwards, the test point is at +12 volts. If it moves in the reverse direction, the test point is at –12 volts. Although the meter is being fed with a voltage of the wrong polarity, the deflection of the meter will be too small to cause any damage, even after many tests have been made. A lack of movement from the pointer means that the test point either is at 0 volts or not connected to anything at all.

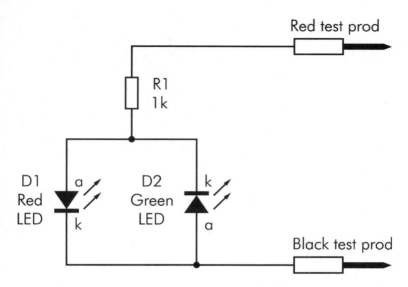

Fig.1.39 The circuit diagram for the simple voltage checker

Of course, all voltages are measured relative to ground, and the negative test prod should therefore be connected to the signal ground pin of the port.

A range of test meters should be available from any electronic component store. These days most do-it-yourself superstores sell two or three test meters including a choice of analogue or digital instruments.

Seeing the light

With a little do-it-yourself it is possible to make a simple tester that shows the state of RS232C lines using a couple of light emitting diodes (LEDs). The circuit diagram for the tester is shown in Figure 1.39. A LED is a true diode, and unlike a filament bulb it will only light up if it is fed with a DC supply of the correct polarity. This property is used here to have one or other of the LEDs switch on, depending on the polarity of the input voltage. In use, the black test prod is connected to the signal ground pin and the red test prod is connected to the test point. With a +12 volt input signal it is red LED D1 that conducts and lights up, while green

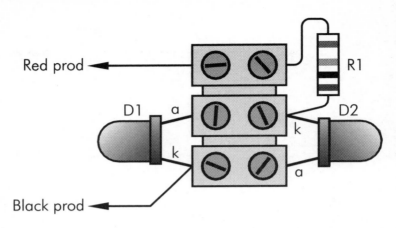

*Fig.1.40 The three components can be mounted on a 3-way
            connector block*

LED D2 remains switched off. With a –12 volt input level the roles are
reversed, with green LED D2 switching on and D1 failing to light up.

The current limiting circuit at each RS232C output should prevent the
LEDs from passing excessive currents. However, it is better to play safe
and include a resistor (R1) to ensure that an excessive current can not
flow. If there should happen to be a supply output on one of the port's
terminals, this resistor will ensure that one of the LEDs does not go up in
the proverbial "puff of smoke". Although the maximum current available
from an RS232C output is quite low, it is more than adequate to cause a
modern LED to light up quite brightly.

It should not be difficult to build the tester on a small circuit board, or a
connector block can be used if you wish to avoid soldering. A small
block of the type used for lighting circuits is more than adequate for this
application. A suitable connector block, together with the other parts,
should be available from a large electronic component store. Connector
blocks are also sold by do-it-yourself superstores. These blocks are
usually sold in 12-way strips, but only a 3-way block is needed here. A
12-way type is easily cut down to size using a sharp modelling knife.
There is no need to use fancy LEDs for D1 and D2, and "bog standard"
5-millimetre diameter components are perfectly adequate. The power
rating of resistor R1 is unimportant, and any type having a rating of 0.25
watts (250 milliwatts) or more will suffice.

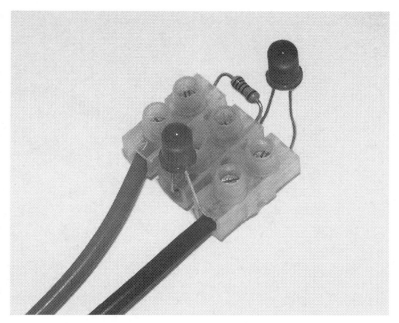

Fig.1.41 The completed connector block assembly

The wiring is shown in Figure 1.40, while Figures 1.41, 1.42 and 1.43 show three views of the finished tester. The cathode (k) lead of an LED is normally indicated by having that lead slightly shorter than the anode (a) lead. Many LEDs also have the case slightly flattened next to the cathode lead. Make sure both LEDs are connected the right way around, or the unit will give misleading results.

In use

With some form of tester you are not reduced to "fumbling in the dark", and can instead work out a sensible strategy to get the port outputting data. Start by checking the state of each handshake output on both ports. You are looking for outputs that are at the +12-volt "on" state so that they can be used to hold handshake inputs of the troublesome port at the "on" state. If the port that is refusing to output data is only being used as an output, its own handshake outputs are probably the best option. They should not be set to the "off" state, because the port is not receiving any data that will fill the receiver buffer.

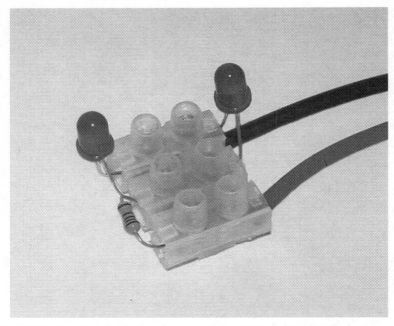

Fig.1.42 Another view of the components on the connector block

Try connecting each handshake and status input to an output in the "on" state, in turn, to see if the port can be coaxed into sending data. This will not always be successful, and it may be necessary to have two or more of these inputs at the "on" state before data is transmitted. These are the handshake and status inputs, and therefore the ones that are likely to be causing the problem:

Clear to send (8, 5)

Data set ready (6, 6)

Carrier detect (1, 8)

Ring indicator (9, 22)

Each pair of numbers in parentheses is the pin number for a 9-pin PC serial port followed by the pin number for a standard 25-pin serial port. The inputs that are most likely to cause problems are clear to send and data set ready. One or both of these will be used as the main handshake

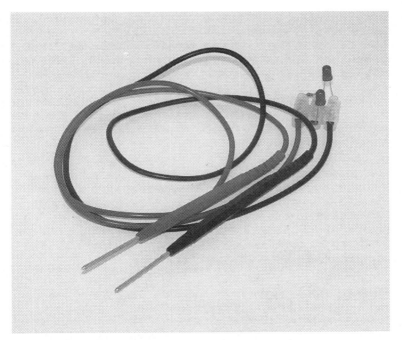

Fig.1.43 The finished tester, complete with test prods

line or lines, and no data will be sent unless one or both are set to the "on" state. Even where the application does not warrant handshaking, it is possible that the port will not send any data unless these lines are taken to the "on" state. You know that handshaking is not required, but the software controlling the port may not, and could be looking for the appropriate input signals.

Normally the clear to send and data set ready terminals are respectively coupled to the request to send and data terminal ready outputs of the other port. These connections are often omitted when handshaking is not needed, and a simply three-wire connection is used. If this results in a lack of activity from one or other of the ports, adding the missing connections is one possible solution to the problem. However, this means switching to a 5-way cable where the two additional connecting wires will not do anything useful. Taking the clear to send and data set ready inputs to +12 volts is all that is needed.

The easy way to do this is to use an output of the same port to provide the "on" signal. There are only two handshake outputs and no status outputs, so it is a matter of using either the data terminal ready or request to send output. If the system can genuinely operate without handshaking, both of these should be permanently at +12 volts. Where possible, check that the outputs are at the "on" state. Both of these outputs are implemented on the vast majority of serial ports, but it is possible that one or other of them will be absent. Where they are both present and at the appropriate voltage, add a link between the clear to send and request to send terminals of the port.

Then add a link between the data terminal ready and data set ready lines. If only one handshake output is at the "on" level, then connecting both handshake inputs to that terminal should give the desired result. It is worth checking the normally unused pins of a 25-pin serial port to see if any of these are used as a +12-volt supply output. Pins 9 and 10 are the most likely to be used in this way. If a +12-volt supply is available, connecting the handshake inputs to this terminal is the most reliable way of ensuring that they stay in the "on" state.

Output detection

If connecting the handshake inputs to the "on" state genuinely does not produce any output, it is unlikely that the problem is anything to do with the cabling. Either the port hardware is faulty, or (more probably) there is a problem with the software that is driving the port. How do you ascertain whether the port is producing an output signal? A lack of response from the receiving device could be due to a broken data lead in the connecting cable or a fault in the receiving device. Unless you have some form of tester there is no way of telling whether the port is producing any data.

Ideally an oscilloscope would be used to check the transmit data line of the port to see if there is any activity from it. Assuming you do not have access to this type of equipment, a test meter should give a rough indication of what is going on. Under standby conditions the transmit data line should be at −12 volts, and it will rapidly change between −12 and +12 volts when data is being transmitted. The voltage changes when data is being transmitted are far too rapid for a test meter to follow. Analogue test meters and most digital types will read the average output voltage. A few digital types seem to read whatever the test voltage happened to be at the instant it was sampled.

The average voltage will be something close to zero, with the +12 and –12-volt pulses more or less cancelling one another out. With the sampling method a series of rather random looking test voltages will probably be produced. The exact readings obtained are not relevant. What you are looking for is a change from a steady reading of about –12 volts to a different reading or readings when data is transmitted.

The simple LED tester described previously is actually better than a test meter for this type of checking. Under standby conditions the green LED (D2) should switch on to indicate that the output is at the "off" (–12 volt) level. The two LEDs should flash on and off when data is transmitted, but the flash rate will be so high that it will not be perceivable by the human eye. Instead, both LEDs will appear to be switched on continuously, albeit at less than normal brightness. With most test meters there is no clear differentiation between a low voltage and an output that is rapidly switching between the "on" and "off" states. Both conditions produce a low voltage reading. The LED tester clearly differentiates between the two. Neither LED lights up with a low test voltage, while both LEDs appear to light continuously when a pulsing output is tested.

It is perhaps worth mentioning that the logic testers sold by most electronic component shops may seem to be ideal for testing RS232C interfaces, but virtually all of them are unsuitable for this application. Firstly, most of these gadgets do not have a built in power source, and must be powered from the circuit under test. No power source is available from most RS232C ports. Secondly, logic testers are only designed for use with normal logic signals. Most logic testers have protection circuits at their inputs, but there is a slight risk of the voltages used by RS232C ports causing damage. Do not use a device of this type for testing serial ports unless the instruction manual specifically states that it is safe to do so. A simple LED tester of the type described previously is a better choice for this type of testing.

2. Uncontrolled data

Coaxing data from a serial port can be a problem, but the more common cause of problems is a lack of flow control. In other words, the data just keeps on flowing with the handshake lines having no effect. The most common cause of this problem is the use of a simple three-wire connection that does not implement the handshake lines. This often occurs because someone has purchased a serial cable having the right connectors, not realising that there are various ways in which the two connectors can be linked. In other cases, the user buys a simple cable under the impression that no hardware handshaking is required, when it is in fact needed in order to obtain reliable results.

It is usually pretty obvious when there is a problem with the handshaking. With a printer for example, things start out correctly but start to go badly wrong after the first page or two. The printing is correct initially because the printer's buffer is able to store the data that can not be printed immediately. Eventually the buffer becomes full and the printer tells the PC to stop sending data. If the computer continues to transmit data, it becomes inevitable that some or all of that data will be lost. Either the data already in the buffer must be overwritten by the new stuff, or the newly arriving data must be discarded rather than being added to the buffer. In most cases the existing data is retained in the buffer and anything that can not be accommodated by the buffer is discarded.

The initial data in the buffer is therefore printed out properly, but much of what follows is simply lost. If the printer is being fed with ASCII characters this results in a large part of the document being lost, but anything that does make it into the buffer will be printed out. These days most printers do not deal in simple ASCII characters, but instead print out complex bitmaps, etc. This tends to give rather unpredictable results once the initial contents of the buffer have been printed. Many printers seem to spew out numerous blank or largely blank pages. With others, you get the normal output initially followed by what is often just a single page of garbage.

In cases where the printer or other device just produces garbage right from the start, it is unlikely that the problem is due to a lack of proper handshaking. It is far more likely that there is a mismatch in the word format and (or) the baud rate, and it is a good idea to check these points first. With luck, the receiving device will have error lights or even a liquid crystal display that gives some indication of what is going wrong. A light marked "error" switching on is not much help, but an error message such as "buffer overrun" makes it clear what is going wrong. In this example, the buffer is not able to accommodate all the data that is being received, and the problem is clearly due to a lack of effective handshaking. With a message such as "parity error" or "framing error", it is far more likely that the problem is related to the baud rate or word format.

Where the problem does definitely seem to be due to a lack of effective hardware handshaking, one possible solution to the problem is to try using software handshaking. There is a big advantage to this approach if the link is being provided by a three-wire cable. Using hardware handshaking will require the use of a new cable having more wires, whereas a basic three-wire link should be adequate for software handshaking. Apart from the cost of buying some new multi-way cable, using software handshaking could bypass a lot of hassle.

The drawback of the software method is that it can only be used when it is available at both ends of the link. It is available using any modern version of Windows, but was not properly supported in MS/DOS and early versions of Windows. However, some programs implement their own version of software handshaking even if it is not implemented by the operating system. A fair proportion of peripherals support software handshaking, including most printers that sport a serial port. I have encountered some peripherals that could only be used successfully with software handshaking, so with troublesome equipment it is probably worth trying this method sooner rather than later. The "in and outs" of software handshaking are covered later in this chapter.

Hardware control

If you wish to go ahead with hardware handshaking and only have a three-wire link at present, the first step is to replace the cable with one that implements at least basic handshaking. This means a minimum of cross coupling of the request to send and clear to send lines, and the data set ready and data terminal ready lines. Where this does not give satisfactory results, try the methods of interconnection suggested previously for null modem leads. Where the standard methods do not give the desired result, it is a matter of trying everything in the hope of success, or adopting a more methodic approach.

With the methodic approach, the first thing you need to discover is how the flow of data from the output port is controlled. In other words, which handshake input or inputs are responsible for actually switching the flow of data on and off? There are four handshake and status inputs, any of which could be involved in flow of data from the port. These were listed previously, but for the sake of convenience they are listed again here.

Clear to send (8, 5)

Data set ready (6, 6)

Carrier detect (1, 8)

Ring indicator (9, 22)

As before, the numbers in brackets show the pin numbers for a 9-pin PC serial port first followed by the pin numbers for standard 25-pin RS232C ports.

With all four inputs taken to the "on" state the port should output data continuously until the complete document (or whatever) has been sent. Monitor the transmit data output and try taking each of the inputs to the "off" (–12-volt) state to see if this shuts off the flow of data. One slight complication here is that an output at –12 volts is required, and it is possible that none of the handshake outputs of the port will oblige with a suitable signal. With most ports, connecting an input to ground is sufficient to give an "off" state, so it is worth trying this method first. If this does not work, the transmit data output of the other port should go to the "off" state if no data is being transmitted. One of the handshake outputs of the other port might also provide a suitable voltage.

In theory, it should be possible to halt the flow of data by taking one of the handshake inputs to the "off" state. The most likely candidate is the clear to send input, but with an awkward port it could be one of the others. You may find that more than one of the inputs can be used to halt the flow of data. With a really awkward port you might find that two of the inputs must be taken to –12 volts in order to halt the flow of data. Having determined what lines or combination of lines can switch off the data flow, write down your findings so that any confusion is avoided later when you wire the custom serial cable for the link.

The testing now moves to the other end of the link, and the next step is to find the handshake output on the receiving device that is used to indicate that a hold-off is required. This is a matter of feeding data into the port and monitoring the two handshake outputs to see what happens when the receiver buffer becomes full. The handshake outputs are the data terminal ready and request to send outputs. You are looking for a change on these outputs that can be used to halt the flow of data from the other port. For example, suppose the data terminal ready output goes "off" when the buffer is full and that taking the clear to send input of the other port "off" halts the flow of data. A link from one to the other should provide successful handshaking.

It should only need one connection from the receiving device to the transmitting one in order to provide effective handshaking. Of course, this assumes that the system is used for half duplex operation. Full duplex operation, with communications in two directions, requires separate handshaking for each data link. The same testing procedures can be used to devise a suitable handshake implementation for communications in the second direction.

Other facilities

The peripheral device may use the handshake lines and the status outputs to implement additional features, such as indicating that a printer is out of paper. The instruction manual for the peripheral should really give details of how any special features of this type are handled by the serial interface, complete with connection details for a suitable serial cable. Unfortunately, details of the way in which the serial port is utilised are often very skimpy or even completely lacking. If a custom serial cable is not included with the peripheral, it is worth checking to see if it is available as an optional extra. Where cables of this type are available they can be difficult to obtain and quite expensive, but if you can locate one it is probably worthwhile buying it. The manufacturer's custom serial cable should provide hassle-free connection to your PC.

If a suitable ready-made cable is not available and the instruction manual is of little help, you may well find that the peripheral is perfectly usable without the added facilities that are available. In the early days of computing, most printers worked perfectly well using links to the computers that were very basic. Most of the "frills" provided by modern printers and printer drivers are of limited practical value.

Where it is important to implement the additional facilities, it is a matter of doing some further tests to see how the system operates. For instance, suppose that the printer uses a handshake output to indicate that it is out of paper. Checking the states on the handshake outputs with the printer loaded with paper and then empty should show which output is being used. If the request to send output is already being used for hardware handshaking, the data terminal ready output is the only one available for this type of thing. It is then a matter of connecting the appropriate output to each spare input of the PC's serial port, in turn, to see which one provides the correct response from the PC.

3. Missing characters

The third type of problem encountered with serial interfaces is similar to the lack of flow control described previously, but it is less severe. When outputting simple ASCII text it may appear at first as though everything is working fine. However, on closer examination it becomes clear that there is an occasional missing character, or perhaps a small group of missing characters. With other types of printing the errors will probably be more obvious, but the printed pages will usually be largely complete. This contrasts with results when there is a complete lack of flow control, and many of the pages are totally absent.

The missing characters are produced by the handshaking operating too slowly. Typically, the receiving device waits until its buffer is full and then sets the handshake output to indicate that a hold-off is required. However, by then the sending device may have started sending the next byte of data, and having started it will finish sending that byte. The sending device may have another byte in its transmission buffer, and it may even send that before responding to the signal from the handshake line.

This type of problem is difficult to deal with because there is a fundamental flaw in the system. It may not be possible to obtain satisfactory results using the two items of equipment concerned. There is a possible workaround the problem, which is to use a lower baud rate. This generally slows things down, and it might enable the handshaking to operate before transmission of a new byte of data is commenced. In practice, even if it does provide the desired result, the baud rate might have to be reduced to the point where the link is so slow as to be of little practical value.

Another possibility is to use software handshaking, if this option is available. There is no guarantee that software handshaking will work any better than the hardware variety. Having made a mess of the hardware version of handshaking, the designer may well have repeated his or her error in the software implementation. However, in practice it is often the case that software handshaking will work perfectly well with equipment that refuses to operate properly using the hardware variety. It is certainly better to give software handshaking a chance, rather than pressing on with a poorly implemented hardware version that will probably never work perfectly.

Handshake selection

If you decide to use software handshaking, how do you go about implementing it on your computer and peripheral? Selecting the handshaking method under Windows 9x is easy, but the route to the window that controls this setting is not as short as it might be. A computer running Windows ME is used to illustrate this example, but things are much the same using any version of Windows 95 or 98. The first task is to launch the Windows Control Panel. One way of doing this is to select Settings from the Start menu, followed by Control Panel from the submenu that appears. If you have the My Computer icon on the Windows desktop,

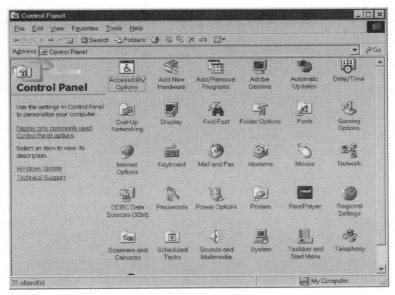

Fig.1.44 The Windows Control Panel

double-click on this and then on the Control Panel icon or menu entry. Either way, a window something like the one shown in Figure 1.44 will appear.

The exact appearance will depend on the set-up of your PC, but there should always be an icon or a menu entry called System. Double clicking on this should bring up the System Properties window, which will probably default to the General section (Figure 1.45). This provides some basic information about the version of Windows that you are using and the computer's hardware. Operating the Device Manager tab produces the section that gives access to the hardware settings (Figure 1.46). The various categories listed here cover virtually all the internal hardware. Additionally, some external peripherals such modems as may be included.

In this case it is the Ports section that is of interest, and double clicking on its entry will expand it to show the standard ports that are installed on the PC (Figure 1.47). Do not worry if some of the PC's ports are not included in the list. Normally it is only the serial and parallel ports that are listed here. Other ports such as game and USB types either have their own entry or are grouped with other hardware. Game and MIDI

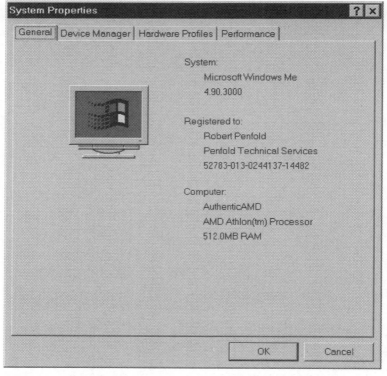

Fig.1.45 The General section of the System Properties window

ports for example, are usually grouped with the sound system, because in many PCs they are part of the soundcard. The PC used in this example has the standard complement of two serial ports and one parallel type.

Double clicking on an entry for a port will produce its properties window. Figure 1.48 shows the property window for serial port 2 (COM2), but the one for serial port 1 (COM1) is essentially the same. Initially the General section is shown, and this should confirm that the port is present and working properly. It is the Port Settings section that is required in this case, and operating the appropriate tab should produce something like Figure 1.48. The Flow Control menu near the bottom of the screen offers three options, which are Xon/Xoff, Hardware, and None. As explained previously, Xon/Xoff is an alternative name for software handshaking,

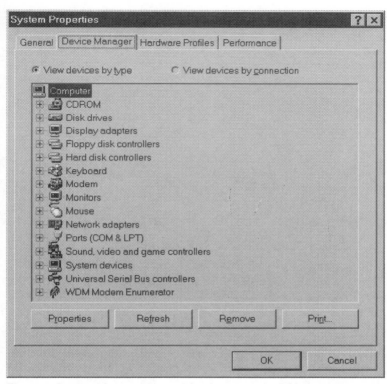

Fig.1.46 Device Manager has entries for most of a PC's hardware and some peripheral devices

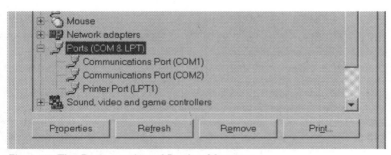

Fig.1.47 The Ports section of Device Manager

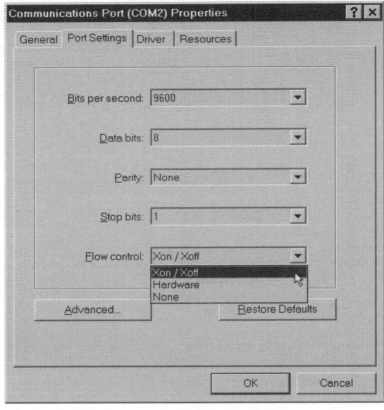

Fig.1.48 Selecting the required method of flow control

and is the one that should be selected if you wish to use this method of flow control.

Obviously, the Hardware option is chosen when hardware handshaking is to be used, and the None option is used where both the peripheral and the PC can handle a continuous flow of data. It is essential that the None option is selected when a simple three-wire link is used. With either of the other two options, the PC would look for handshake signals that the peripheral would not supply. This would probably result in the PC refusing to send any data from the port, because it would not be getting a signal from the peripheral to indicate that it was ready to receive

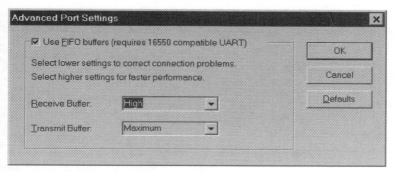

Fig.1.49 The buffers sizes can be altered

data. Selecting hardware handshaking when the software variety is needed, or vice versa, is likely to have the same result.

If there are problems with flow control it is worth operating the Advanced button, which brings up a window like the one of Figure 1.49. This provides some basic control over the transmitter and receiver buffers. FIFO incidentally, stands for "first in first out". Each menu gives the option of four buffer sizes. Normally a large buffer is used since this helps to give fast data transfers, but a smaller buffer size can sometimes cure flow control problems. However, where the problem is due to poor design at the peripheral end of the system, tweaking the PC's serial port is unlikely to eliminate the problem.

Peripheral setting

Setting the handshake method on the peripheral is something that will vary considerably from one device to another. With something like a laser printer, there may well be a liquid crystal display, pushbuttons, and a menu system to select the required port settings. Many of these menu systems are quite involved, so life is much easier if you have the instruction manual. Without one you may still be able to find the required settings by methodically searching the menu system.

With other units there are DIP-switches to select the port settings. A DIP-switch is simply a bank of miniature switches (Figure 1.50). The switches are set to the correct combination of "on" and "off" settings for the particular set-up you require. With some gadgets there are only a few of these switches, while with others there can be several banks of them. I have seen some printers where the DIP-switches run virtually the full

Fig.1.50   An 8-way DIP-switch

width of the unit, with literally dozens of switches covering a wide range of settings. Whether the unit you are using has a few switches or dozens, there is little chance of altering the set-up successfully unless you have the instruction manual. The only exception is where the circuit board has markings next to the switches that shows their functions. A variation on this scheme of things is to have a diagram somewhere inside the printer, often on a lift-up cover that shows the functions of the switches.

If you can not find the instruction manual and there is no built-in help available, it is worth trying the manufacturers web site. Many manufacturers now place downloadable versions of instruction manuals on their web sites, or failing that, there may be a section of the site devoted to things like DIP-switch settings. It is also worth looking at the FAQ (frequently asked questions) section, which now seem to be a feature of practically every equipment makers web site. It is unlikely that you will be the only user experiencing set-up problems, and there may well be something of use in this section of the site.

Switch confusion

It is necessary to take due care when dealing with DIP-switches, because the switch diagrams can be ambiguous. In the example of Figure 1.51, if the black rectangles are taken to represent to miniature control knobs, then the switch has these settings:

Switch no.	1	2	3	4	5	6	7	8
Setting	On	Off	On	On	On	Off	Off	Off

On the other hand, if the pale grey rectangles represent the control knobs, the DIP-switch has these settings:

Switch no.	1	2	3	4	5	6	7	8
Setting	Off	On	Off	Off	Off	On	On	On

Where the diagrams are a bit ambiguous there might be a chart that gives details of the switch settings in a more certain fashion. Sometimes there is an additional diagram that clarifies matters. The diagram of Figure 1.52 for example, makes it clear that the black rectangles represent the miniature control knobs. With something like serial port settings,

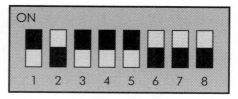

Fig.1.51 A typical DIP-switch diagram

there is little prospect of damaging anything if the settings are wrong. The equipment will simply fail to work properly until the settings are corrected. Consequently, where there is no other option available you can simply try one interpretation and then test the equipment to see if it functions correctly. If it does not, try the other interpretation of the switch settings.

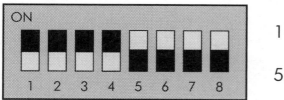

1 to 4 = ON

5 to 7 = OFF

Fig.1.52 A diagram such as this clears up any confusion over DIP-switch settings

Jumpers

There is an alternative to DIP-switches in the form of jumpers. These seem to be less used than was once the case, but they are still to be found on PC expansion cards, including those that provide additional ports. They may still be found on some peripheral devices. When a jumper is placed onto a pair of metal pins it places a short-circuit across them. Sometimes there are just two pins, and the jumper is either placed over the pins or omitted. In practice, the jumper is usually placed onto one pin but not the other if the short-circuit is not required. This leaves the pins unconnected, but the jumper is left in the equipment where it will not become mislaid or even get thrown away. An alternative method of using jumpers is to have three pins, with the jumper used to link the

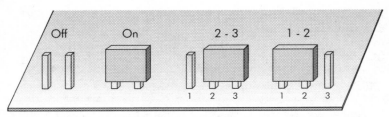

Fig.1.53 Jumpers can be used in conjunction with two or three pins

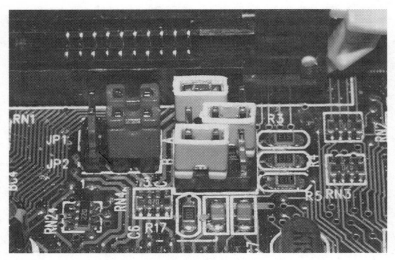

Fig.1.54 Two sets of jumpers on a circuit board

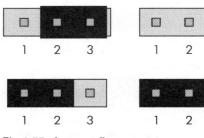

Fig.1.55 Jumper diagrams can be confusing

central pin and one or other of the other two. Both methods of using jumpers are illustrated in Figure 1.53, and Figure 1.54 shows two small blocks of pins complete with some jumpers.

Diagrams showing how to configure jumpers, like those for DIP-switches, can be a bit ambiguous. In the example of Figure 1.55 there is little doubt

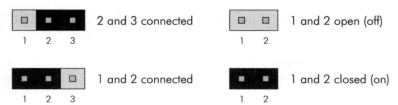

Fig.1.56 There is often an explanatory diagram for the jumper setting diagrams

about the settings of the jumpers on the sets of three pins, but the settings for pairs of pins are less clear. Does the black fill indicate that the jumper is present or omitted. With luck, there will be an additional diagram (Figure 1.56) or some notes that help to clarify matters. Again, if there is no other option it might be a matter of using trial and error.

Baud rate, etc.

Baud rates and word formats are not necessarily subjects you will need to get involved with when dealing with serial ports. Some equipment is supplied complete with a device drivers disc that sets up the serial port to suit the hardware connected to it. Some devices actually use the serial port in a non-standard fashion, and things like the baud rate and word format are then irrelevant. The software "does its own thing" with the port, and any adjustment to the port settings that you may make will not affect the interfacing to the peripheral. However, with a lot of serial interfacing it is still necessary to make sure that the receiving device has suitable settings, and that those on the PC precisely match them.

It is not essential to understand how a serial interface operates in order to set it up correctly. Provided both ends of the system have the same settings, everything should work perfectly well. On the other hand, when sorting out problems it is definitely an advantage if you have at least a basic understanding of what is going on. You may prefer to skip this next section, but the basics of serial interfacing and the terminology used are not difficult to grasp.

Bit-by-bit

A serial interface sends all eight bits of data over a single line, and it must therefore send bits one at a time. This is the reason that serial interfaces tend to be relatively slow. A standard parallel interface transfers whole bytes (sets of eight bits) at a time, and there are other parallel interfaces that send two or even four bits at a time. A serial interface literally transfers data on a bit-by-bit basis. As pointed out previously, an RS232C port has provision for a clock signal to synchronise the sending and receiving devices, but in practice this method is little used. It is not used with PC serial ports at all.

A PC serial interface is asynchronous, which means that there are no additional connecting wires to carry any form of synchronisation signal. Of course, the transmitting and receiving circuits must be kept correctly synchronised somehow. Synchronisation is achieved by using standard transmission rates and sending additional bits with each byte of data.

The two example waveforms of Figure 1.57 show how this system operates. As pointed out previously, the signal voltages are not at any form of standard 5-volt logic levels, but are instead at plus and minus 12 volts. The actual voltages can be anything from about plus and minus 3 volts when loaded and used with a long cable, to about plus and minus 24 volts direct at the pins of the port and unloaded. It pays to bear this point in mind when making voltage checks on RS232C ports. Serial interface chips do actually operate at normal logic levels, but they interface to the RS232C connector via special line drivers and receivers. These provide level shifting so that the interface operates at the correct voltage levels, and they also provide an inversion. Hence positive and negative voltages respectively represent logic 0 and logic 1, which can be a little confusing if you are used to working with 5-volt logic levels. These use 0 volts and a positive voltage to respectively represent logic 0 and logic 1.

RS232C serial interfaces operate at a number of standard transmission rates, or baud rates as they are known. The baud rate is simply the number of bits sent per second if there is a continuous data stream. All the standard baud rates are listed here:

50	75
110	150
300	600
1200	2400
4800	9600
19200	

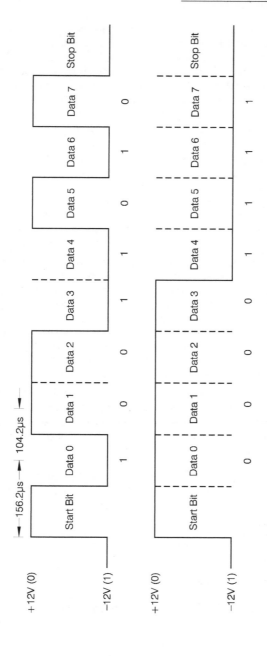

Fig. 1.57 Example waveforms and times for a serial signal

Note that PCs are often used at higher rates than 19200 baud, even though these are non-standard. In particular, a rate of 115200 baud is often used, and this is this highest rate available using a normal PC serial port. Some are supposed to be able to operate at 23400 baud or even higher, but I have never encountered an ordinary PC serial port that can handle these rates. There is good reason for using the highest possible rate, and that is simply a matter of speed. To be more precise, it is a general lack of speed that forces the use of speeds beyond the normal maximum.

Unless you need to use very long connecting cables, it is definitely advisable to use the highest baud rate that both ends of the system can accommodate. Including the synchronisation bits it typically requires 10 bits to send each byte, so even at 115200 baud the system can only transfer 11 to 12 kilobytes per second. At 50 baud the system can only handle about five bytes per second. Any reasonably competent typist can enter data via the keyboard at a faster rate than this!

The synchronisation signals are called stop and start bits, which are, as one would expect, sent immediately before and after the data bits. The start bit indicates to the receiving circuit that it must sample the signal line after a certain period, and this time is equal to the period of 1.5 bits. In the example of Figure 1.57 the transmission rate is 9600 baud, which works out at approximately 104.2 µs per bit (1000000 µs divided by 9600 baud equals 104.2 µs). Sampling the input line after 156.2 µs (1.5 bits) therefore results in the logic level being tested in the middle of the first bit. This is always the least significant bit (D0).

The input line is then tested every 104.2 µs until bits D1 through to D7 have been read into the receiver register. The data line is then returned to its standby state for 104.2 µs to produce the stop bit, which really just provides a guaranteed minimum gap from one byte of data to the next. This gives the receiving device time to deal with one byte of data before it starts to receive the next one. It also permits a simple form of error checking. If the input line is found to be at the +12 volt level during the stop bit, clearly an error has occurred. This is usually termed a framing error, and the usual cause is a mismatch in the sending and receiving baud rates.

Word formats

The serial signal in this example has one start bit, eight data bits, one stop bit, and no parity checking, which is probably the most common word format. However, there are many others in use, with anything from five to eight data bits, one, one and a half, or two stop bits, and odd or even parity checking. There is always a single start bit incidentally. In a PC context you will normally require eight-bit data transfers. Some early printers only used the basic ASCII character set, and could therefore be used with seven-bit word formats. These days it is very unlikely that you will encounter a printer of this type, and eight-bit operation is essential.

Normally it is better to use one rather than two stop bits because this gives a slightly faster maximum transfer rate. However, two stop bits can be used if the peripheral has minor flow control problems, or if it simply does not support single stop bit operation. Parity checking is a simple method of error checking that relies on an extra bit being sent at the end of bytes, where necessary, so that there is always an even or an odd number of bits. This method of checking is not very reliable since a double glitch can result in data being corrupted but the parity being left intact. It is little used in practice and I recommend avoiding word formats that involve either type of parity checking.

Serial interfaces have a reputation for being difficult to deal with, and this is at least partially due to the numerous baud rates and word formats in use. It is not simply enough to get the transmitting and receiving devices connected together correctly. Unless both ends of the system are set to use the same word format and baud rate it is unlikely that the system will function correctly. It will certainly fail to operate at all if the sending and receiving baud rates are different. You may get away with using the wrong number of stop bits or an incorrect parity setting, but at the very least a warning light will probably start flashing on the peripheral.

A great deal of time is probably wasted by people trying to sort out a problem with the cabling when it is actually a mismatch in the word format or baud rate that is the cause of the trouble. Always make sure that both ends of the system are set to the same word format and baud rate. Double check these settings rather than waste time trying to sort out cabling problems that might not exist. If there is a problem with the cables, the likely result is no transfer of data at all, or things working properly at first and then going completely wrong. With a baud rate or word format problem the data is likely to be corrupted from the first byte onwards. If the receiving device has status lights or some form of display, this is likely to report problems such as framing and overrun errors if there is a mismatch with the baud rate or word format. Problems with the cabling should not produce these types of error unless there is an intermittent fault.

Settings

Setting the word format and baud rate on the peripheral device relies on the same methods that are used for selecting the handshake method. In other words, a display plus a menu system, a bank of DIP-switches, or pins and jumpers. These methods were covered in some detail previously and will not be discussed again here.

On a PC these settings are handled using the same properties screen that is used for selecting the type of handshaking used. Launch the Windows Control Panel by selecting Settings from the Start menu, and then Control Panel from the submenu. Double-click on the Systems icon or menu entry to bring up the System Properties window, and then operate the Device Manager tab. Double-click on the Ports entry to expand it, and then double-click on the entry for the required port. This produces the properties window for the port, and selecting the Port Settings tab produces the control window for the port.

Baud rate

It is then a matter of using the menus to select the required settings. In most cases both the PC and the peripheral will be able to handle a range of baud rates and word formats, so how do you decide which one to use? As already pointed out, it is best to use the highest baud rate available. Even this will not produce a particularly fast transfer rate, but it will at least give the best rate that the equipment can handle. The baud rate menu (Figure 1.58) offers a full range of standard baud rates from 110 baud to 19200 baud.

There is also a range of faster rates, but some peripheral devices do not support anything beyond 19200 baud. Where higher rates are supported by the PC and the peripheral, bear in mind that most PC serial ports will not operate at a rate of more than 115200 baud. The baud rate menu does actually offer some higher rates, but these are non-operational with an ordinary PC serial port. There is no harm in trying one of these settings, but it is not worthwhile persisting with a high rate if it gives unreliable results or simply fails to work at all. Use the fastest rate that gives reliable data transfers, and resist the temptation to push the baud rate too high.

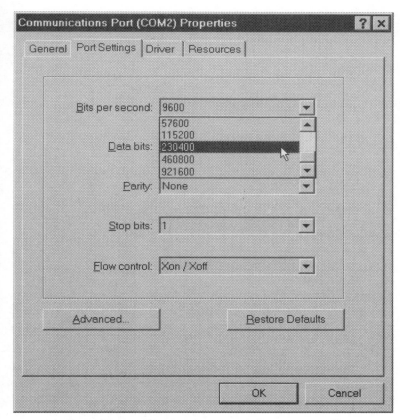

Fig.1.58 Not all the listed baud rates are usable with most PCs

Data bits

Anything from four to eight data bits can be selected, but as already pointed out, in a computer context it is normally eight-bit operation that is required. However, if you should need a seven-bit word format for use with an old ASCII printer, or five-bit operation for use with a Teletype system, the appropriate number of data bits can be set using this menu. I have never come across any equipment that uses four or six-bit data transfers, but they are there if some obscure item of equipment should require them.

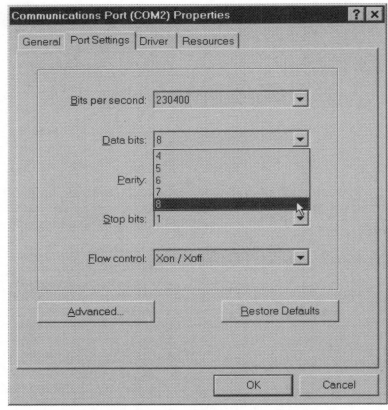

Fig.1.59   Only eight data bits are normally used with PCs

Parity

You do not really need parity checking in order to know whether the system is producing glitches. If the data is being corrupted, it will probably become all too apparent almost at once. Parity checking is of most use where there is a risk of the occasional glitch, and even one or two errors could have dire consequences. An obvious example is when printing out accounts, where one or two incorrect figures could have serious consequences. In practice, it is unusual for a system to operate with only one or two errors here and there. Mostly a data link will work reliably

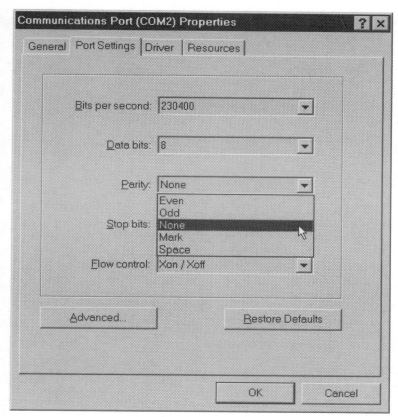

Fig.1.60 Several parity options are available

or it will produce a significant percentage of errors. Also, there is no guarantee that parity checking will detect every glitch, which greatly reduces its practical value.

Some peripherals insist on using parity checking, but with most it is optional or not implemented at all. Where there is no necessity to use parity checking it is probably best not to do so. If parity checking is used, it does not matter whether the odd or the even variety is selected. However, make quite sure that both devices use the same type of parity checking. The Windows parity menu (Figure 1.60) offers "Mark" and "Space" options. When transmitting, these set the parity bit at +12 volts

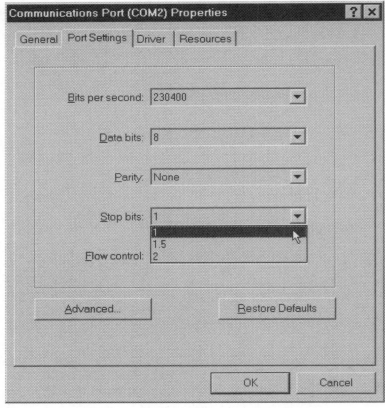

Fig.1.61 One stop bit potential gives the fastest transfer rates

or –12 volts, not at whatever state the parity process dictates. As far as I am aware, the only practical application of this is to deliberately generate parity errors so that the parity checking on the receiving device can be tested.

Stop bits

There are three options available from the Stop bits menu (Figure 1.61), which are 1, 1.5, and 2 stop bits. As pointed out previously, one stop bit has the advantage of giving slightly faster data transfers. Using two stop bits gives groups of 11 bits rather than 10 bits per byte of data, slowing things down by around 10 percent. Unless the peripheral device can only operate with two stop bits, or you are trying to cure minor flow control problems, always opt for one stop bit. The 1.5 stop bit option is only needed for a few specialised applications such as some Teletype systems.

Note that the options set via these menus are used for transmission and reception via that port. A PC serial port does not have the ability to use different baud rates, etc., for transmission and reception. Since very few applications require split operation this is not really a significant drawback. Most PCs have two serial ports as standard (COM1 and COM2). These have their own properties windows that are accessed via Device Manager. The two ports can therefore have different baud rates and word formats, and are totally independent. Any additional serial ports will have their own entries in Device Manager, and can also have different baud rates and word formats to the other serial ports.

The PC serial ports are clearly very versatile, and can accommodate virtually any standard baud rate or word format, including a number of old and obscure ones. Peripherals are not always as accommodating, and may have only a limited range of options available. I have encountered a few devices that had the serial port settings pre-set, with only a single word format and baud rate being available. If the peripheral is very restrictive, it is clearly a matter of setting the PC to suit the peripheral rather than the other way round.

Loop the loop

If you are in a position where the peripheral and cable do not work properly with one PC, but work fine when tried with another PC, it can be useful to check that the PC's serial port hardware is functioning correctly. Most general-purpose PC checking programs have sections that deal with the serial and parallel ports, and these can be very useful if you require confirmation that the port is faulty. These programs mostly offer two levels of testing.

The more superficial tests simply check that the appropriate port registers are present and behave as expected, but make no attempt to read or write data. If a port fails this type of test, or the checking software simply fails to find the port at all, there is almost certainly a major fault in the port hardware. However, with an integral port always double check that the port is switched on in the BIOS Setup program. If a port is switched off in the BIOS it is "invisible" to any software, and is effectively not there. Using the BIOS Setup program is covered in the next chapter.

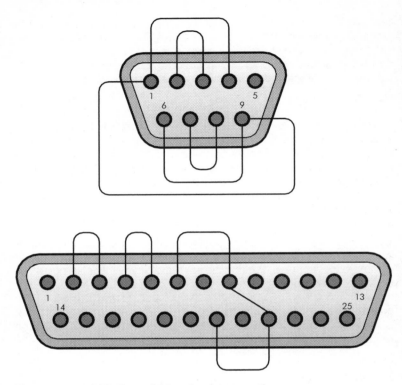

Fig.1.62 9 and 25-pin serial loopback connections

The more detailed tests change the states of some output lines and attempt to read the states of these via some input lines. This loopback testing as it is called, requires the appropriate connections across certain pins of the port. In some cases connections are needed from one port to another, but most testing of this type is carried out using just the port under test. The required connections vary somewhat from one test program to another, and the companies that produce diagnostics software can often supply matching loopback connectors. Details of the required interconnections should also be published in the manual for the program, and (or) on the software manufacturer's web site.

The loopback plugs illustrated in Figures 1.62 (serial) and 1.63 (parallel) work with the popular CheckIT program and some others. If you have a

Pin 1 to pin 13
Pin 2 to pin 15
Pin 10 to pin 16
Pin 11 to pin 17
Pin 12 to pin 14

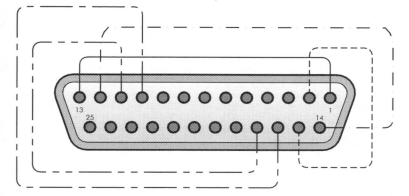

Fig.1.63 *Typical loopback connections for a PC parallel port*

Fig.1.64 *A home-made 9-pin serial loopback connector*

1   Serial port troubleshooting

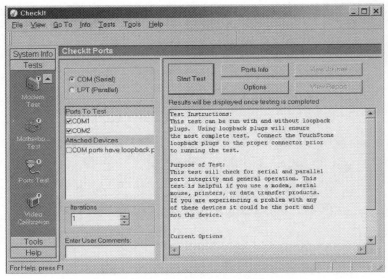

Fig.1.65 The port testing section of the CheckIT program

soldering iron, it is easy to make your own low cost loopback plugs. For a serial type you need a nine or 25-way female D connector, and for a parallel type a 25-way male D connector is needed. The links are easily added using multi-strand insulated connecting wire. Fix the connector to the worktop with Bostik Blu-Tack or something similar so that you do not have to chase the connector around the worktop while trying to make the connections! Figure 1.64 shows a completed nine-pin serial loopback connector.

Figure 1.65 shows the port testing section of the CheckIT program. The radio buttons enable the serial or parallel ports to be selected for testing. A checkbox gives the choice of testing with or without a loopback connector fitted. Of course, where a loopback connector is available it is better to select this option because it gives more comprehensive testing. A window giving a progress report appears once the testing is underway (Figure 1.66). A list of results is available once the testing has been completed (Figure 1.67), and the user is alerted by a warning message if any of the tests have been failed.

It is only fair to point out that this type of testing is not necessarily conclusive, even if the loopback option is used. With an RS232C port, it

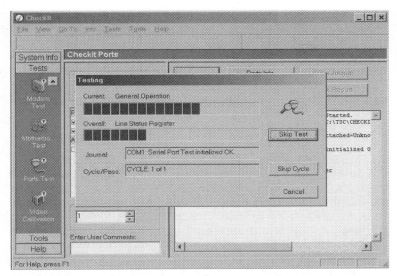

*Fig.1.66 Once testing is underway, the program gives a progress
report via a popup window*

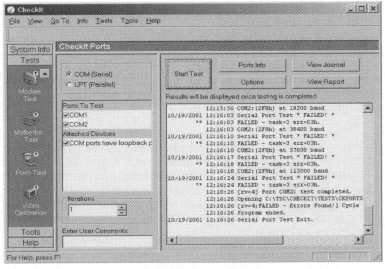

Fig.1.67 A list of results is provided once the testing is finished

is possible that conclusive results will be provided using the loopback option, because all or most of the input and output lines will be checked. The same is not true when testing a parallel port, where loopback testing usually omits checks on many of the lines. In particular, it seems to be normal for one data output to be tested, leaving the other seven untested. If one of these outputs is inoperative it will result in the port outputting garbage, but this will not be detected by the loopback testing.

Finally

Most aspects of serial port interfacing have been covered in this chapter, and the techniques described here are sufficient to get the vast majority of serial port peripherals working with a PC. Note that some of the general information on computer interfaces provided in chapter 2 applies to serial ports. In particular, the information about hardware conflicts, IRQs, and input/output addresses is applicable to serial ports. This section of chapter 2 should be consulted if you have problems with a serial port that worked perfectly until a new piece of hardware was added to the PC. This is probably the most common manifestation of a hardware conflict.

Points to remember

RS232C serial ports are relatively slow and awkward to use. Where there is the option of using a parallel port or a USB type instead, use the alternative port. It will almost certainly provide much better results and should be free of hassle.

Few items of hardware have a full implementation of an RS232C serial port. The slightly cut down version used on a PC is the nearest thing to a standard implementation. Some peripherals are equipped with extremely basic serial ports. This can lead to problems when you try to use a terminal of the peripheral's serial port that is not actually implemented. This is the cause of many serial port cabling problems.

Connecting a modem to a PC is usually hassle-free, because a DTE unit is being connected to a DCE type. RS232C serial interfaces are designed to be used in this way, with a communications device such as a modem. No cable trickery should be called for. A "straight" serial cable is required, and these are readily available.

Apart from modems, most serial port peripherals are DTE devices, like the PC itself. A null-modem cable is then needed, and this has cross-couplings that fool each unit into "thinking" that it is connected to a DCE device. There is no single cable and method of connection that suits all peripherals that have a DTE serial port. Some units will work perfectly with an "off the shelf" null-modem cable, but others require a custom cable.

Making your own cable is not difficult, but getting everything working perfectly can be very time consuming. If a serial port deviates too far from the accepted standards there is no guarantee that it can be made to work properly in conjunction with a PC.

If the link seems to work initially, perhaps with the first few pages from a printer being fine, but then everything goes haywire, there is probably a lack of effective handshaking. The peripheral's buffer becomes full, but it is unable to halt the flow of data from the PC. The buffer overflows and data is lost.

In most cases it is possible to sort out the hardware handshaking and get everything working properly. However, it might be quicker to try software (XON/XOFF) handshaking, which will usually work using a basic three-wire connection. Note that the cable must provide full-duplex operation, so that the peripheral can sent handshake messages to the PC.

When a PC's serial port fails to transmit any data at all, the PC is probably looking for the appropriate handshake signals, but is not receiving them. The settings for the port might be incorrect, but even using the right settings it is sometimes necessary to take some of the handshake inputs to the "on" state before anything will be sent. Note that this can be necessary even when no hardware handshaking is being used.

1   Serial port troubleshooting

If the data stream is largely correct, but the odd byte is missing here and there, the most likely cause is that the handshaking is working too slowly. There may be no effective solution to this problem. Try using a lower baud rate and (or) a word format that has two stop bits. Changing from hardware to software handshaking will often cure the problem.

Error messages such as "framing error" and "overrun error" are usually the result of an incorrect baud rate or word format. If the data is totally scrambled, it is more likely to be the baud rate that is wrong. Where the data is largely or totally intact, the word format is the likely cause of the errors. Note that a mismatch in the number of stop bits will often cause an error message, but it will not usually prevent the data from being decoded accurately. Other mismatches in the word formats are likely to produce numerous decoding errors.

Generally, it is best to opt for the highest baud rate that is supported by both the PC and the peripheral. This may still provide a relatively low data transfer rate. The properties window for a serial port usually offers baud rates well beyond the normal maximum of 19,200 baud. Bear in mind that most PC serial ports can not operate at rates beyond 115,200 baud, even if higher rates are offered in the properties window.

Parity checking is not guaranteed to detect all decoding errors, and it is normally just an unnecessary complication. It might be worth using it in situations where it is imperative to keep any errors to a minimum.

There are plenty of programs that will test a PC's hardware, including the standard ports. Where possible, use loopback testing because this is more thorough than the standard test procedures. It is not difficult to make loopback plugs if you are handy with a soldering iron.

Parallel ports, USB, etc.

Printer ports

A PC printer port is not just used with printers, and it used with a range of devices including scanners, external drives, and a range of specialist units. In view of its multipurpose capabilities, the alternative name of "parallel" port is perhaps more apt. Despite its versatility, the primary role remains that of a printer port, and most users will never use it for anything else. In common with serial ports, the parallel variety is due to be phased out in due course, with the USB taking over as the standard interface for PC peripherals. New PCs still have at least one parallel port as standard and additional ports can be provided by expansion cards. There are still plenty of devices on sale that can only be used with this type of port. Consequently, it is likely to be some time yet before serial or parallel ports disappear from the PC scene.

Printer connections

We will consider the parallel port in its intended role before moving on to its use as a general-purpose interface. A PC printer port uses a 25-way female D connector (Figure 2.1), which is easily distinguished from a 25-way serial port as the latter uses the male version of the connector. Most PC serial ports use a 9-pin connector these days, leaving no room for confusion. The connector at the printer end of the system is a 36-way Centronics type (Figure 2.2), and this type of port is often referred to as a "Centronics" port.

The pin functions at the PC end of the system are shown in Figure 2.3. D0 to D7 are the lines on which the data is sent, and with eight of them it is possible to send complete bytes of data at a time. This makes a parallel port potentially much faster than a normal serial port. In fact, a standard printer port can handle up to about 200,000 bytes per second,

Fig.2.1 The parallel port is the 25-way D connector

*Fig.2.2 The parallel port on a printer invariably has a 36-way
Centronics connector*

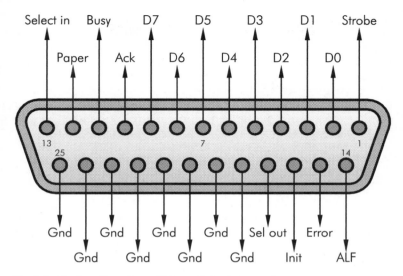

Fig.2.3 Pin functions for a PC parallel printer port

which is equivalent to a serial port operating at about 2,000,000-baud. Modern PCs have enhanced parallel ports that can operate at up to 2,000,000 bytes per second, which is equivalent to about 20,000,000 baud! Where possible, it is clearly better to use a parallel port rather than a serial type.

With standard parallel interfacing there is no equivalent to the baud rate of a serial interface. The Strobe terminal is an output that is normally high (logic 1 or +5 volts), and it is pulsed low (logic 0 or about 0 volts) each time fresh data is placed on the data lines. This is used to indicate to the receiving device that new data is available. The receiving device then places the byte of data in its buffer until it is ready to deal with it. This process is sometimes termed "grabbing a byte". A limit is set on the rate at which data can be sent, and this ensures that a new byte of data is not sent before the previous byte has been placed in the receiving unit's buffer. It is this factor that sets the 200,000 bytes per second limit, and it is up to the software in the PC to ensure that the maximum rate is not exceeded.

Handshaking

Although the electronics can keep up with 500,000 bytes per second, printers and most other peripheral devices can not manage a sustained rate at anything approaching this figure. Without some form of handshaking the buffer at the receiving device would soon become full and data would be lost. Since a normal parallel port provides communication in one direction, only hardware handshaking is applicable. For reasons I have never fully understood, there are two handshake terminals on a parallel port, and these are the Ack (Acknowledge) and Busy terminals. These are outputs on the printer and inputs on the PC parallel port.

The printer sets its Acknowledge output low when it is ready to receive data from the computer. The Busy line is set low by the printer when its buffer is full and it needs a halt in the flow of data. Both inputs are implemented by a PC printer port, and both outputs may be present and working on the printer, but only one or the other is needed to control the flow of data. These lines seem to have been used in different ways by various manufacturers over the years, and in the past it was sometimes necessary to experiment with these interconnections in order to obtain satisfactory results. I had one home computer where it was necessary to couple the Acknowledge output of the printer to the Busy input of the computer in order to obtain a properly controlled flow of data.

Probably the intended method of operation is to have a pulse on the Acknowledge line to indicate that the last byte of data has been received and processed, and that the next byte can be sent. The Acknowledge pulse is probably intended as a means of ensuring that data is not sent at too high a rate for the electronics in the printer to cope properly. If the electronics in the printer is not as nifty as it might be, this pulse can be extended in order to slow everything down. The Busy line is then used as the true handshake line that provides a hold-off when the printer's buffer is full.

In practice the Acknowledge line is sometimes ignored, which should not produce any problems provided the sending device does not send data at an excessive rate. There should be no problems when using a PC with any reasonably modern printer. The Acknowledge and Busy lines should be implemented properly at both ends of the system, and there should be a properly controlled flow of data provided they are linked together. If you are into "antique" computers or printers it might be necessary to experiment with the connections to these lines in order to get things working satisfactorily.

Pin functions

There are several additional inputs and outputs on the PC's parallel port that can provide additional features. For the record, this is a full list of the pin functions, with a brief explanation for each pin or group of pins.

Strobe (pin 1)

Pulsed low each time a new byte of data has been placed on the data lines. This indicates to the printer that fresh data is available.

D0 to D7 (pins 2 to 9)

Bytes of data are sent on these eight lines.

Acknowledge (pin 10)

Pulsed low by the printer to acknowledge receipt of the previous byte of data, and to indicate that the next byte can be sent. It is probably not intended as a true handshake line, but has sometimes been used in that way. The flow of data can be held off indefinitely by extending the Acknowledge pulse.

Busy (pin 11)

This line is set low by the printer to indicate that its buffer is full and that no more data must be sent until this line is returned to the high state. The Busy line is intended to operate as the main handshake line that controls the flow of data to the printer.

Paper (pin 12)

This line is known by various names such as "paper out" and "paper end". It is set high by the printer when it runs out of paper. Most Windows printer drivers will respond to this line by placing a warning message on the screen.

Select in (pin 13)

This line is set high by the printer to indicate that it is switched on and ready for use.

Auto line feed (pin 14)

The computer sets this line high to produce a line feed. Probably not of much use, if any, with modern printers.

Error (pin 15)

This input is set low by the printer when it detects some form of error. This usually means the paper has jammed, but it could be another error such as a lack of ink or toner powder. Most Windows printer drivers will produce a suitable onscreen message in response to a signal on this line.

Initialise (pin 16)

The computer sets this output low to initialise (reset) the printer. This takes the printer to its normal start-up state, removing any changes made to its settings since switch-on.

Select out (pin 17)

This is another output at the computer end of the link. The computer can set this line low in an attempt to activate the printer if it is not already receiving a high signal on the Select in line. Usually the computer will wait for a pre-set period for a response from the printer. If no response is received, the printer driver should display an onscreen message pointing out that the printer is not responding. A lack of response usually just means that you have forgotten to switch on the printer.

Ground (Pins 18 to 25)

These are all signal ground connections, and are usually in addition to a connection between the chassis of the two devices via the screen of the connecting lead. Using eight ground connections when one would suffice might seem like a case of overkill. However, with many printer leads a wire connected to ground is used between one data line and the next, and possibly between other lines as well. Having extra ground terminals at each end of the leads eases the problem of making connections to all these ground lines.

The point of the extra ground connections is to provide screening between the data lines. Parallel interfaces can handle fast signal transfers, but only over short distances. A normal printer cable is only about 1.5 to three metres in length. Even with quite short cables such as these, there can be major problems with capacitance in the cable coupling a signal from one line to another. This stray coupling is most likely to cause problems with the data and Strobe lines, but it has the potential to cause problems with any of the lines.

The screening provided by the additional ground lines should be sufficient to prevent significant coupling from one signal line to another. The cables

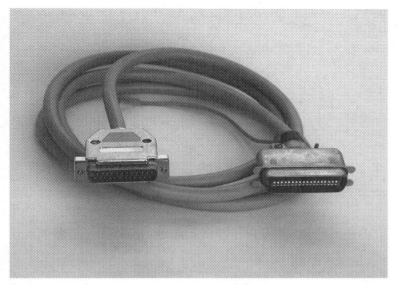

Fig.2.4 A PC printer lead is a standard item that is easy to obtain

still have to be relatively short, since the capacitance in the cable tends to slow the rate at which signals go from one logic level to another. With a long cable, the rate of change becomes too slow to give reliable operation. Special low capacitance printer cables having lengths of 10 metres or more are produced, but are quite expensive. They are also relatively difficult to obtain.

Old and new

There should be no need to make a custom cable if you simply need to connect a PC parallel port to a printer having a Centronics port. Despite the increasing use of USB ports, a PC printer lead (Figure 2.4) probably remains the most common form of PC data lead. PC printer leads of various lengths should be available from any computer store or at your local computer fair. Although most computer peripherals are supplied complete with data cables, it is very unusual for printers to be supplied with data cables. Most users deal with this by using their existing cable when they buy a new printer. This can eventually lead to difficulties. The obvious problem is that after many years of use it is quite likely that the old cable will degrade to some extent, possibly to the point where it fails to work properly.

Less obviously, older printer cables often have something less than a full set of interconnections. This does not matter when a PC is used with some printers, especially the older and simpler types. These printers usually rely on the data lines being present, together with the Strobe, Acknowledge, and Busy lines, but need little or nothing else apart from the Ground lines. Modern printers often require most or possibly all of the lines to be implemented. Without a full set of interconnections it becomes inevitable that errors will occur.

For example, with the Select in terminal of the PC's printer port left unconnected it will go permanently high or low. Either way, it will mislead the printer driver. If the Select in line goes high, the printer driver will work on the basis that the printer is always online, and will try to print to it even if it is switched off. With this line permanently low, the printer driver will "think" that the printer is always switched off and will never try to print to it. If you have this sort of printing problem and you are using an old cable, it would definitely be a good idea to try a new cable having the full set of interconnections.

Bi-directional

Before USB came along there was a problem for makers of PC peripherals if their gadgets required two-way communication with the computer. The obvious choice was an RS232C port, but even at high baud rates, this type of interface is far too slow for many purposes. There are other types of two-way interface that can be used, but these are not standard PC ports. They are practical propositions, but involve the added expense of an interface card for the PC. A parallel port offered a cheap alternative, but only if some means of using it for two-way communication could be found.

Initial attempts used the data lines, etc., to output data to the peripheral in the normal way. One or more of the status inputs (Error, Paper, and Select in) was used to input data. The problem with this method was that there were too few inputs to permit data to be read one byte at a time. Data was usually read using what was effectively a form of serial interfacing. This enabled data to be sent to the peripheral at a high rate, but the rate of transfer was much lower when data was sent from the peripheral to the PC.

Eventually the bi-directional printer port was devised, and virtually all PCs now have this type of parallel port. It is only older PCs that lack this facility, and in this context an older PC means anything prior to the arrival of the Pentium processor. Actually, it is not quite as clear cut as that and a few 80486 based PCs did have bi-directional printer ports. Most of the very early Pentium PCs lacked this facility. Bi-directional ports have their origins in the IBM PS/2 series of PCs, which were launched before the Pentium processor came along. It took some time for the idea to work its way into the PC "clones". Hence, there is no clearly defined point at which all new PCs had this feature.

Provided you are using a PC that has a clock speed of 200MHz or more it should certainly have a bi-directional printer port. Modern printer port cards also support bi-directional operation, but may not be usable in the most advanced modes due to a lack of proper support in the computer's BIOS program. Of course, older printer cards do not support any form of bi-directional operation. Where a parallel port card lacks switches or jumpers to set any bi-directional modes, it is reasonable to assume that the card lacks these modes.

With proper bi-directional operation the data lines default to operation as normal outputs, but under software control they can be switched to operate as inputs. This permits data to be written and read as complete bytes, offering high-speed data transfers in both directions. Some bi-directional operating modes permit data to be transferred at up to 2 megabytes per second, which is more than adequate for most purposes. In these high-speed modes the normal functions of the handshake and status lines are changed. Consequently, the enhanced modes can only be used with devices that are specially designed to support them.

Although bi-directional operation is possible, a port of this type is not strictly speaking a full duplex type. At any one time, the port can only input or output data, unlike a serial port, which can send and receive simultaneously via separate data lines. On the other hand, by alternating between sending and receiving it is possible to handle up to one megabyte per second in each direction. This still represents a very useful rate of transfer. In addition, many practical applications do not require data to be simultaneously sent and received.

Modes

Over the years, bi-directional printer ports have evolved, and new standards have been introduced. These are designed to give greater speed and versatility, but having more than one standard inevitably complicates matters. These are the available modes:

Normal/Standard

This mode is the original one, which operates the port as a straightforward printer type. Bi-directional operation is not supported when this mode is selected. This mode is not available with most modern PCs and printer cards. It is known by various names including Normal and Standard.

SPP

SPP stands for standard parallel port. Do not confuse this mode with the Standard/Normal one. Confusingly, a modern PC may have a Standard or Normal mode listed in its BIOS Setup program, and no SPP mode. This mode is then the SPP mode, even if it is not described as such. SPP is the standard bi-directional mode, and it seems to have little or no support from the BIOS program. The hardware and software designers are free to use the port in any way they think fit. In the SPP mode a port defaults to the output mode, and it is therefore usable as a normal printer port.

EPP

This is another bi-directional mode, but unlike the SPP mode, it seems to have a certain amount of support from the BIOS program. EPP stands for enhanced parallel port, or possibly extended parallel port. By either name, it offers exactly the same facilities.

ECP

ECP stands for enhanced capabilities port, and this is the most advanced mode, although in practice it seems to offer little more speed than the EPP mode. This mode has the ability to use DMA (direct memory access), which could give improved performance in some applications, but can also lead to complications such as hardware conflicts. The ECP standard has been tweaked a few times over the years, so there is now more than one standard. This is another possible cause of problems.

Apart from the data lines, the normal pin functions are abandoned when using the enhanced modes, and some are left unused. Fortunately, the user does not normally have to get involved in the technicalities of enhanced parallel ports. On the other hand, you can not simply connect your new peripheral to the PC and expect it to work flawlessly using the parallel port in one of these advanced modes. Unless your PC is quite old, it is unlikely that it will require any changes to its set-up in order to use the SPP mode. The EPP and ECP modes are a different proposition, and it is unlikely that the parallel port will default to either of these. There is no need to alter the mode setting unless the peripheral's instruction manual specifically states that the parallel port should be set to the EPP or ECP mode. It is not always essential to use an enhanced mode, but the instruction manual will often recommend using one or other of these modes. This is simply because devices like external CD-RW drives will often operate very much slower if the parallel port is not set to an enhanced mode. Therefore, if the parallel port and the peripheral support enhanced operation, it definitely makes sense to make the change.

Changing mode

Changing the mode of a built-in parallel port is achieved via the BIOS Setup program. With an expansion card, the mode is usually set via DIP-switches or jumpers. Whatever method is used, it is not a change that the support software for the peripheral device can make for you. The instruction manual for your PC should give details of how the mode of the parallel port can be changed.

Unfortunately, some manufacturers do not include this type of information because they prefer not to encourage users to tinker with their PCs. Other manufacturers simply provide some form of "Quick Start" guide plus any instruction manuals that came with the main components used in the PC. The manual for the motherboard should tell you what you need to know, but do not expect it to go into great detail. Most motherboard manuals are very brief and to the point, and in some cases there is a certain amount of pidgin English.

It is not usually too difficult to change the mode of a parallel port, even without any guidance from an instruction manual. The BIOS Setup program is normally entered during the initial checking routine that occurs just after the computer is switched on. It must be entered before the computer starts to boot into the operating system. By far the most common method of entry is to press the Del key, but several other keys or combinations of keys have been

Fig.2.5 Pressing the Del key is the normal way into the BIOS Setup program

used in the past, and no doubt some of these are still in use. Usually a message appears on the screen telling you which key to press (Figure 2.5). The BIOS can only be entered while this message is on the screen.

Operating the appropriate key or keys may produce an instant result, but with a modern PC it is likely that all or part of the checking process will be completed before the Setup program appears. A reluctance for the PC to switch over to the BIOS Setup program seems to be a common problem. If the PC simply goes straight on to the boot process, let it boot into the operating system and then restart the system so that you can try again. This time try repeatedly pressing the appropriate key until the computer switches to the BIOS Setup program.

BIOS?

Before looking at the BIOS Setup program, it would perhaps be as well to consider the function of the BIOS. BIOS is a acronym and it stands for basic input/out system. Its main function is to help the operating system handle the input and output devices, such as the drives, and ports, and also the memory circuits. It is a program, and it is stored in a ROM on the motherboard. These days the chip is usually quite small and often sports a holographic label to prove that it is the genuine article (Figure 2.6). Because the BIOS program is in a ROM on the motherboard, it can be run immediately at start-up without the need for any form of booting process. The BIOS program carries out the initial checks at switch-on and then initiates the booting process for the disc-based operating system.

The BIOS can provide software routines that help the operating system to utilise the hardware effectively, and it can also store information about the hardware for use by the operating system, and possibly other software. It is this second role that makes it necessary to have the Setup program. The BIOS can actually detect much of the system hardware and store the relevant technical information in memory. However, some parameters have to be set manually, such as the time and date, and the user may wish to override some of the default settings. The Setup program enables the user to control the settings that the BIOS stores away in its CMOS memory. A battery powers this memory when the PC is switched off, so its contents are available each time the PC is turned on. The BIOS ROM uses a different type of memory that retains its contents when the PC is switched off, but it does not require a backup battery.

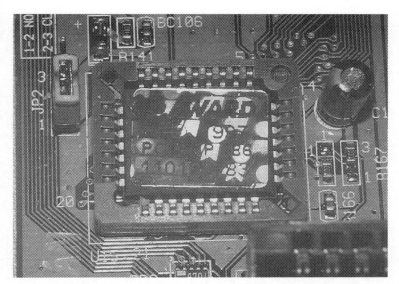

Fig.2.6 The BIOS Setup program is in a ROM chip on the motherboard

In the past, it was not normally necessary to use the BIOS Setup program unless an internal repair or upgrade was made, such as a change of hard disc or the addition of a DVD drive. These days the BIOS Setup program is a more common port of call because many ports and other facilities are now an integral part of the motherboard, rather than being provided by expansion cards. Using switches or jumpers to control things like the port settings is now quite rare, and the modern trend is to control as many parameters as possible via the BIOS. This probably helps to keep down costs, and it is certainly easier to alter settings via a program rather than trying to change switches or jumpers in inaccessible places deep inside the PC.

On the downside, the BIOS Setup program can be a bit intimidating. In the early PCs the BIOS was only used to store some basic information about the drives, the amount of memory fitted, the time and date, and a few other pieces of information. A modern BIOS contains hundreds of settings, many of which are highly technical and govern things like the timing of the memory circuits. The secret of success is to only alter the settings you understand, and to leave everything else unchanged. Under no circumstances start playing with settings that you do not understand. It is unlikely that unsuitable settings would damage any of the hardware,

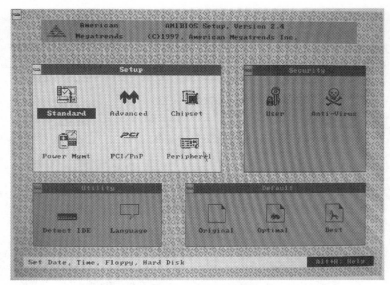

Fig.2.7 The AMI BIOS has a sort of basic WIMP environment

but this can not be totally ruled out. Inappropriate settings could certainly leave the computer in an unusable state, and it could take some time to sort everything out and get it working perfectly again.

Navigating the BIOS

There are several BIOS manufacturers, and their BIOS Setup programs each work in a slightly different fashion. The Award BIOS and AMI BIOS are two of the most common, but there are others in widespread use. The AMI BIOS has a Setup program that will detect any reasonably standard mouse connected to the PC, and it offers a simple form of WIMP environment (Figure 2.7). It can still be controlled via the keyboard if preferred, or if the BIOS does not operate with the mouse you are using. The Award BIOS is probably the most common (Figure 2.8), and as far as I am aware it only uses keyboard control. There are a few more categories in the main menu of an up to the minute Award BIOS (Figure 2.9), but otherwise the choices are much the same with an old BIOS or a modern example.

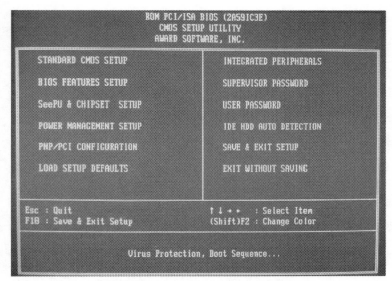

Fig.2.8 The Award BIOS is probably the most common

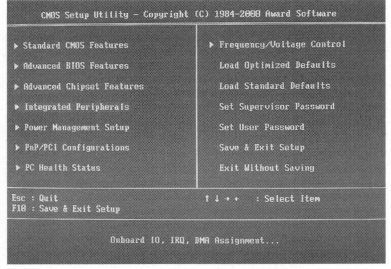

Fig.2.9 A modern BIOS Setup program has more menu options

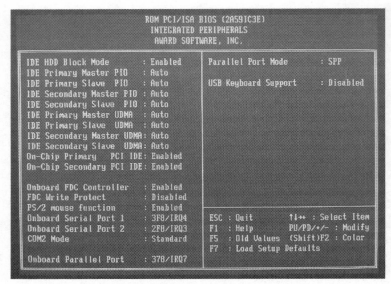

Fig.2.10 A typical Integrated Peripherals menu

Apart from variations in the BIOS due to different manufacturers, the BIOS will vary slightly from one motherboard to another. This is simply due to the fact that features available on one motherboard may be absent or different on another motherboard. Also, the world of PCs in general is developing at an amazing rate, and this is reflected in frequent BIOS updates. The description of the BIOS provided here has to be a representative one, and the BIOS in your PC will inevitably be slightly different. It may be necessary to do some searching through the menus in order to find the section that deals with the integrated ports.

If you are using a PC that is something less than the latest thing in PC technology, the BIOS Setup program will be relatively simple. There should be no difficulty in finding the menu that deals with the integral ports. A modern BIOS is too complex to have all the settings in a single menu, so the initial screen is effectively a menu of the available menus. There should be an option called something like "Integrated Peripherals", and this is the one where the port settings are controlled. Figure 2.10 shows a typical Integrated Peripherals menu.

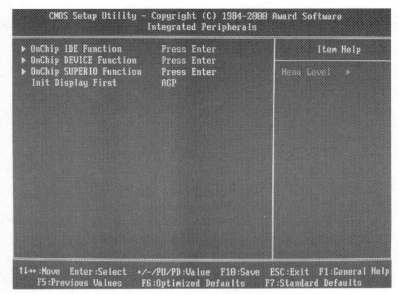

Fig.2.11 An example of an Integrated Peripherals submenu

With a modern BIOS it can be more difficult to find the appropriate menu. There are so many settings that can be altered via the BIOS Setup program that some of the menus have several submenus. Having access to a detailed instruction manual for the PC or the manual for the motherboard makes life much easier with a BIOS of this type. However, it should still be possible to find the required settings without the aid of an instruction manual. As before, there should be a menu called something like Integrated Peripherals, but selecting this option will not give direct access to the port settings. Instead, a menu offering a few submenus will appear (Figure 2.11). If in doubt, select each menu in turn until you find the one that deals with the parallel port. In this example, the OnChip Device Function and OnChip SUPERIO Function seem to be the most likely candidates. In fact, the latter controls the parallel port settings (Figure 2.12).

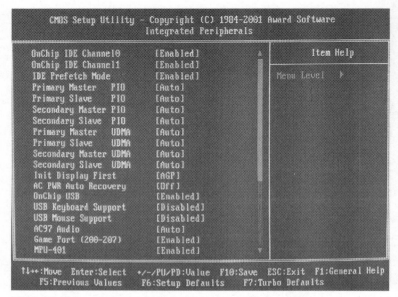

Fig.2.12 This submenu gives access to the port settings

Scrolling

Some menus can be a bit confusing at first sight, and in the Integrated Peripherals menu of Figure 2.13 the section dealing with the parallel ports appears to be missing. In fact several sections seem to be totally absent. However, if you look to the right of the menu options you will see something that looks a bit like a Windows scrollbar. Rather than using submenus, this version of the Award BIOS uses scrollable menus. Mouse control is not possible with this BIOS, but it is possible to scroll up and down using the appropriate two cursor keys. Figure 2.14 shows the menu scrolled down to reveal the menu options for the built-in parallel port.

When you finally locate the correct menu it is clearly the Mode setting that is of interest, and this BIOS Setup program offers four choices. The default is Normal (Figure 2.15), but as the instruction manual for the PC's motherboard makes clear, Normal in this case actually means the SPP mode. As explained previously, with many of the more recent BIOS versions the SPP mode is referred to as the Normal or Standard mode. A straightforward output mode is not included with a BIOS of this type,

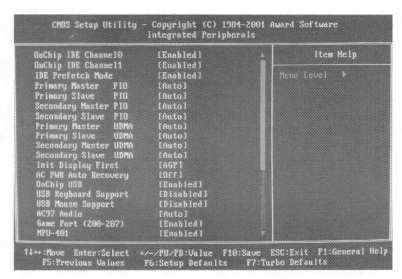

Fig.2.13 A number of settings seem to be absent from this menu

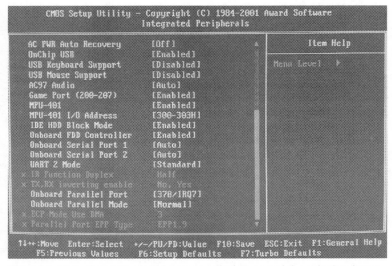

Fig.2.14 Here the menu has been scrolled to reveal the missing items,
including the parallel port settings

```
Onboard Parallel Port          378/IRQ7
Onboard Parallel Mode          Normal
ECP Mode Use DMA               3
Parallel Port EPP Type         EPP1.9
```

Fig.2.15 The parallel port defaults to the Normal (SPP) mode

or indeed with practically any modern BIOS. This is of no practical consequence because an SPP port defaults to operation as an output port. Unless a piece of software switches it to the input mode, it will work perfectly well as a standard PC printer port.

The next option is ECP/EPP, where the BIOS and port hardware supports EPP and ECP operation. If you are using a peripheral that requires an enhanced mode but the instruction manual is less than clear about the one that you require, then this "catch all" option is probably the best choice. Two more options become available when this mode is selected (Figure 2.16). First, the direct memory access (DMA) mode for ECP operation must be selected. Unless there is a good reason to do so, simply leave this at the default setting. There are two versions of the EPP mode available, which are versions 1.7 and 1.9. Usually, the latest version will be set by default, and this is normally the best one to use. Only opt for the earlier version if the instruction manual for the peripheral specifies this version, or if something less than perfect results are obtained using the default setting.

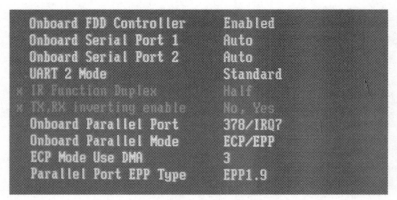

```
Onboard FDD Controller         Enabled
Onboard Serial Port 1          Auto
Onboard Serial Port 2          Auto
UART 2 Mode                    Standard
IR Function Duplex             Half
TX,RX inverting enable         No, Yes
Onboard Parallel Port          378/IRQ7
Onboard Parallel Mode          ECP/EPP
ECP Mode Use DMA               3
Parallel Port EPP Type         EPP1.9
```

*Fig.2.16 More options become active when the ECP/EPP mode
is selected*

```
Onboard Parallel Port          378/IRQ7
Onboard Parallel Mode          EPP
x ECP Mode Use DMA             3
Parallel Port EPP Type         EPP1.9
```

Fig.2.17 The EPP version can be selected

The other two options provide separate ECP and EPP operation. With the EPP mode selected it is possible to alter the version used (Figure 2.17), and with ECP operation the DMA mode can be altered (Figure 2.18). With any mode selected, it is possible to alter the address and interrupt request (IRQ) settings. The general subject of system resources is covered later in this chapter, and it is not something that will be considered further here.

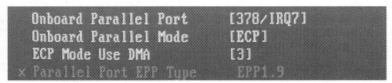

```
Onboard Parallel Port          [378/IRQ7]
Onboard Parallel Mode          [ECP]
ECP Mode Use DMA               [3]
x Parallel Port EPP Type       EPP1.9
```

Fig.2.18 The ECP mode DMA channel can be altered, but this will not normally be necessary

Parallel cables

A parallel printer cable having a Centronics connector at the printer end, as already pointed out, is an "off the shelf" item that should be available anywhere that sells computer bits and pieces. Apart from a few printers that are old enough to have become collectors items, a modern PC printer lead should work properly with any printer that has a Centronics style port. The situation is very different with other peripherals that connect to the parallel port. The obvious way of doing things is to use a normal printer lead for all parallel port peripherals, but in practice this type of lead is little used for anything other than printers. Possibly the Centronics connector is deemed rather large and cumbersome for most parallel port peripherals, many of which are quite small.

Many peripherals use a 25-way cable having a 25-way D connector at each end. Pin 1 connects to pin 1, pin 2 connects to pin 2, and so on. In other words, a lead that is very similar to a "straight" RS232C serial lead having the full set of 25 interconnections. Some of these leads probably are serial leads, effectively used in reverse with the male connector at the computer end of the system. However, there is no real standardisation of non-printer parallel cables, and manufacturers can use whatever method of connection they deem most suitable. With the exception of printers, practically all PC peripherals are supplied complete with a data lead, so there should be no problem unless this lead becomes lost or damaged.

When you are faced with the problem of a missing or damaged parallel lead, you should seek advice from the manufacturer or the retailer that supplied the equipment. If a standard lead is required, the retailer or manufacturer should be able to give details of the lead so that you can track one down. In fact the retailer will probably be able to supply a suitable lead. With a non-standard lead, it should be possible to obtain a new lead from the manufacturer or their agent, but it will probably cost the exorbitant prices associated with spare parts. Even so, it is probably worthwhile paying out for the replacement lead as it should avoid any hassle.

Cloning

Things are likely to be very difficult if the peripheral needs a non-standard lead that is no longer available from the manufacturer. It should be possible to make your own cable provided the connector at the peripheral end of the cable is a normal "off the shelf" item, and not a special "one off" designed specifically for that particular piece of equipment. You will still have the problem of finding details of the interconnections. The manufacturer might be able to help, and with problems of this type it is worth checking the manufacturer's web site. You will probably not be the only person having problems, and the Support or FAQ section of the site might have some guidance. Failing that, a general search of the Web using appropriate search criteria might turn up some useful details.

If you have a cable but it is damaged, some tests on the cable should show the method of connection used. The obvious problem here is that a non-working cable will have one or two of the interconnections absent. Where the fault is intermittent, you may still be able to trace the full set of connections. It will probably not matter too much if there are one or two broken connections that can not be traced. With (say) 23 interconnections successfully traced, it is usually pretty obvious where the missing one or two connections fit into the scheme of things. Where the interconnections are anything less than completely straightforward, always make a table or diagram showing all the connections. This makes life much easier when making the copy of the cable.

Avoid the temptation to simply try any cable that has the right connectors, or to make custom cables where you are really just guessing at the interconnections. Most computers and peripherals are designed to be reasonably foolproof, but this is not to say that it is impossible to damage them using incorrect connections. If you end up trying what amounts to random connections between a parallel port and a peripheral, there is a very real risk that one or both will be damaged.

Sound systems

The original PCs had very elemental sound systems that just consisted of an output line driving a small loudspeaker. There were some clever programs that could get this basic arrangement to do things that appeared to be impossible for such minimalist hardware. Perhaps most impressive of all, there was a program that could get the PC to "talk" by using the loudspeaker and the output line as part of a speech synthesis system. The basic sound system is still found in modern PCs, but it usually does nothing more than produce one or two beeps during the initial testing when the computer is switched on. Everything else is handled by a separate and sophisticated sound system that uses external loudspeakers or headphones.

Originally the sound system was handled by an expansion card, and often it still is. Many PC motherboards now have the sound system built in, but the facilities on offer are much the same either way. As a minimum, there is usually some form of sound sampling and playback facility, plus a wave synthesiser for handling multi-track playback of MIDI files, etc. MIDI is covered later incidentally, and will not be discussed further here. Unless you are using an upmarket sound card, the audio ins and outs are via 3.5-millimetre stereo jack sockets. Most sound cards have four of these (Figure 2.19), but with an integral sound system it is more normal to have just three (Figure 2.20). These are the four that are present on a soundcard, together with a brief description of each one:

Microphone (pink)

The microphone input is often a monophonic type rather than a stereo input. One input is usually sacrificed to provide a power output. This can produce difficulties with some types of microphone, as discussed

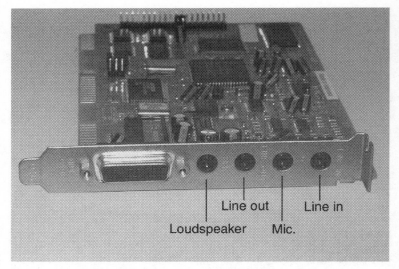

Fig.2.19 Most soundcards have four audio connectors

later.

Line input (blue)

A microphone provides relatively low output levels and therefore needs a sensitive input for satisfactory results. The Line input is for higher signal levels, such as those provided by CD players, tuners, etc.

Line output (green)

This is a stereo output at a high enough level to drive equipment such as cassette recorders and amplifiers. If you are using active loudspeakers, they should be driven from this socket. It is not intended for use with headphones, but it will often give tolerable results if you are happy with relatively low volume levels.

Headphones (orange)

This output will usually give satisfactory results with any normal headphones, including those sold for use with personal stereo units and headphones intended for use with hi-fi systems. The output level is not high enough for use with loudspeaker systems that lack an integral amplifier, apart from the very high efficiency units sold for use with

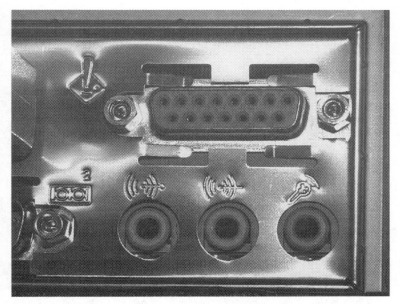

Fig.2.20 There are usually three audio connectors for an integrated audio system

personal stereo units. Even with these, you might find it difficult to hear speakers above the sound of the PC's cooling fans!

With some soundcards there is a fifth output socket that can drive passive loudspeakers, but more usually this in fitted in place of the headphone socket. It should perhaps be explained here that passive loudspeakers are the type that lack an integral amplifier, while active loudspeakers have a built-in amplifier. In order to drive passive loudspeakers properly the soundcard must include a stereo power amplifier, and most soundcards used to include a small power amplifier. This facility seems to be something of a rarity these days.

With some soundcards and integrated audio systems it is possible to alter the function of the Line output so that it will act as a headphone output, or in a few cases it can function as a loudspeaker output. The switching is usually via a jumper on the soundcard, or on the PC's motherboard in the case of an integrated audio system. Where appropriate, the instruction manual for the soundcard or motherboard should include instructions for altering this setting. With an integrated audio system, there is only room for three audio sockets in the input/ output block on the motherboard. It is usually the headphone output that is omitted, but as explained previously, it may be possible to set this socket as a headphone output.

Microphone problems

A common problem with PC sound systems is that they function perfectly for some time, but fail when you eventually try to record sound via a microphone or use a voice recognition system. This is not usually due to a fault in either the soundcard or the microphone. As pointed out previously, there is a lack of standardisation with PC microphone inputs. The problem is usually due to incompatibility between the microphone and the audio system. Due to the lack of true standardisation, a microphone that works perfectly well with one card might give no signal at all when used with another.

A common method of testing an item that appears to be faulty is to swap the suspect item with one from another PC that is fully operational. If the fault transfers to the other PC, then the suspect item is almost certainly faulty. If the problem with the faulty PC persists, the fault lies somewhere else in that PC. The substitution method of testing is unreliable when applied to microphones due to large differences between various microphone inputs. If a microphone has been working well but ceases to do so, trying it with another PC might give a helpful pointer. If the microphone works when tried with another PC, the microphone is not faulty. It is presumably the microphone input of the sound system that has become faulty. Beyond that, it is unlikely that substitution testing with be of any value. Without technical information and test equipment, it can be difficult to sort out problems with PCs and microphones.

The microphone problem stems from the fact that the microphone inputs of early SoundBlaster cards, and many of the compatible cards of a similar age, are intended for use with a carbon microphone. This is a rather crude form of microphone, as used in early telephone handsets. The audio quality of a carbon microphone is usually quite low, but the output signal is at a very high level by microphone standards. Hence, the microphone inputs of most early soundcards, and some recent ones come to that, are relatively insensitive.

Although the microphone connector on the card is a stereo 3.5-millimetre jack socket, this is normally a monophonic input. The third terminal is used to provide power to the carbon microphone, and not to provide a second stereo channel. By no means all soundcards have this type of microphone input. Some have a monophonic input with one terminal of the input socket left unused, while others do actually have a stereo microphone input.

Carbon microphones are little used with soundcards these days, and in all probability they never have been used to any extent with PCs. The normal choices at present are electret and dynamic microphones. Electret microphones require a power supply to operate, and this is often in the form of a built-in battery. However, some electret microphones are designed for use with a SoundBlaster style microphone input, and use the soundcard as the power source. A fair percentage of microphones used in headsets for PC use are of this type (Figure 2.21). Dynamic types do not require a power source, but often have very low output levels.

Fig.2.21 A headset having an electret microphone powered from the PC

There is clearly plenty of scope for incompatibility problems when using the microphone input of an audio card. If you use a low output microphone with an insensitive input there will probably be too little audio signal to be of any practical use. If you use a microphone that requires power from the soundcard, it will only work if the card actually provides a suitable power source. This type of microphone will probably fail to produce any output signal at all if it does not receive power from the soundcard. Using a stereo microphone will clearly not give the desired result if the card only has a monophonic microphone input.

Sorting out microphone problems tends to be difficult. In theory, it should be possible to obtain information about suitable types of microphone from the soundcard's instruction manual or the manufacturer's web site. With an integrated audio system it is the instruction manual for the motherboard that should be consulted. In practice, the information

Fig.2.22 The volume control icon

available on this subject is often sketchy to the point of being virtually non-existent. You often end up trying any microphone you can lay your hands on in the hope that it will work. In general, the safest option is a dynamic microphone that has a fairly high output level. This type of microphone will work properly regardless of whether the soundcard provides a power supply output, and it will give usable results with an insensitive input.

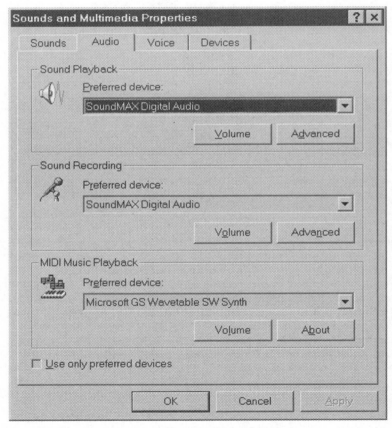

Fig.2.23 The Sounds and Multimedia Properties window

If a microphone fails to give a satisfactory signal level or no signal at all, investigate the software side of things before giving up on it. A little loudspeaker icon usually appears on the Windows taskbar when the soundcard drivers are installed (Figure 2.22). Double clicking on this may produce nothing more than a simple volume control, but it sometimes produces

Fig.2.24 The recording mixer window

a screen that provides various audio controls. A facility of this type might be available from the Control Panel, either via the Multimedia icon, the Sounds and Multimedia icon, or by way of an icon for the audio card. This depends on the configuration of your PC and the version of Windows in use.

It might require some delving into the Control Panel, but it should be possible to find the panel that deals with the audio system, and it will probably look something like Figure 2.23. Operating the Volume button for the recording section will produce a control window like the one of Figure 2.24. If it is possible to select the recording source, make sure that the microphone input is enabled. This usually means placing a tick in the appropriate checkbox, as in this example. By default the system might only record from the "line" input socket. If there is a slider control for the microphone, make sure that this is well advanced and not fully backed off.

There is sometimes a switch that can be used to boost or reduce the recording level by 20 decibels. In other words, it boosts or reduces the signal by a factor of 10. If there is a lack of microphone signal, make sure any switch of this type is set to give the higher level of sensitivity. If, on the other hand, there are problems with distortion due to overloading when the microphone is used, set the switch for lower sensitivity.

Your chances of success are much higher if you use a microphone that is intended for operation with a PC. These have characteristics that enable them to work satisfactorily with a wide range of soundcards and integrated audio systems.

PC compatible microphones of various types are available from the larger computer stores and computer fairs. In addition to the headsets mentioned earlier, lapel and desktop microphones (Figure 2.25) are available. You are not guaranteed perfect results every time with one of these microphones, but you do at least minimise the risk of problems. If you wish to use a high quality electret microphone that is not designed for PC use, choose one that has an integral

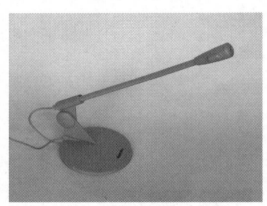

Fig.2.25 A desk microphone designed for use with a PC

battery. Even if the microphone socket lacks a power output, it should still work with a microphone of this type.

Plug problems

The wrong type of plug is the most likely cause of problems with microphones that are not specifically designed for use with a PC. Some microphones are fitted with a 3.5 millimetre monophonic jack plug, which is much the same as the stereo variety but it has only two terminals. Figure 2.26 shows both types of plug. Microphones of this type will usually work properly with a PC microphone input, but with low output microphones and insensitive microphone inputs there may be a grossly inadequate signal level. There is no easy solution to this problem.

If the soundcard uses the "spare" terminal to provide power to the microphone, there is a potential problem when using a microphone having a monophonic plug. The power supply output will be short-circuited to ground when the microphone is plugged in. In practice, this should not matter, because the supply is always limited to a very low output current. There is no risk of any damage occurring even if the supply is short-circuited for prolonged periods. Note that this is not true of most other power supply outputs of a PC.

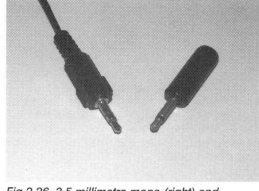

Fig.2.26 3.5 millimetre mono (right) and stereo jack plugs

The normal connector for a microphone is a standard jack plug, which is also called a quarter-inch or 6.35-millimetre jack plug. This is just a scaled-up version of a 3.5-millimetre plug, or to be more accurate, the 3.5-millimetre type is a scaled-down version of the original 6.35-millimetre type. A huge range of audio adapters is available, and it should be possible to obtain one that will enable a standard jack plug to be used with a 3.5-millimetre socket.

Adapters that provide the opposite conversion (3.5-millimetre plug to 6.35-millimetre socket) are by far the most common type, and there are several other types of jack adapter, so be careful to obtain the right adapter. Alternatively, you can make your own adapter by wiring a standard jack line socket to a 3.5-millimetre stereo jack plug. Yet another option is to remove the original plug and replace it with a 3.5-millimetre type. In many ways this is the best option, but it could invalidate the microphone's guarantee.

Stereo recording

As pointed out previously, most soundcards and integrated sound systems do not have a stereo microphone input. If you are using a soundcard, it is worth checking its instruction manual. Some soundcards have jumpers that give two or three options for the microphone input, and one of these might provide stereo operation. In most cases though, there is no built-in provision for anything more than a single microphone. This does not mean that it is impossible to use two microphones for stereo operation, but it will be necessary to resort to some external help in order to obtain an extra microphone input.

There are two basic approaches to this problem. The more simple method is to use a stereo microphone preamplifier ahead of the Line input. A suitable preamplifier might be difficult to track down, but should be available from one of the larger retailers that deal in all-things electronic. The drawback of this method is that the Line input is then unavailable for use with a cassette deck, a tuner, or whatever. A more expensive but more versatile option is to use a stereo mixer ahead of the Line input. Even a fairly simple mixer is likely to have inputs for at least one pair of microphones and two or three high level inputs for use with cassette decks, etc. The more you are prepared to pay, the more inputs and facilities you can have. However, for most purposes a basic audio mixer is all that is needed.

If you opt for an external mixer it will probably be possible to buy an "off the shelf" cable to connect its output to the Line input of the PC. The smaller and cheaper audio mixers often utilise 3.5-millimetre jack sockets, or Phono sockets (as used on most hi-fi equipment). Leads suitable for connecting these to a PC Line input socket should not be difficult to track down. The larger and more expensive mixers often use standard jack sockets or even the professional (and very expensive) XLR connectors. Finding suitable leads for these is likely to be more difficult, but if necessary you can use a ready-made lead plus a suitable adapter.

Screened leads

Making your own audio leads is not difficult but does require a miniature soldering iron and some solder that is suitable for electrical work.

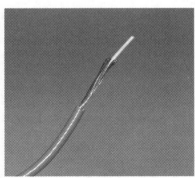 Screened cable is needed, but any screened cable for audio use should suffice for line level signals. Expensive low-noise cable is not needed. Twin screened cable is needed for a stereo connection, and there are two types of twin screened lead. These are the individually screened and overall screened varieties. As the name suggests, each wire of an individually screened cable has its own screen. With an overall screened lead the wires have a common

Fig.2.27 The most common form of screened cable

screen. The wires are therefore screened from the outside world but are not shielded from each other.

The individually screened type is preferable because it is less likely to compromise the stereo channel separation, particularly at high frequencies. Without individual screening, capacitance in the cable tends to couple the signals from one wire to the other. On the other hand, the overall

Fig.2.28 A braided screen is combed into separate wires

screened type should be adequate for an application such as this where the cable is carrying a fairly high signal level, and the cable will presumably be no more than a few metres long. It is also somewhat easier to use.

Screened audio cable is usually quite thin, and there should be no problem in removing the outer sleeving using ordinary wire strippers. This will reveal the screen in the form of numerous fine wires, which will be either side by side (Figure 2.27) or woven into a braiding. If the wires are woven into a braiding, it will be necessary to "comb" them with a fingernail so that the wires are separated (Figure 2.28). The wires are then twisted together and tinned with solder. If the wires are not woven into a braiding they can simply be twisted together and tinned with solder without any pre-forming. The insulation is stripped from the ends of the two wires and the bare ends are tinned with solder (Figure 2.29).

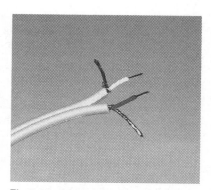

Fig.2.29 A twin screened lead ready for connection to the miniature jack plug

The screen always carries the ground connection, and it connects to the metal chassis of each plug. The two wires carry the left and right signals, and connecting them to one of the plugs the wrong way around will result in the left-hand channel coming from the right-hand loudspeaker and the right-hand channel coming from the left-hand loudspeaker. Figure

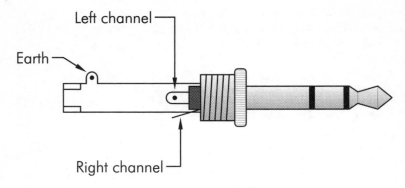

Fig.2.30 The standard tag functions for a stereo jack plug

2.30 shows the functions for the three tags of a 3.5-millimetre jack plug, and this should help you to get things right first time. Alternatively, you may simply use trial and error to get it right. Making the connections to the plugs should be easy provided the wires and the tags are all tinned with plenty of solder prior to attempting the connections. The two flanges at the very rear of the plug are squeezed together using pliers so that they grip the cable and provide strain relief.

Up-market

If you intend to do a lot of recording with your PC it is probably worthwhile upgrading the sound system. There are up-market soundcards specifically designed to turn a PC into a versatile recording and editing system. Although most of these are far from cheap, they offer what is generally a far better range of features and higher performance than a "bog standard" soundcard. These up-market cards usually come complete with some useful recording and editing software. Replacing an existing soundcard with an up-market type is a straightforward upgrade.

Things can be more difficult where the PC has an integrated sound system. It will almost certainly be necessary to switch off the sound circuits on the motherboard in order to get the new soundcard to work properly. With some budget motherboards this is not possible, but the vast majority of on-board sound systems can be deactivated. The computer's manual should give detailed instructions on switching off

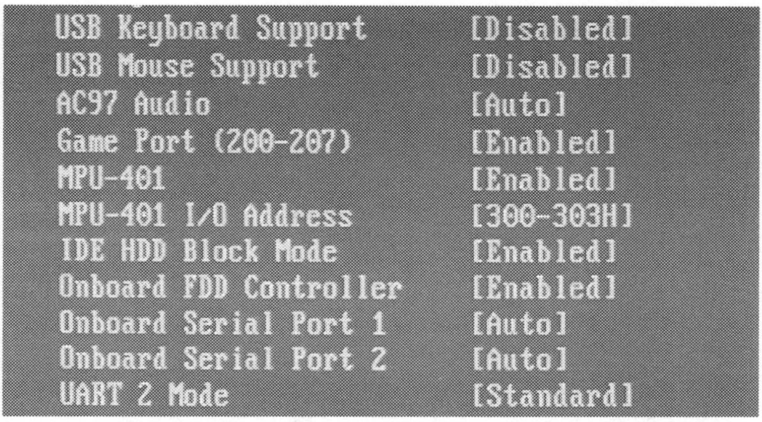

```
USB Keyboard Support        [Disabled]
USB Mouse Support           [Disabled]
AC97 Audio                  [Auto]
Game Port (200-207)         [Enabled]
MPU-401                     [Enabled]
MPU-401 I/O Address         [300-303H]
IDE HDD Block Mode          [Enabled]
Onboard FDD Controller      [Enabled]
Onboard Serial Port 1       [Auto]
Onboard Serial Port 2       [Auto]
UART 2 Mode                 [Standard]
```

Fig.2.31 Typical options in the audio section of a BIOS Setup program

any integrated sound system. It may involve opening up the case and altering a jumper setting, but in most instances it can be switched off via the BIOS Setup program.

Where this feature is available, it will usually be found in the Integrated Peripherals section or a submenu of this section. Figure 2.31 shows a typical set of options for an integrated sound system. It is the AC97 Audio setting that is of importance here. In this example there is an Auto setting that is used by default. This might detect a soundcard and automatically switch off the on-board sound system, but it is better to make sure by using the Disabled setting.

Loudspeakers

Active loudspeakers are normally driven from the Line output socket of the sound card or integral sound system. Like the Microphone and Line inputs, this is normally a 3.5-millimetre stereo jack socket. Active loudspeakers for use with PCs are usually supplied with a lead that has a 3.5-millimetre plug at each end. This lead is used to connect the Line output to the input of the main loudspeaker (the one that contains the amplifier). The lead that connects the main speaker to the secondary speaker is a simple two-way type that uses 3.5-millimetre monophonic jack plugs, or the stereo variety with one terminal of each plug left unused. Again, a suitable lead is almost invariably supplied with the loudspeakers.

115

Fig.2.32 *The standard functions of stereo jack plug terminals*

If you suspect either lead is damaged it is easy to do a continuity check, as described later in this chapter.

Before testing the leads you can do a simple check to see if there is anything wrong with this part of the audio system. Disconnect the loudspeaker lead from the audio card and try touching the non-earth terminals of the plug with the blade of a small screwdriver. Figure 2.32 identifies the three terminals of the jack plug. Make sure that you are touching the blade of the screwdriver and not just the insulated handle, because this test relies on mains "hum" and other electrical noise being picked up by your body. This signal should produce a 50-hertz "hum" and other general noise from the loudspeakers provided the volume control is well advanced. If you have an item of audio equipment that has a 3.5-millimetre stereo output socket, such as a personal stereo unit, use this as the audio source.

Either way, a lack of sound from one or both of the loudspeakers indicates a fault in a cable or the loudspeaker units. If the cables pass the continuity test, presumably the loudspeakers are at fault. If the loudspeakers are mains powered, as most are, check the fuse in the mains plug and ensure that everything is connected together properly.

Power adapters

With units that are powered from a mains adapter, make sure that the adapter is connecting to the main loudspeaker unit properly. The power plugs used with these units are a common cause of problems, and many of them are not designed for use as power connectors. For example, many of these units use miniature jack sockets, which were only designed for use with low-power audio signals. Switch cleaner aerosols are available from electronics component suppliers and some do-it-yourself superstores. Spraying both connectors using one of these cleaners might improve reliability. Cleaning connectors by scraping them using penknife, sandpapering them, etc., is not a good idea. It might provide a temporary fix, but it will damage the metal plating on the connectors. This virtually guarantees that the problem will soon return.

Where cleaning the connectors makes no difference and intermittent contact is still obtained, the problem is almost certainly due to a faulty lead or damage to the main speaker unit. Testing leads is covered later in this chapter. The standard problem at the loudspeaker end of the system is that one terminal of the power connector breaks away from the printed circuit board. Most PC loudspeakers are not particularly expensive these days, and it is unlikely to be worthwhile having a professional repair done on a unit that is outside the guarantee period. With the loudspeaker unplugged from the power adapter and the PC, it might be possible to open it up, solder over the broken connection, and reassemble everything. This is not exactly a high-tech repair, and should not be beyond the average do-it-yourself enthusiast. Realistically, the only alternative is to replace the loudspeaker system.

Many households now have quite a collection of mains adapters, making it essential to always get each gadget paired up with the right adapter. These units are not all the same, and they come in a wide range of voltage and current ratings. There are also regulated and unregulated types. The output voltage of a regulated supply will be close to the stated output potential at any current up to the supply's maximum rating. With an unregulated supply, the output potential is much higher than the voltage rating except when maximum output current is being drawn. In practice, the output voltage is often about double the stated level under no load, and is still well above the nominal output voltage under full load. Using a regulated supply instead of an unregulated supply will probably result in the gadget failing to work, but is not likely to cause any damage. An error the other way around would give an excessive supply voltage and could render the gadget beyond economic repair.

Another point to bear in mind is that two supplies having the same type of plug might have them wired differently. Using the wrong supply can therefore have dire results even if the voltage and current ratings are correct, due to the supply being connected with the wrong polarity. This more or less guarantees serious damage to modern electronic equipment unless a fuse or other protection circuit in the adapter cuts off the power before any major damage occurs.

Never use a mains adapter with any device unless you are sure that it suitable. I have never damaged anything by using an unsuitable adapter, but I have had one or two near misses. I have known people damage various items from Christmas lights to Zip drives and laptop computers by using inappropriate power supplies, so it is certainly something that needs to be taken seriously.

Picture interference

A common problem with loudspeakers is that interference appears on the screen when they are in use. A cathode ray tube (CRT) uses magnetic fields to control the beam of electrons that produces the picture. Any magnetic field close to a monitor that uses a CRT can affect the picture. The loudspeakers contain fixed magnets and electromagnets, but in most cases it is not the loudspeakers themselves that cause the interference. The problem seems to be caused by the 50-hertz magnetic field generated by the mains transformer in the power supply unit. With any peripheral that is powered by an external power supply, it is important to keep the supply well away from the monitor. Probably most people have these units down on the floor and well away from the monitor, so they do not usually cause problems anyway.

Loudspeakers that have an integral mains power supply are a different matter. The standard arrangement is to have a loudspeaker on each side of the monitor, and if space is limited, the gap between each loudspeaker and the monitor is usually minimal. Although most loudspeakers for PC use are magnetically shielded, the shielding is invariably less than perfect. Hence, there is interference on the screen with the loudspeakers very close to the monitor.

Usually the only way around this problem is to move the loudspeakers away from the monitor. Moving the loudspeakers by as little as 200 to 300 millimetres is often enough to reduce the problem to an insignificant level. If this is not practical due to a lack of space on the computer desk, perhaps the loudspeakers could be moved onto small wall-mounted shelves or other pieces of furniture. Results with stereo signals are generally better with the loudspeakers well separated, so moving them away from the monitor might give better results all round.

Soundcard problems

If the loudspeaker system is functioning correctly but there is a lack of sound when they are used with your PC, the obvious conclusion is that the soundcard or integrated audio system is faulty. This could be the cause of the problem, but the majority of problems with PC audio systems

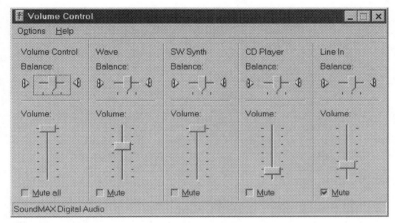

Fig.2.33 A typical Windows audio mixer for playing sounds

are due to the device drivers not being installed properly, or some other software problem. First, check that the volume control in the Windows taskbar is not set at minimum. On more than one occasion I have been asked to help sort out problems with a PC audio system, only to discover that the silence was caused by the Windows volume control being set at minimum!

Next go to the Sound and Multimedia Properties window, and then operate the Volume button in the Sound Playback section. This should produce a window containing a mixer, similar to the one for recording. It will probably have provision for more signal sources, and there will typically be about half a dozen level controls (Figure 2.33). Make sure that the volume controls for any signal sources you are using are well advanced. Also, make sure that the overall volume control has a suitably high setting. Signal sources can be muted by ticking the appropriate checkbox, and it is a good idea to have unused sources switched off. This avoids having unnecessary noise added to the output signal by these sources. Has the signal source you are using been accidentally turned off?

If the controls are all set correctly, the next step is to check that the sound card is properly installed. Go to the Windows Control Panel by selecting Settings from the Start menu, followed by Control Panel from the submenu. Then double-click on the System icon to bring up the System Properties window, and operate the Device Manager tab to

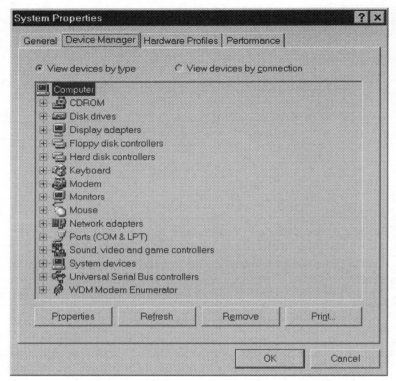

Fig.2.34 Virtually all the hardware is included in Device Manager

produce a window like the one in Figure 2.34. The Sound entry will already be expanded if there is a problem with the soundcard, and there will be one or more of the dreaded yellow exclamation marks in evidence. You can double-click on the Sound icon to check the individual entries if this section is not already expanded. This should give something like Figure 2.35.

Soundcards are potentially confusing due to the number of entries they have in Device Manager. In this example there are four entries, although the bottom one is actually for the modem and is nothing to do with soundcard. The first entry is usually for the game port that is a feature of practically all soundcards. The next is for the MIDI driver, which enables the card to emulate a MIDI synthesiser. Game ports, MIDI, and MIDI files

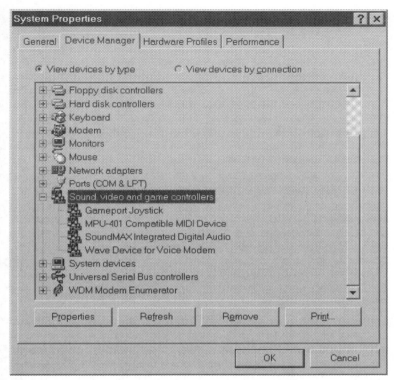

Fig.2.35 There are usually several drivers for the sound system

are covered later in this chapter. The next entry is for the wave synthesiser, which is the one that enables digital audio such as WAV files to be played. With some soundcards there are actually two entries for wave synthesis. This occurs where the card offers both basic wave synthesis and some more advanced version.

Soundcards have traditionally been very troublesome, but in fairness to the manufacturers of the current cards, it has to be admitted that the modern cards are much easier to deal with. With a PC that uses an old soundcard that fits into an ISA expansion slot it is not too surprising if the card periodically "goes walkabout". Before doing anything drastic it is worth rebooting the computer to check that there is a genuine problem. Occasionally Windows fails to detect a device properly during the boot-up sequence, rendering the device non-operational. Rebooting should result in the soundcard being detected and normal operation being restored.

If not, try reinstalling all the drivers for the soundcard. It is best to remove the old drivers and reboot the computer before reinstalling the drivers. To remove a drive, left-click on its entry in Device Manager, operate the Remove button, and then operate the Yes button when asked if you are sure that you wish to remove the driver. Note that you can not simply select and remove a category. Each device driver must be removed individually, and a category will disappear from Device Manager once all its contents have been removed.

If the sound system still refuses to work, try removing relevant device drivers again, and then shut down the computer. Next remove the soundcard, or switch on the computer, go into the BIOS Setup program and switch off the sound system if it is an integrated type. Reboot the computer and check that the device drivers have all been removed from Device Manager. If necessary, delete them again and reboot the PC. When the drivers are definitely gone, switch off the PC and refit the soundcard. If the audio system is an integrated type, go into the BIOS Setup program and switch it on again. Finally, reboot the computer and reinstall the device drivers.

If reinstalling the sound system from scratch does not cure the problem, it is likely that there is a hardware fault and that a new soundcard or motherboard is needed. However, before resorting to expensive repairs it is a good idea to check the manufacturer's web site to see if updated versions of the device drivers are available. It is quite normal for audio and video device drivers to go through a number of revisions in order to iron out various "teething" problems and incompatibilities. A surprisingly large number make it into the shops with device drivers that are no use at all with most PCs.

Game port

Game ports were originally provided by a game port expansion card, or by a multifunction input/output card that included other ports. These days the game port is usually included on the audio card, or on the motherboard if it has an integrated audio system (refer back to Figure 2.20). With PCs that have PC99 colour-coded connectors, it is a sort of yellow-orange hue. The standard connector for the game port is a 15-way female D connector, and games controls invariably have a captive lead fitted with the appropriate connector (Figure 2.36). There is a strong

Fig.2.36 Game controllers normally have a captive lead

trend towards using a USB interface for games controllers, and a USB port offers greater versatility than the now rather dated game type. However, there are still huge numbers of game port devices in circulation, and it is likely that this type of port will remain in common use for some years yet.

The game port has several inputs together with four +5-volt supply outputs (Figure 2.37). A variable resistor can be connected between each Position input and the positive supply rail, and one way of using these is to have two of them per joystick. One input indicates the horizontal position of the stick and the other provides the same function in the vertical plane. This type of joystick can be used to move an onscreen object to a certain position on the screen rather than simply indicating movement in a certain direction. The game port can accommodate two joysticks of this type.

These potentiometer joysticks, as they are often called, have never been very popular though. One problem is that the Position inputs of the

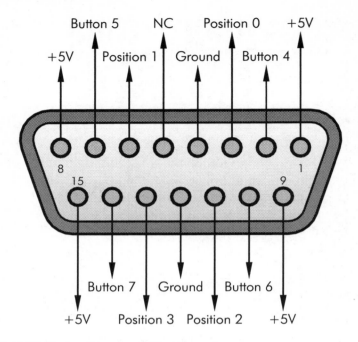

Fig.2.37 Pin functions for a PC game port

game port work in a fairly crude fashion, and the tolerance on the variable resistors used in the joysticks are often quite high. In order to get usable results it is usually necessary to go through a simple calibration process, and even then, some of these joysticks could not utilise the full screen area. Results also tend to be a bit wobbly using this type of joystick. Another drawback of potentiometer joysticks is that they tend to be less durable than the simple switch type, which is important in an application such as this.

Many PC games controllers are not of the potentiometer variety, and instead use a switch between each position input and the +5-volt supply. With four switches needed to indicate movement to the left, right, up, and down, this permits only one joystick per game port. Many controllers use a more sophisticated arrangement that has two resistors and a couple of switches per input. This method can accommodate two joysticks per port. The switch and resistor type is probably the most common form of game port controller.

The four Button inputs are for "fire" buttons on the joystick or joysticks. Although there are only four of these inputs, using some simple electronics in the game controller it would probably be possible to accommodate up to sixteen switches. This method seems to be little used in practice though. Many controllers have more than four buttons, but the extra buttons just duplicate one or more of the four normal buttons. Different button layouts suit different types of game, and most controllers are designed to be as accommodating as possible. Clearly, there are numerous ways in which the game port can be used with controllers, and usable results will only be obtained if the operating system and software are set for use with the right type of controller.

Controller installation

Three criteria have to be met before a games controller will function properly. First, it must be compatible with the games software you are using. Surprisingly perhaps, not all games programs actually support any form of controller. Obviously game controllers are not applicable to some types of game, but support is absent with some software that would seem to be well suited to this method of control. Where some form of controller is supported, is the program compatible with the controller you are using?

The second requirement is that the game port is activated and installed properly into the operating system. In the past it was quite normal for games to run under MS/DOS, and it was then unnecessary to have the game port installed in Windows. It was not normally necessary to have a MS/DOS device driver either, since the game program directly accessed the port hardware. Things are different these days, and only "golden oldie" game programs run under MS/DOS. The game port will only function with Windows if a device driver for it has been properly installed.

Fig.2.38 The game port's driver is included in the sound section of Device Manager

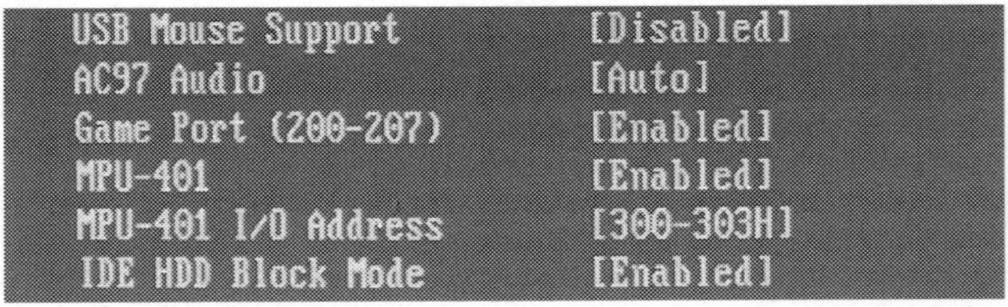

USB Mouse Support [Disabled]
AC97 Audio [Auto]
Game Port (200-207) [Enabled]
MPU-401 [Enabled]
MPU-401 I/O Address [300-303H]
IDE HDD Block Mode [Enabled]

Fig.2.39 An integrated game port can be switched on and off via the BIOS Setup program

Gaming Options
Controllers
Controller IDs
Voice Chat
Use this application to configure and test game controllers.
Game Controllers:
Controller
Status
Refresh
Add...
Remove
Properties
OK

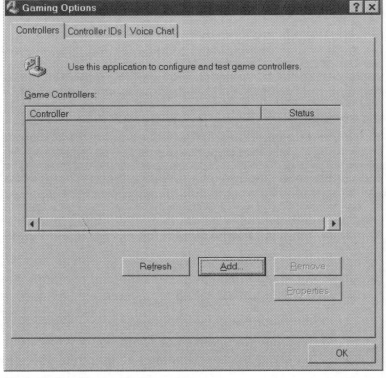

Fig.2.40 The Gaming Options window

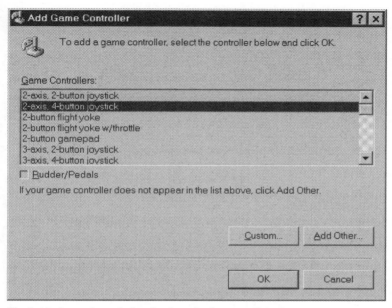

Fig.2.41 A number of standard controllers are listed

If a driver for the game port has been installed, it should be easy to find it in Device Manager. It should be included with the other drivers for the soundcard (Figure 2.38). Most soundcard installation programs install a full set of device drivers by default, and the Windows Plug and Play system would probably pick up the game port if the installation program did not install the driver. Accordingly, it is unlikely that this driver will be absent if the port is present and working. If it is absent, try rerunning the installation program for the soundcard.

Sometimes the installation program reports that it can not install the driver because it is unable to detect the port hardware. The hardware could be faulty, but in most cases it is disabled. With a soundcard, check the instruction manual to see if there is a switch or jumper on the card that enables the port to be switched on and off. With an integrated audio system it is possible that there will be a switch or jumper to control the game port, but this is unlikely. There are usually four settings for the sound system in the BIOS Setup program (Figure 2.39), and one of these controls the game port. Make sure that the Enabled option is selected here.

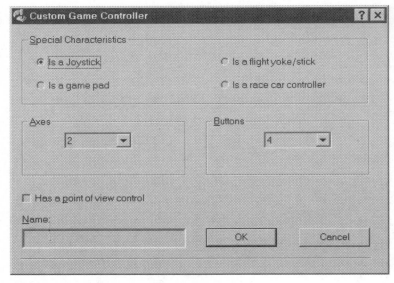

Fig.2.42 The Custom Game Controller window

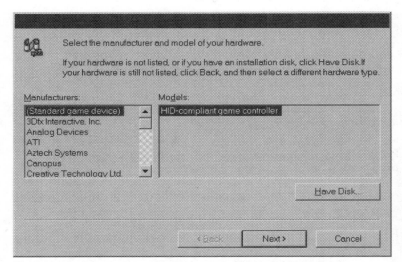

Fig.2.43 Further game controllers are available via this window

The third requirement is that the controller itself is installed in Windows. It is possible that the controller will be supplied with an installation disc, but with most "run of the mill" controllers it is necessary to install them manually. First select Settings from Start menu, and then choose Control Panel from the submenu. The Windows Control Panel should have an icon or entry called something like Gaming Options. Double-click on the icon or entry to bring up the Gaming Options window (Figure 2.40). Left-click on the Controllers tab if it is not selected by default.

The main section of the window will show a list of installed game controllers, but initially it will be empty. To install a new controller, first left-click on the Add button. This will produce a new window like the one shown in Figure 2.41. A list of standard controller types is provided in the main part of the window, and where appropriate, one of these should be selected. The instruction leaflet supplied with the controller should indicate which one to use, if the unit is compatible with one of the standard types.

Custom controller

Where the unit is not a standard type, one option is to operate the Custom button. This produces a window like the one of Figure 2.42, where the appropriate settings can be selected. The instruction leaflet for the controller should list the correct settings if this method of installation is needed. Another option is obtained by operating the Add Other button, which produces a window like the one of Figure 2.43. Here various

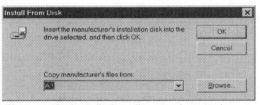

Fig.2.44 An installation disc can be used with non-standard controllers

manufacturers are listed on the left, and a list of controllers for the selected manufacturer appears on the right. Probably of more importance, there is a Have Disk button that enables the device to be installed using the device driver supplied by the manufacturer. This button produces the small window of Figure 2.44. Here the path to the device driver can be typed into the textbox or it can be located using the Browse option. Installation then progresses along standard Windows lines.

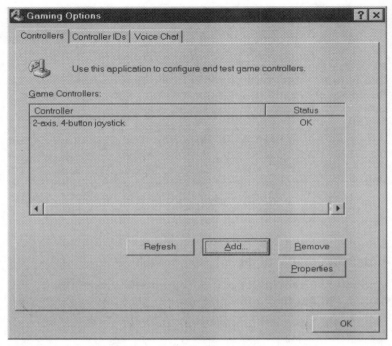

Fig.2.45 Once installed, the new controller should be listed

Having added a controller by one means or another, left-click the OK button to return to the Gaming Options window, that should now have an entry for the newly installed controller (Figure 2.45). If the controller is connected to the game port and Windows detects it properly, OK will be shown against its entry. Otherwise, some form of error message such as Not Detected will be displayed. You will then have to check that the device is connected to the port correctly and operate the Refresh button to try again. If the message simply says something like Unknown, this probably means that the controller is not one that can be detected, and it does not necessarily mean that there is a problem.

To check the controller is functioning properly, left-click on its entry to select it and then operate the Properties button. If the Test section does not appear by default, left-click on the Test tab. This produces a window like the one shown in Figure 2.46. The appropriate "light" should appear

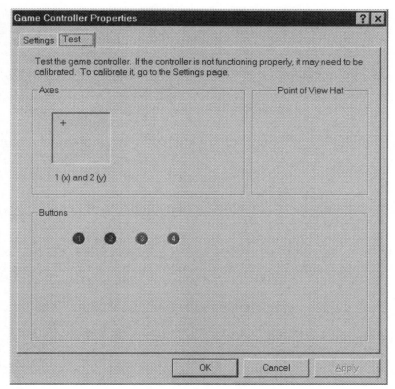

Fig.2.46 This window enables the controller to be tested

to switch on when its button is operated, and the upper section of the window should respond to the axis control. Some types of controller require calibration before the axis control with work accurately. First operate the Settings tab, and in the new version of the window (Figure 2.47) operate the Calibrate button. This launches the new window of Figure 2.48, where the controller can be calibrated.

The calibration process is very simple. First, a button on the controller is pressed while the stick is properly centred. Next the stick is moved in circles so that the calibration program can gauge the maximum and minimum readings, and then a control button is pressed. Finally, a control button is operated while the stick is accurately centred, and that completes

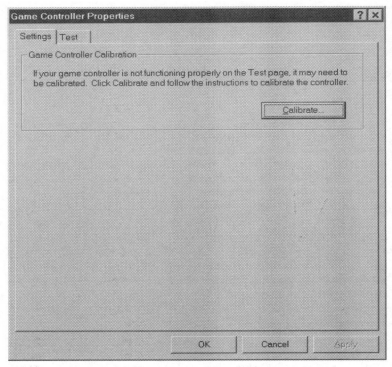

Fig.2.47 There is a Calibrate button in the Settings section

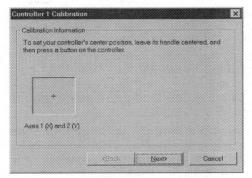

the calibration process. Note that it is not only potentiometer joysticks that need calibration. Satisfactory results may not be obtained using switch types unless the calibration process is completed.

Fig.2.48 The window used for calibration

MIDI Port

MIDI (musical instruments digital interface) enables electronic instruments such as synthesisers and sound samplers to be connected together to form a complex music making system. The standard connector for a MIDI interface is a five-way (180-degree) DIN type. The MIDI standard also allows for the use of XLR connectors, which are a high-grade professional type. However, manufactures of MIDI equipment that use XLR connectors must make suitable adapters available, so that their equipment can be used with standard (DIN type) MIDI leads. Predictably, apart from a few upmarket MIDI expansion cards, PC MIDI ports do not use DIN or XLR connectors. Instead, the game port doubles-up as a MIDI port. A special MIDI cable or adapter is therefore needed to connect a PC to MIDI devices.

As noted previously, soundcards cause a certain amount of confusion due to the number of device drivers that are usually associated with them. MIDI usually contributes at least its fair share of drivers, and most soundcards have two or three of these. One of the drivers is for the MIDI port, and it will produce a Roland MPU-401 compatible port. This enables the PC to communicate with MIDI synthesisers, keyboards, etc., and it is needed if you wish to use the PC with an external MIDI system. You can for example, use the PC to run a real-time sequencer program that enables it to act as a sort of multi-track recorder.

Note that the soundcard does not produce any sound via the MIDI port. In the early days of MIDI it was not unknown for uninformed users to connect the output of a MIDI port to the input of an audio system. All this produced was some "clicks" and general noise from the loudspeakers. MIDI is a form of digital interface that has similarities to an RS232C port. It operates on the basis of sending coded messages that carry information such as switch on a certain note with the specified loudness, or switch off a certain note. A synthesiser or other MIDI equipped musical instrument is needed in order to turn these messages into music.

Virtually all soundcards have one or two additional MIDI drivers that produce virtual MIDI synthesisers. These can be used with any software that has the ability to drive a MIDI device, and they get the soundcard to operate as a MIDI synthesiser. If the card has wavetable and FM synthesis there will probably be a separate driver for each type of synthesis. One of these will be used by default, but somewhere in the menu system, most MIDI software gives the option of using the other form of synthesis.

When playing MIDI files you have to bear in mind that the quality of the results is not solely dependent on the quality of the source files. If the playing is a bit crude with some inept timing, this is due to a lack of quality in the source file. If the sound quality is rather poor with unconvincing instrument sounds, this is due to a lack of quality in the sound synthesis. Where two or three types of synthesis are available, it is certainly worthwhile trying them all to see which one works best. Some types of sound synthesis are much more convincing than others. In most cases, one type of synthesis will provide noticeably better results than the others on offer, and it makes sense to ensure that the higher quality method is used by default.

MIDI problems

When using the internal MIDI synthesis, MIDI files should play through the loudspeakers in the usual way. If there is a complete lack of sound, start by checking that the device driver for some form of MIDI synthesis is actually installed. The best way to do this is to go to the Windows Control Panel and double-click on the Multimedia and Sounds icon or entry. Note that the Multimedia and Sound settings are handled separately in some versions of Windows. It is then the Multimedia section that is required. Left-click the Audio tab of the properties window, which should produce something like Figure 2.49. Activate the menu in the MIDI Music Playback section to reveal the available options for playing MIDI files. In this example there are only two options, which are a form of wavetable synthesis, and the MPU-401 MIDI port.

The wavetable option is needed for sound playback via loudspeakers connected to the soundcard. The PC used for this example has a fairly basic integrated audio system, but some PCs will have more than one form of sound synthesis to choose from. The MIDI files should be played correctly using any of the available synthesis options, but as explained previously, one will probably give significantly better results than the others will.

The MPU-401 option should not be used if playback via the soundcard is required. This option sends MIDI messages via the MPU-401 compatible port, and does not produce any audio output from the soundcard. Some soundcards will actually play along in unison with the messages sent to the MIDI port. However, there is no guarantee that this will happen, and strictly speaking the soundcard should not play MIDI files unless it is specifically selected as the MIDI output device.

Operating the Volume button produces the mixer window for audio playback, and one of the volume controls should be for the synthesiser. This will probably be called something like a software synthesiser rather

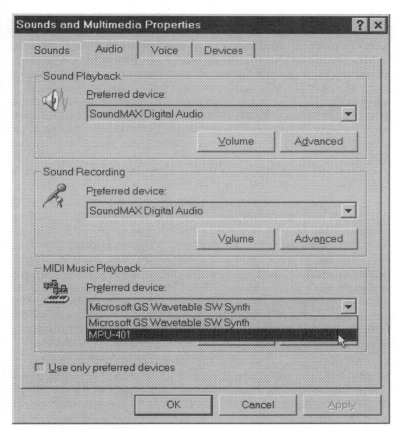

Fig.2.49 The MIDI Music Playback menu lists the available playback options

than a MIDI synthesiser. Make sure that the volume control for this device is well advanced and that the Mute checkbox is not ticked. With an integrated audio system, make sure that the audio system is enabled in the BIOS Setup program. If the MIDI playback facility still fails to work but the audio system works with other file types, either there is a hardware fault or the drivers for the synthesiser are not installed correctly. Check the entries for the soundcard in Device Manager to see if any problems are reported. Whether or not they are, try deleting the relevant entries and reinstalling the soundcard's device drivers.

MPU-401

The MIDI port of a soundcard or integrated audio system is compatible with the Roland MPU-401 interface, but some are more compatible than others are. The genuine Roland MPU-401 is a sophisticated piece of electronics that provides more than just some simple port hardware. It contains so-called "intelligence" that takes some of the workload off the PC's microprocessor. This was very useful in the days when PCs were relatively slow and needed all the help they could get from the other hardware. This sort of thing is less important these days, because most PCs have an excess of computing power when used in many applications. In fact the built-in facilities of an MPU-401 interface could actually slow things down when applied to a modern PC.

A MIDI port that has full MPU-401 compatibility will include the built-in intelligence, and should be usable with any applications software that works properly with the real thing. The MIDI ports of soundcards and integrated audio systems have the basic MPU-401 port hardware but almost invariably lack the built-in "intelligence". These are sometimes called "dumb" MIDI ports. This lack of full compatibility is not really a major drawback, since most modern MIDI software only uses the basic hardware, or perhaps has the option of using either a full MPU-401 interface or a "dumb" type. Some soundcard device drivers provide a software emulation of the built-in "intelligence". This method should work well enough provided you are using a reasonably powerful PC. Where appropriate, it is clearly necessary to set the software for use with a basic MIDI port if that is all the soundcard can provide.

Cables

As pointed out previously, normal MIDI cables can only be used with a PC MIDI port via a special cable, which is really an adapter rather than a simple cable. These do not seem to be as readily available as most other PC leads, but they are produced. Your chances of success are probably better with one of the large retailers of electronic musical instruments rather than a computer store. On the face of it, there is no difficulty in making your own leads provided you are reasonably competent with a small soldering iron. Figure 2.50 shows the pin functions for the 15-way D connector when it is used as a MIDI port.

In reality there is problem in that the soundcard does not include all the hardware for a MIDI interface. The main omission is that the opto-isolator on the MIDI input is missing. It is part of the MIDI hardware standard that all inputs include this isolation circuit. The basic idea is to have the coupling made via light rather than a direct electrical connection. This has each unit in the system electrically isolated from the others, which can help to avoid problems with "hum" loops and digital "noise" entering the audio circuits of the system.

There can also be problems if some units in the system are not earthed, but instead use double-insulation

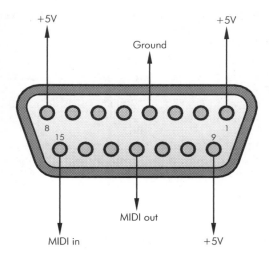

Fig.2.50 Pin functions of the game port when it is used as a MIDI port

to guard against electric shocks. It is possible to have large voltage differences between the chassis of different units when using equipment of this type. Although the current available is strictly limited, the high voltages are still capable of zapping some of the semiconductors when two units are wired together. Opto-isolation keeps the high voltages at bay and prevents any damage from occurring.

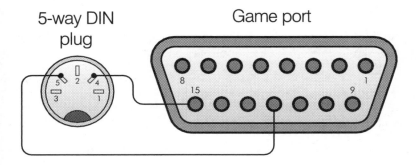

Fig.2.51 The connections required for a MIDI output lead

If you buy a PC MIDI lead or adapter, it should include the opto-isolator at the input. There could certainly be problems in using a lead or adapter that lacks this feature.

An opto-isolator is needed at inputs but not at outputs. If you only require a lead to connect the game port's MIDI output to a MIDI instrument, it is not difficult to make your own lead. The two connections required are shown in Figure 2.51. Strictly speaking, a 220-ohm resistor should be added into one lead, but in practice the lead will work perfectly well without it. Probably the best cable for MIDI use is a good quality twin screened type intended for audio use. The screen should be earthed to the metal shell of the 15-way D connector, but it must not be connected to the 5-way DIN plug. Those wishing to build their own PC MIDI adapter should be able to locate plenty of Internet sites that have details of suitable circuits.

MPU-401 problems

Probably the most common mistake when wiring up a MIDI system is to connect inputs to inputs, and outputs to outputs. This is unlikely to cause any damage, but will not get the system working properly. The correct method is to connect the MIDI output of the soundcard to the MIDI In socket of the synthesiser. If you need to use a sequencer program to record tracks played on the synthesiser's keyboard, the MIDI Out socket of the synthesiser must be connected to the MIDI input of the soundcard. Further instruments can be driven from the PC by using the Thru sockets on the instruments and the chain method of connection. In other words, the Thru socket on the first instrument connects the In socket on the next, the Thru socket on that instrument connects to the In socket of the third instrument, and so on.

Another common problem is that MIDI applications software will record from an instrument, but will not play back the sequences via that instrument. There will usually be only one source for recording sequences, which will be the MIDI input. Consequently, this has to be the default source. There will probably be two or three options for playing back sequences though. There will be one or two MIDI playback options that use the soundcard's sound generators, or the MIDI port can be used. The MIDI port is unlikely to be used by default, so go to the Sounds and Multimedia Properties window and select the MPU-401 option for MIDI playback.

Some music software has built-in facilities for selecting the destination for MIDI output. This facility can only work by overriding some of the

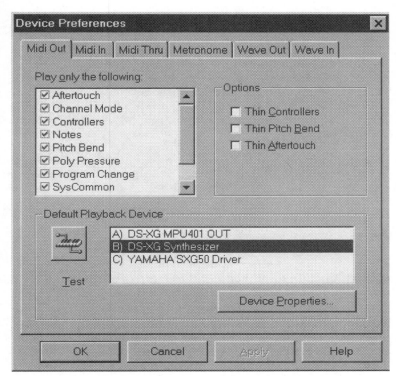

Fig.2.52 The MIDI playback device can be changed using most MIDI software

Windows sound settings, so check this point if some MIDI software works properly while other software produces no output via the MIDI port. It can be useful to play a MIDI sequence using the Windows Media Player that is supplied with recent versions of Windows. If a sequence plays properly via an external instrument using this player, but not when using a MIDI program, there is clearly a problem with the set-up of the MIDI program. MIDI applications software usually has a menu that includes a Preferences or Configuration option. Either of these should enable the output of the program to be directed to the MIDI port. Figure 2.52 shows one section of the Preferences window of Midisoft Studio and, amongst other things, this enables the desired MIDI output device to be selected.

There is nothing wrong with the interface, the MIDI PC cable, or the software if the first instrument in a chained system works properly. A

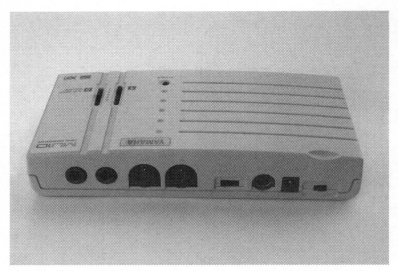

Fig.2.53 This MIDI sound module has MIDI and serial inputs

lack of response from other instruments in the system is due to a hardware fault in one of the instruments, a faulty cable carrying a Thru connection, or an instrument not being set up correctly. If any instrument in the system fails to respond, including the first one in a chained system, do not overlook the possibility that its MIDI ports are not switched on.

With a sound module the only way of communicating with the device is via the MIDI ports, so it is unlikely that there will be any way of deactivating the ports. The exception is where there is more than one way of communicating with the device, such as a choice of a serial interface or the MIDI ports. Figure 2.53 shows the rear panel of a Yamaha MU10 sound generator, which has MIDI and serial ports. A switch provides the choice of normal MIDI operation or three types of serial operation. Many keyboard instruments have the option of switching off the MIDI ports, and often default to the "off" setting.

You need to make sure that any MIDI instrument is set up to operate on the channel or channels you are using. For initial testing it is best to use Omni mode, because the instrument will then respond to data on any of the 16 MIDI channels. Take some time to make sure that all the instruments in the system are set up correctly, rather than wasting time looking for cable faults, etc., that do not exist.

SCSI

Some scanners and other devices interface to the computer via a SCSI port (small computers systems interface, and pronounced "scuzzy"). This is a form of high-speed bi-directional parallel port, but SCSI is totally incompatible with normal PC bi-directional ports. A few motherboards have a built-in SCSI interface, but this is something of a rarity. A built-in interface is only intended for built-in devices, which in practice means a hard disc or some other form of disc drive. There are numerous ISA and PCI expansion cards that provide SCSI ports, and many peripherals that require this type of interface are supplied complete with a suitable card and connecting cable (or they are offered as an optional extra). The card should be supplied with any necessary driver software to integrate it with the common operating systems, although modern versions of Windows will detect and load driver software for some SCSI interfaces.

There are several complications when dealing with SCSI, and sorting out problems with this type of interface is often less than straightforward. It has evolved over the years and there are now several versions in common use. Some manufacturers have produced SCSI equipment that does not strictly adhere to the agreed standards, and this has tended to further complicate matters. As a result, some equipment works fine with its matching SCSI interface card, but other SCSI equipment can not be used with the card due to non-standard cabling or other problems. The first two scanners that I bought worked fine with the supplied SCSI cards, but neither card was usable with any other SCSI equipment. With SCSI equipment it is essential to carefully read through the instruction manuals to determine exactly what you have. Check the "fine print" to see if there are any little gems of information there that you need to know about. Where possible, buy peripherals complete with a SCSI card that is guaranteed to be a correct match for the peripheral.

Versions

In order to deal with SCSI interfaces you need to have at least a basic knowledge of the various versions. The original specification was followed by versions two and three. Version two exists in standard, fast, and wide versions. The SCSI-3 variations are Wide, Ultra, and Ultra2. Devices that are designed for use with a SCSI-2 or SCSI-3 interface may not work properly with an original SCSI interface. Things are better in the opposite direction, and a standard SCSI device should work with a modern SCSI interface. However, as already pointed out, you need to be wary of non-standard interface cards that are generally incompatible with other SCSI devices.

Provided a SCSI expansion card genuinely conforms to one of the standards, there should be no major problem in replacing the card if it becomes faulty. On the other hand, buying a new peripheral having a modern SCSI interface could cause problems. The existing SCSI card might have to be replaced by a more up to date type in order to get the peripheral working properly.

SCSI devices are connected together using the "chain" method. In other words, each SCSI device has an input port and an output port, and if there is only one device in the system, its input connects to the output of the controller. If there is a second device, this has its input connected to the output port of the first device. A third SCSI unit would have its input connected to the output of the second device, and so on. This is essentially the same as the chain method of connection used for MIDI systems. Up to eight devices can be used in each chain, or 16 with the more recent versions, but in both cases the interface card counts as one of the devices. Unless you are prepared to become a SCSI expert it is advisable to settle for just the interface card and one peripheral.

SCSI cables

A SCSI cable is usually a substantial 50-way type, but a 68-way cable is used for Wide versions of this interface. A 50-way Centronics connector (Figure 2.54) was originally used, but a form of D connector is often used these days. The cables always use "straight" connection, with no crossed-over wires. Assuming you settle for just one SCSI peripheral, the cabling is just a matter of connecting the output of the controller to

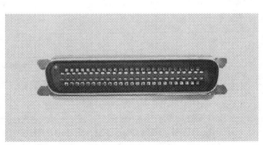

the input of the peripheral. The connectors are polarised and will only fit the right way around.

The SCSI interface makes use of termination resistors, and there should only be termination resistors at each end

Fig.2.54 A 50-way Centronics connector

of the system. By default these resistors are normally in-circuit, and with only a controller and one peripheral they should be left in-circuit. They are only removed or switched out on a unit that is not at one end of the "chain". When fitting a new SCSI controller card or hard disc drive you should obviously consult the instruction manual and check the hardware to ensure that the termination resistors are properly switched into circuit.

Presumably, because SCSI is not a standard PC interface, most hardware testing software does not provide any help with this type of port. With any installed hardware that seems to be malfunctioning, it is a good idea to check its entry in Device Manager. This will often detect a hardware fault and indicate that there is a problem. It will also indicate any problems with the device driver. If there is a problem with the device driver, try deleting it from Device Manager and reinstalling it. A newer version might be needed if this does not help. Whenever you encounter problems with drivers, it is worthwhile checking the manufacturer's web site for an updated version. There will often be a newer and (hopefully) fully operational version for download.

Bear in mind that many pieces of hardware do not have a universal Windows driver that will work with Windows 95, 98, 98SE, etc. It now seems to be quite normal to have a specific device driver for each version of Windows. Even if a generic driver for Windows 9x is available, a totally different driver is normally needed for Windows NT, etc. Some installation programs will detect any mismatch between the driver you are trying to install and the operating system in use. Most will then display a suitable error message and bring things to an abrupt halt. Others will quite happily continue with the installation process, even if it could have dire consequences for the Windows installation. Always read any installation notes thoroughly before installing any drivers, and make sure that only the appropriate software is loaded.

SCSI cards

Adding a SCSI peripheral to a PC involves adding an interface card, and that card grabs some of the computer's resources. Such is the complexity of a modern PC that spare resources are usually in short supply, and the SCSI card might try to utilise resources that are already allocated to other equipment. This produces what is termed a hardware conflict. This type of problem is more likely to occur with a peripheral that uses an expansion card than one that uses an existing port, and it is not exactly a rarity when adding a SCSI card. The general subject of hardware conflicts and sorting them out is covered later in this chapter.

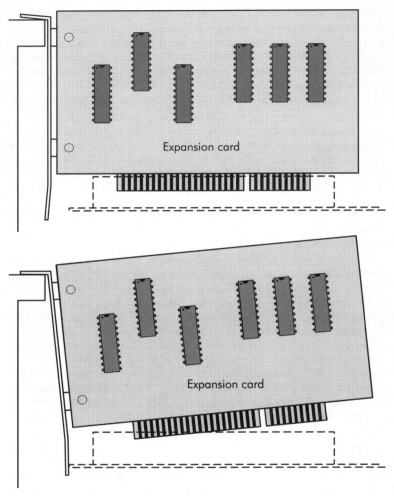

Fig.2.55 A mounting bracket can cause problems if it does not have the correct right-angled bend

If there seems to be no problems with the installation of the drivers, it is then a matter of resorting to the usual testing methods. First, look for any signs of damage to the interface card, the connecting cable, or the peripheral itself. Is the interface card properly installed in the PC? A common problem is that of the expansion card tending to ride up at the rear. Sometimes this happens as soon as the card is bolted into place, but it does sometimes happen that the card is all right for some time, and then it pops up out of place. The usual cause of the problem is the mounting bracket not having the proper right angle fold at the top. Initially the card fits down into the slot correctly, as in the upper diagram of Figure 2.55, but when the fixing bolt is tightened the card tends to go out of alignment, as in the lower diagram of Figure 2.55.

With the expansion card fitted into the slot at an angle, the terminals of the slot tend to be short-circuited by the expansion card, bringing the whole computer to a halt. A visual inspection of the expansion cards will usually reveal this problem. It is also worthwhile pressing on the expansion card to see if it will push down further into the expansion slots. If a card pushes further into place but almost immediately pops back up again, there is almost certainly a problem with the mounting bracket. The cure is to remove the card, carefully bend the mounting bracket to the correct shape, and then reinstall the card, making sure that it is fully inserted into the expansion slot.

A similar problem can occur with a card that looks as though it is properly seated in its expansion socket, whereas it is in fact too high up and not making electrical contact with the slot. Although this is difficult to spot visually, because you can not see how much of the card is within the expansion slot, it should be revealed by firmly pressing down on the expansion cards one by one. If a card presses down into the slot, but springs back up again when you take your hand away, it is not properly seated in its slot. This problem is another one that usually stems from distortions in the card's mounting bracket. The expansion card will normally fit into the slot properly if the mounting bracket is carefully formed into the correct shape. Some expansion cards are fixed to the mounting bracket via flanges on the bracket and a couple of mounting bolts. In order to get the card to fit into the computer reliably it is sometimes necessary to loosen the two fixing nuts, adjust the position of the bracket slightly, and then retighten the nuts.

USB

USB (universal serial bus) was designed to address the problems with the existing computer interfaces used with Macintosh computers and PCs. A lack of proper standardisation caused problems with most of these interfaces, but particularly problematic with the SCSI and RS232C varieties. A parallel system such as SCSI offers very high data transfer rates, but the cables tend to be bulky and expensive. A high-speed serial port offers reasonably fast data transfers, and can use relatively simple and inexpensive cables. A serial system was therefore adopted, and after a few "teething" problems USB 1.1 was launched, and finally worked properly.

USB 1.1 has a maximum data transfer rate of 12 megabits per second, but this is not quite as good as it seems because any one device in the system can only utilise half of the bandwidth. Even so, data can be uploaded or downloaded at a rate of over 600,000 bytes per second, which is sufficient for most purposes. It is certainly high enough for printers, external modems, digital cameras, scanners, and most other popular peripherals. After a slow start, USB interfaces are now a common feature on computer peripherals. In order to broaden the usefulness of USB ports, version 2.0 was devised and it is now starting to appear in real-world devices. It is backward compatible with USB 1.1, and offers a much higher maximum transfer rate of 480 megabits per second. This is more than adequate for virtually all peripherals, including fast disc drives and video devices.

USB advantages

USB was designed to have advantages over the alternative types of port, and it has been successful to a high degree. These are the main advantages:

Built-in

USB has the advantage of being built-in to a PC, unlike the main alternatives of SCSI and Firewire. Apart from the greater convenience, this avoids the cost of an expansion card, and the problems that can arise when trying to install the card.

Speed

Like an RS232C interface, a USB type provides two-way operation, but with much faster transfer rates. A modern parallel port can provide fast two-way operation, but requires the use of bulky and expensive cables.

Expandability

PC parallel and serial ports are only intended for use with one device per port. With the aid of switching units it is possible to use more than one device on each port, but only in a relatively crude and inconvenient fashion. USB is designed to handle numerous devices, and in theory at any rate, up to 127 peripherals can be connected to a PC via this interface.

Power

A few serial and parallel ports to have power supply outputs, but this is not a standard feature and it is something that is not supported by PC versions of these ports. A USB port has a +5-volt supply output, and a version 1.1 port can supply up to 0.5 amps. This works out at only 2.5 watts, and large peripherals still require their own power supply. However, it is sufficient for smaller devices, such as joysticks and modems.

Plug and Play

USB properly supports the Windows Plug and Play feature. With some of the more simple devices, Windows will detect their presence at boot-up and automatically load the necessary device driver. It is necessary to go through the usual installation process when dealing with units that are more complex. A disc contain the device drivers should then be supplied with the peripheral. Either way, the new device should always be detected properly provided there are no hardware faults. Using other ports, Plug and Play tends to be a bit iffy, or even non-existent.

Standardised

The slow speed of an ordinary serial port is a major drawback, but the lack of standardisation and built-in complexities make it difficult to use. There can be problems when using a serial interface with a modem, but the likelihood of problems are many times greater when it is used for other peripherals. In fairness, the RS232C standard was only designed for use with communications devices such as modems, and it was never intended for printers, etc. A USB port is suitable for non-technical users because it requires no setting up of baud rates or word formats. All data is handled using the same system.

Simple cables

A USB link uses a four-way cable, and two of the wires carry the ground and +5-volt connections. The other two wires form what is termed a "twisted pair", and they carry the data. There are no handshake lines to deal with, and it should never be necessary to make a custom cable. The complexities of a USB link are handled in the software rather than by having numerous connections between the two units. For example, a system of addressing is used so that the computer can send data to the appropriate device when there are two or more peripherals connected to the same USB port. A system of coding is used so that the peripherals treat received data in the correct way. This complexity is handled by the device drivers and the firmware in the peripherals. Users just plug everything in, load the device drivers where appropriate, and then start using the equipment.

Plugging/unplugging

Connecting any device to a computer while either of the units is switched on is not normally to be recommended. Disconnecting devices under the same circumstances is usually discouraged as well. There is a real risk of damage to the computer and the peripheral if you simply plug in and unplug things as the fancy takes you. However, USB is designed for connection and disconnection "on the fly", thus removing the need to switch everything off before adding a USB device to or removing it from the system.

Conflicts

USB makes it easy for peripherals to share system resources. In theory at any rate, it is possible to add dozens of peripherals to the USB ports without any risk of problems with hardware conflicts.

USB hubs

It is possible to use the chain method of connection with USB peripherals, but in practice they usually lack an output that can be connected to the next device in the chain. The usual way of using more than one device per USB port is to use a device called a hub. This is a box having two or more USB ports on the front, and a cable at the rear that connects to a USB port on the PC. The simplest USB hubs are non-powered devices that have two ports (Figure 2.56). With most PCs the USB ports are in the cluster of connectors at the rear of the PC where they are difficult to get at. Some PCs have one or two more USB ports in a concealed compartment on the front panel. This is a more convenient place when the ports are used with gadgets such as USB microphones and pointing devices. It is now quite common for monitors to have a built-in USB hub that also gives easy access to two or more ports. If your system lacks these facilities, a simple two-port hub is useful if you need a couple of easily accessible USB ports.

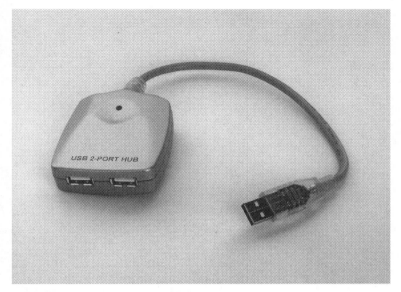

Fig.2.56 A simple twin port USB hub

The larger USB hubs have four or more ports and have their own power supply. The USB hubs built into monitors are normally of this type. The practical significance of the hub being powered is that the full 0.5 amps of current should be available from each port. With a non-powered hub only 0.5 amps can be drawn in total, since that is all that is available from the PC port to which the hub is connected. In order to be certain of satisfactory results, only one device that draws power from the USB port should be used with this type of hub. In practice, it is likely that there will be no problem if two low-power devices are used, such as a USB mouse and a microphone. However, there is no guarantee that both devices will work with a non-powered hub.

A to B

When dealing with USB cables you will encounter A to B and A to A leads. The connector that fits the USB port in the PC is an A type, and the one that connects to the peripheral is a B type connector. An A to B lead is the type used to connect a peripheral to the computer, but smaller devices often just have a captive lead terminated in an A connector. An

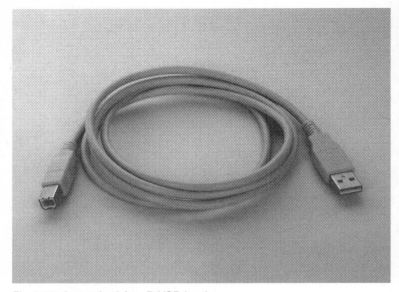

Fig.2.57 A standard A to B USB lead

A to A lead is used to connect two computers together, for file transfer or simple networking. This is not a standard type of lead though, and it is more of an adapter than a simple lead. The small box in the middle of the lead contains some electronics and matching software is needed to get this arrangement working properly. In effect, both computers are connected to the same peripheral, which is the "box of tricks" in the middle of the cable. B to B cables are available, and presumably permit two peripherals to be linked. Practical applications for these cables are something less than obvious.

The A connector is wider and flatter than the B connector (Figure 2.57), and both of them are polarised. Consequently, there is no risk of connecting anything the wrong way around. If you make a mistake, the connector will not fit into place. Matters are complicated slightly by manufacturers being allowed to "do their own thing" with the B connectors. Non-standard type B connectors are only permitted if manufacturers supply suitable leads with the peripherals and make spare leads available. Small USB devices such as digital cameras are often supplied with a lead having a "shrunken" version of the B connector (Figure 2.58).

USB problems

It took some time for USB to gain acceptance, and the main reason for this was a lack of proper support from the operating systems of the time. In particular, the USB port hardware did not work properly with the early versions of Windows 95. Device Manager would show the dreaded yellow exclamation

Fig.2.58 This USB lead has a small B connector to fit a digital camera

marks against the USB entries. The USB ports usually installed properly with the final version of Windows 95 (OSR2), but there were often problems when trying to use USB peripherals with this operating system. Microsoft does not support USB with Windows 95, and you need to use Windows 98 or later for trouble-free USB operation with a PC running Windows.

With some PCs you find that the USB ports are reported by Device Manager as being present and correct, but there are no ports anywhere to be found on the PC! This is a consequence of USB's long "gestation period". Many PCs having the hardware for two USB ports were produced at a time when there was no proper support available from the operating system. There should have been a back-plate with the two USB sockets fitted on the rear of the computer. A lead attached to the sockets would then have been connected to the port hardware on the motherboard. The USB connectors, etc., were often omitted because USB was not actually used to a significant degree at the time.

It is possible to add the missing back-plate assembly provided the appropriate type for your PC is available. The connectors on the motherboard differ slightly from one manufacturer to another, so you need to be careful to buy a back-plate assembly that precisely matches the motherboard in your PC. If your PC has a spare PCI expansion slot, it might be easier to disable the on-board USB ports and fit a USB expansion card. The only drawback of this method is that it will be a little more costly than adding the back-plate assembly.

Enabling USB

If a suitably modern version of Windows is in use but Device Manager still indicates a problem with the USB ports, it is possible that the port hardware is faulty. It is worth trying one or two things before getting a repair done, which in most cases will require replacement of the motherboard. Start by deleting the entries for the USB ports in Device Manager. Shut down the computer, restart it, and then reinstall the drivers for the ports. It is also worth checking the section of the BIOS Setup program that deals with the USB ports. This will usually be in the Integrated Peripherals section, and there will be three settings associated with the USB ports (Figure 2.59).

The OnChip USB option is the one that permits the USB ports to be switched on and off. The Disable option should be used if a USB expansion card is to be used instead of the on-board ports. It might also be worthwhile disabling the ports if they are not going to be used and the PC is suffering from a lack of system resources. Obviously the Enabled setting must be used if the ports are to be utilised.

The other two settings enable support for a USB keyboard and a USB mouse to be switched on. Normally the operating system looks for the keyboard on the keyboard port, and the mouse on a serial port or the PS/2 mouse type. The lack of a keyboard on the normal port will produce an error message from the BIOS POST (power on self-test) program. The operating system may fail to detect and use a USB mouse or keyboard. Placing the relevant BIOS setting at Enabled should ensure that a USB mouse or keyboard is used correctly and that error messages are avoided. Do not set either of these at Enabled unless the appropriate

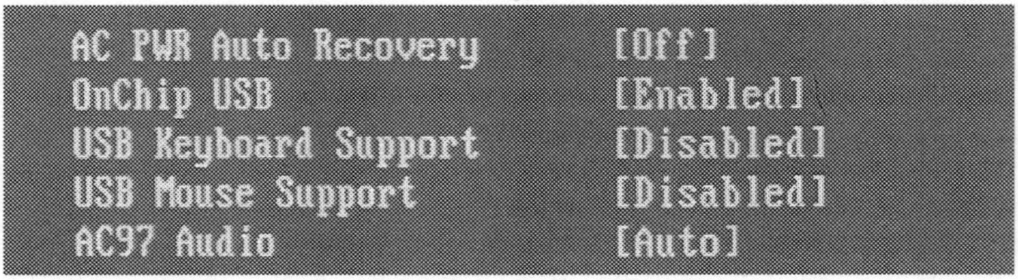

```
AC PWR Auto Recovery        [Off]
OnChip USB                  [Enabled]
USB Keyboard Support        [Disabled]
USB Mouse Support           [Disabled]
AC97 Audio                  [Auto]
```

Fig.2.59 The integral USB ports of a PC can usually be switched on and off via the BIOS Setup program

USB device is in use. Keyboards and mice are the only USB devices that need specific support from the BIOS.

Resources

A PC can accommodate a fair amount of hardware, but there are limits to the number of gadgets that can be used. One of the main reasons for USB being introduced is that it enables a PC to be used with an almost endless range of peripherals without any danger of two devices trying to use the same hardware resources. Conflicts are avoided because the peripherals on the serial bus all share the same resources, which are those of the USB port. The sophisticated protocols that control the flow of data ensure that two devices do not try to use the port's resources at the same time.

A peripheral that connects to any of the built-in ports is less likely to cause hardware conflicts than an internal alternative or a device that requires an expansion card. An external unit that uses a built-in port is merely exploiting the existing hardware, and it should use no additional resources. An internal device or one that uses an expansion card will always require additional resources, which may or may not be available. The advantage of USB is that it takes things a stage further and enables several peripherals to share the same port. With serial and parallel ports it is generally necessary to use more ports in order to accommodate extra devices. A PC can only accommodate a few of these ports, which limits the potential for expansion. The "sky is the limit" with USB.

It is still possible to encounter problems with hardware conflicts when adding an external peripheral. If the peripheral uses an expansion card rather than a built-in port, it is clearly possible that the card will try to use resources that are already in use. Conflicts can also occur when using an existing port, particularly when using RS232C and parallel printer ports. In theory, this should not happen, but some devices "steal" resources that are intended for the standard ports. This may work fine if the port is not in use or has a certain type of peripheral connected to it. Things can then go wrong if you connect a peripheral to a port that was previously unused or switch to a different peripheral.

Checking for conflicts

You can check for problems with hardware conflicts by first going to Device Manager. It will be immediately obvious if there is a problem with one of the installed devices. The relevant section will be expanded and

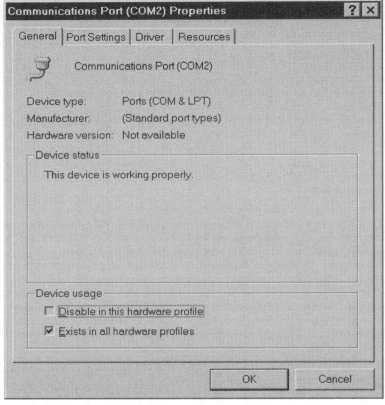

Fig.2.60 The properties window for a communications port

there will be a yellow exclamation mark against an entry in that section. Device Manager may be able to give details of the problem. Double-click on the entry for the faulty device to produce its properties window (Figure 2.60). Then left-click on the Resources tab to produce a window like the one of Figure 2.61.

All is well in this example, and near the bottom of the window it indicates that there are no conflicts. If there is a conflict, this will be pointed out and some technical details will be provided. Sorting out hardware conflicts is a somewhat involved process, with no guarantee of success. Some items of hardware are simply incompatible and can not be used in

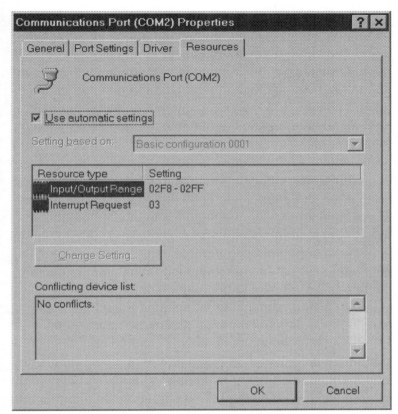

Fig.2.61 The Resources section of the properties window

the same PC. Do not start changing resource settings unless you have the necessary expertise and genuinely know what you are doing. Making mistakes here is a good way of "gumming up" the whole PC.

There is some built-in help available from Windows for those lacking the expertise to sort out this type of thing. Select Help from the Start menu, enter "hardware conflict" into the text box, and then double-click on the entry of the same name that appears in the list below the textbox. This should produce something like Figure 2.62. Left -click where it says, "click here" in the right-hand side of the window to start the Hardware Troubleshooter. This produces a screen like the one of Figure 2.63, and

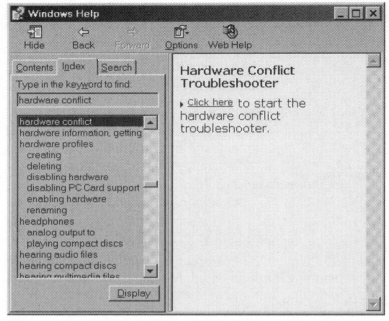

Fig.2.62 Accessing the Hardware Troubleshooter via the Help system

it is then a matter of going through various screens so that Windows can
be fed with the information it requires. It is normally necessary to do
some delving with Device Manager in order to come up with the right
answers, but detailed instructions are provided. With luck, at the end of
the process you will have a solution to the problem.

Addresses

The resources that cause hardware conflicts are IRQs (interrupt requests)
and addresses. Like a computer's memory, the input and output circuits
are controlled by the address lines of the processor. The processors
used in PCs provide some 65536 input/output addresses that are
numbered from 0 to 65535. PCs use a somewhat simplified scheme of
things that only utilises addresses from 0 to 1023. Even given that most
real world input/output circuits require a small block of addresses rather
than a single address, this still provides an adequate number.

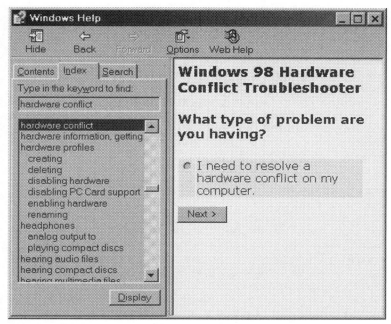

Fig.2.63 A series of questions are answered in order to help Windows make a diagnosis

The numbers used in addresses, whether for memory or the input/output circuits, often look rather strange. For example, the base addresses for the built-in serial ports are normally shown as H2F8 and H3F8. Addresses are often expressed in a numbering system called hexadecimal, which is based on 16 rather than 10. Sixteen single digit numbers are required for this system, but normal numbers only provide 10 of these from 0 to 9. Hexadecimal (hex) therefore uses the normal numbers plus the first six letters of the alphabet (A to F). In an address such as H27F, the H indicates that the value is in hexadecimal. Note though, that other prefixes are also used, including # and &H. The F in the address is part of the number.

It is not normally necessary for users to get involved in the addresses of input/output devices. Occasionally it can be necessary to set the right address range on an expansion card to avoid a conflict. For example, if a printer port expansion card is added, its address range must be different to the one used by the built-in parallel port. Where appropriate, either the address range used by the card must be altered by adjusting the jumper settings, or the BIOS Setup program must be used to alter the addresses used by the built-in port. It is not necessary to understand hexadecimal in order to do this, so do not get fazed by the odd looking numbers.

Note that some computer resources can be shared by the computer's hardware, but addresses do not fall into this category. If two devices share the same addresses, it is likely that neither of them will work, and at least one will certainly fail to work. Both devices are in danger when address conflicts occur, and there is a real possibility of one or the other being damaged. There is a slight risk of address conflicts causing the computer to crash.

Hexadecimal

Printer port addresses cause a certain amount of confusion because the port addresses on one PC can be different to those on another PC. The normal base addresses are H378 for port one (LPT1) and H278 for port two (LPT2). Some early graphics cards included a printer port, and this used a base address of H3BC, presumably in order to avoid possible conflicts with other printer ports in the PC. Operating systems look for installed printer ports and then number them in sequence from the highest address to the lowest. A printer port having H3BC as its base address will therefore be port one. If additional ports are fitted at H378 and H278 they become ports two and three respectively.

Modern motherboards have a built-in printer port, and its base address can usually be altered using the BIOS Setup program. In the past, there was usually a choice of H278 or H378, but most modern boards seem to offer H3BC as well. In fact many motherboards use this as the default address for the port. The Integrated Peripherals section of the BIOS Setup program is normally the one that handles the port addresses (Figure 2.64).

Fig.2.64 The addresses of internal ports are changed via the BIOS Setup program

The address used for the port is not normally of any consequence, but it is something that has to be taken into account when adding a printer port card that fits into an ISA expansion slot. The address used by the expansion card must not be the same as the one used by the motherboard for the built-in port. Where necessary, one or the other must be changed in order to avoid conflicts.

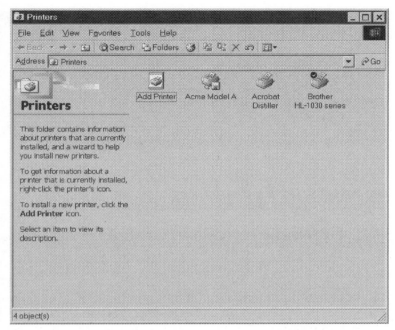

Fig.2.65 The Printers window has icons for the installed printers

Bear in mind that adding a printer card that uses a base address of H3BC will result in the integral port being automatically moved from port 1 to port 2 by the operating system. This could result is data being directed to the wrong port. Either the peripheral concerned can be connected to the correct port, or its port assignment can be changed in Windows. To change the port assignment of a printer, first go to the Windows Control Panel and double-click the Printer's icon or entry. This will produce a window something like Figure 2.65, but the exact appearance will depend on the version of Windows you are using and the printers that are installed on your system. Double-click on the icon for the appropriate printer, and a small window should then appear. Select the Properties option from the Printer menu (Figure 2.66). Another window will then appear, and the appropriate port can then be selected from the drop-down menu (Figure 2.67).

The BIOS Setup program usually allows the base addresses of the two serial ports to be altered, and there may be a similar facility for other

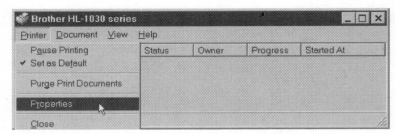

Fig.2.66 The properties window is accessed via the Printer menu

hardware such as the MPU-401 MIDI port. It should not be necessary to alter the settings for the serial ports unless an ISA serial port card is added, and there is no other way of avoiding address conflicts. There is

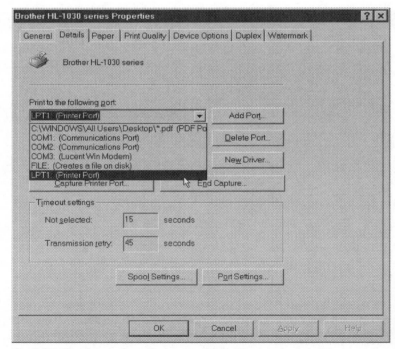

Fig.2.67 The properties window enables any standard port to be selected

sometimes an Auto option in the BIOS Setup program, and with this in use the BIOS should set port addresses that avoid conflicts with any other serial ports. The only problem with this method is that it might require some investigation to ascertain the port numbering, which will not be totally under your control.

It is unlikely that an expansion card, other than a serial or parallel port card, will try to use the standard address ranges of these ports. The situation is different with the normal base address of H300 that is used for the MPU-401 MIDI port. This was not a standard piece of hardware in the original PCs, and the address range used is one that is available for any expansion card. Consequently, it might be necessary to change the MPU-401's base address in order to avoid conflicts with an expansion card. This can be done using the Integrated Peripherals section of the BIOS Setup program.

IRQs

IRQs cause the vast majority of hardware conflicts. The basic idea of interrupts is that a hardware device that needs urgent attention can generate an interrupt by signalling to the processor via its special input terminals. The processor then stops what it is doing, uses a reserved section of memory called the Stack to saves any data it currently holds, and then runs the routine associated with the device that generated the interrupt. When the processor has finished running the interrupt routine, it reinstates the data stored in the Stack and continues where it left off. The point of this method is that it enables the processor to respond very rapidly to devices that need prompt attention, but it does not waste massive amounts of processor time by frequently scanning the hardware.

There are 16 interrupts available, and they are prioritised so that the most urgent one can be serviced first when two or more interrupts occur simultaneously. With a PC this system operates in a less than obvious fashion. This list starts with the highest priority interrupt and works in sequence to the one having the lowest priority.

0, 1, 2/9, 10, 11, 12, 13, 14, 15, 3, 4, 5, 6, 7, 8

Numerous pieces of hardware in a PC can generate interrupts, including things like the mouse port, the serial and parallel ports, and the disc drives. Interrupts can be shared by different pieces of hardware, but only under special circumstances. Consequently, spare interrupt assignments are in short supply. A list of the standard interrupt assignments used by PCs is shown on the next page.

IRQ	Assignment
0	System timer
1	Keyboard
2	Cascade for IRQs 8 to 15
3	COM2/COM4
4	COM1/COM3
5	Unassigned, but often used for LPT2 or a soundcard
6	Floppy drive controller
7	LPT1
8	Real-time clock
9	Unassigned (cascaded to IRQ2)
10	Unassigned, but often used for a soundcard or network adapter
11	Unassigned, but the usual choice for a SCSI interface
12	Unassigned, but normally used for PS/2 mouse port in a modern PC
13	Maths coprocessor
14	Primary IDE hard disc interface
15	Secondary IDE hard disc interface

Although there are 16 interrupt numbers, only 15 are actually usable. The original PCs had one interrupt controller chip providing eight interrupt levels. This was inadequate for later PCs, and a second controller was therefore added. The second controller drives IRQ2 on the first chip, which effectively makes IRQ2 and IRQ9 the same. It is this cascading of two interrupt controllers via IRQ2 that produces the odd sequence in the IRQ priorities list. Note that modern PCs do not use the original interrupt controller chips, but instead have modified circuits that are part of a support chip for processor. All 16 interrupts are usually available, and the priority order is often different to the scheme of things used in the original PCs.

Clearly most of the available interrupt numbers are used by the basic components found in a modern PC. However, there are some available for expansion cards, such as IRQ10 and IRQ11. It may be possible to free up some interrupt lines by disabling hardware that is not in use. For example, the PS/2 mouse port can be switched off if the PC is fitted with

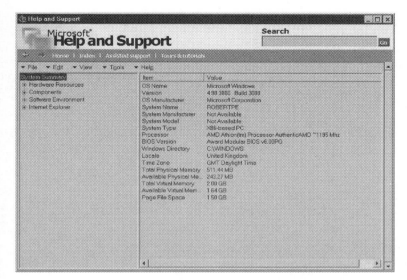

Fig.2.68 Windows can provide some basic system information

a serial or USB mouse. Where only one IDE disc controller is in use, the secondary IDE channel can be disabled, as can any unused ports. The BIOS Setup program usually has facilities to enable and disable input/output circuits on the motherboard.

Sharing

It is sometimes claimed that sharing of IRQs on a PC is not possible, but this is not strictly true. You can get a complete list of the IRQ assignments for your PC by selecting Programs from the Start menu, followed by Accessories, System Tools and System Information from the submenus. This produces a window like the one shown in Figure 2.68, which gives some basic information about the computer. Double-click on Hardware Resources to expand its entry, and then left-click the IRQs entry to select it. The left-hand section of the window will display a full list of IRQ assignments (Figure 2.69), but there will be a short delay while the program scans the hardware.

In this example there are some IRQ numbers that have a single assignment, and others that have several. Some hardware of a modern

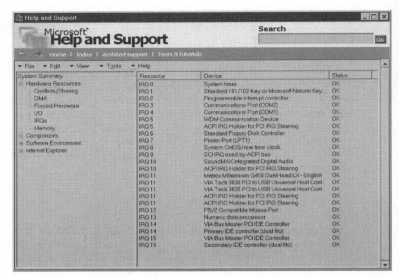

Fig.2.69 Windows can provide a full list of the current IRQ assignments

PC is designed to handle IRQs in a fashion that permits sharing. PCI expansion cards together with a modern operating system should give trouble-free operation with a lack of hardware conflicts. The only important proviso here is that there must be one or two spare IRQs so that the PCI cards have some resources to share. As pointed out previously, the resources of the USB ports are shared by the devices connected to the serial bus, and adding large numbers of devices onto the USB ports should not produce any hardware conflicts. Provided the USB ports have been installed correctly, the devices connected to the ports should work properly.

The situation is different with built-in hardware that connects directly with the buses of the processor, and with ISA expansion cards. These also connect direct to the buses of the processor. In general, sharing of IRQs is not possible with hardware such as this. In practice, there is some sharing of IRQs with hardware such as the serial ports, and it is quite normal for COM1 and COM2 to respectively use the same IRQs as COM3 and COM4. However, in practice this system is unlikely to work if both devices that share an IRQ actually try to utilise interrupts. If only one device utilises them, everything may well work smoothly, although there is no absolute guarantee of success.

Probably the most common example of problems with IRQ conflicts is the mouse ceasing to work when a new piece of hardware is added. Having a mouse on COM2 and a modem on COM4 for example, is asking for trouble. Both devices will make extensive use of interrupts, and both will use the same one (IRQ3). With a mouse on COM1, a modem should be connected to COM2 or COM4. Where two serial ports are needed for peripherals, it is a good idea to use the existing ports rather than buying an RS232C expansion card. Most PCs have a PS/2 mouse port and a couple of USB ports, and these can be used with a mouse of the appropriate type. Buying a new mouse is unlikely to cost any more than purchasing an RS232C expansion card, and should avoid problems with hardware conflicts.

PCI v ISA

Expansion cards that provide additional serial and parallel ports are now available in ISA and PCI versions. ISA and PCI parallel port cards are shown in Figures 2.70 and 2.71 respectively. When there is a choice between an ISA expansion card and a PCI type, the latter has to be

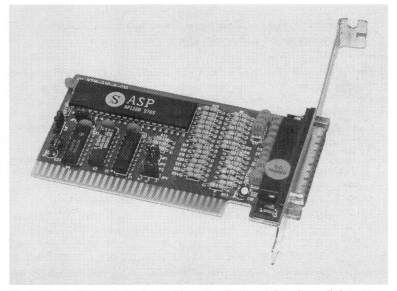

Fig.2.70 An ISA port card provides standard serial and parallel ports

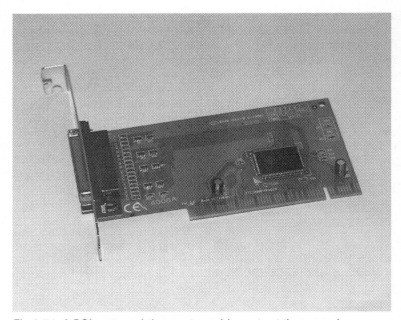

*Fig.2.71 A PCI port card does not provide ports at the normal
addresses without the aid of re-mapping*

regarded as the better choice. ISA expansion slots are being phased
out and an ever-dwindling number of new PCs have any ISA slots. The
few that still have this type of expansion slot almost invariably have just
the one. There would seem to be little chance of carrying ISA cards on
to your next PC, but it is virtually certain that PCI cards will be usable for
many years to come.

When selecting serial and parallel expansion cards, it is important to
realise that ISA and PCI cards provide two rather different types of port.
The advantage of an ISA type is that the card connects direct to the
processor's buses, and it provides traditional ports that have the usual
base addresses. PCI cards are not likely to become obsolete in the near
future, and they have other advantages such as proper Plug and Play
support. However, the PCI bus is really a form of input/output port, and
devices on the PCI bus can not fit into the input/output map in the normal
way. On the face of it, this is unimportant because PCI port cards are
supplied with a disc containing a suitable device driver. This enables
Windows to use the card much as if it was a standard port at the usual

input/output addresses. Provided all the software does things "by the book" and only contacts the ports via the operating system, everything should work fine.

Unfortunately, real-world software does not always do things this way, and it might try to directly control the port's hardware. This will not work at all, because the port's hardware will not be at the usual addresses in the input/output map. It can only be accessed indirectly via the PCI bus, using relatively complex routines. In general, the more common peripherals such as printers and modems are contacted via the usual channels and should not give any problems with a PCI port card. Many devices are less accommodating though, and parallel port scanners and Zip drives mostly use direct access method. It is therefore better to use the more "run of the mill" devices on PCI port cards, and the more specialised peripherals on the PC's built-in ports. With luck, this will avoid any problems.

Re-mapping

The expansion card might be supplied with a software solution in the form of a re-mapping program. This tries to intercept instructions that are directed at the standard port addresses. It then substitutes an appropriate routine to drive the PCI card. There is no guarantee that this type of thing will work properly, but it usually works well enough. One potential problem is that software often controls the hardware directly in order to obtain greater speed. This method of intercepting instructions and substituting appropriate routines might slow things down to an unacceptable degree. This does not seem to be a significant problem in practice, probably due to serial and parallel ports being quite slow in relation to the rest of the PC.

Note that a PCI card is unlikely to use the re-mapping facility by default. The card's device driver should have a properties window that enables the re-mapping to be enabled. This might be available by double clicking on the port's entry in Device Manager, but this often gives access to a cut down version of the properties window. Where this is the case, look for another entry for the card in Device Manager, in amongst the main categories. Double clicking on this entry should give access to the full properties window. If a re-mapping facility is provided, there should be a Configuration section or something similar (Figure 2.72). In this example, the re-mapping can be enabled by ticking the appropriate checkbox, and base addresses of H278 and H378 can be selected for the parallel port. Of course, the address selected must not be in use by

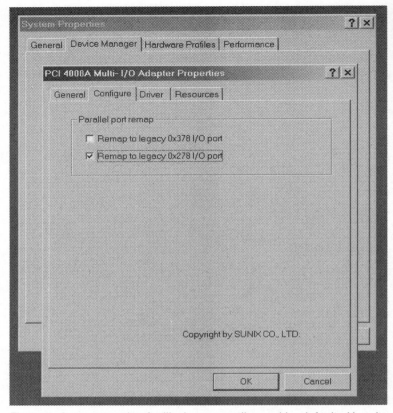

Fig.2.72 Any re-mapping facility is not usually used by default. Here it has been enabled using the card's properties window

another port. Where necessary, check the properties windows for the other ports to determine their base addresses, so that address conflicts can be avoided.

Adapters

Over the years a vast number of adapters have been produced, enabling virtually any type of port to be adapted to suit practically any other type. Most of these are now obsolete, and many of these adapters were too approximate to be of much use. There are still a few adapters produced,

Fig.2.73 A USB to parallel printer adapter

and the ones that permit serial or parallel port devices to be used with a USB port are by far the most popular. They mostly look like an ordinary lead, as does the USB to printer port adapter shown in Figure 2.73. However, there is some sophisticated electronics in the larger of the connectors. These adapters are not really intended as a means of adding more ports to a standard PC, where an expansion card is the normal solution. They can be used in this way if you would prefer not to delve into the interior of your PC, but they are primarily intended for use with Macintosh computers and laptop PCs that only have a USB port.

When using these adapters with a PC you have to bear in mind that, like PCI serial and parallel cards, the port hardware is not at its normal place in the PC's input/output map. This factor could give problems with awkward peripherals. The parallel adapters almost invariably have a Centronics connector at the parallel end, rather than a female D connector. This makes it easier to use the adapters with a parallel printer, since the Centronics connector will plug straight into the printer's input port. It deliberately discourages people from trying to use the adapter with anything other than a printer. Most of these adapters only provide a basic printer port, and do not support any form of bi-directional operation. This renders them unsuitable for many non-printer applications.

Fig.2.74 A manual two-way switching unit

Port sharing

Gadgets that permit more than one device to be connected to a parallel or RS232C serial port were quite popular at one time, but they seem to be used less widely these days. Only one device is actually connected to the PC at any one time, and these units are simply switches. They permit the parallel or serial port to be connected to whichever device you wish to use at the time. The simplest unit is a two-way type that has manual switching (Figure 2.74). There are three 25-way D connectors on the rear panel (Figure 2.75), and there are two ways of using the unit. In order to use two peripherals with one printer port, the INPUT/OUTPUT socket is connected to the PC's printer port. Sockets A and B then connect to the two peripherals. The alternative is to connect sockets A and B to ports on different PCs. The INPUT/OUTPUT socket then connects to a peripheral that is shared by the two PCs.

Switching units of this type are primarily intended for use with parallel ports and printers, but all 25 input/output terminals are switched, and they will therefore work with serial ports and with any serial or parallel peripheral. When used with a parallel port or ports, a 25-way cable having

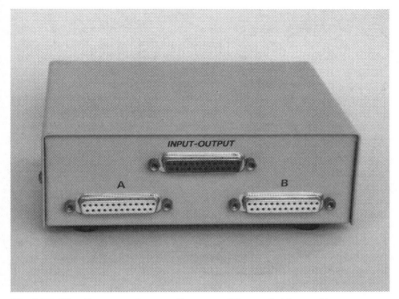

Fig.2.75 The D connectors on the rear of the switching unit

a male D connector at each end is required to connect the switching unit to a PC. This standard cable should be available from the same shop as the switching unit. Parallel peripherals connect to the switch box using whatever cable would be used for direct connection to the PC's parallel port.

Things are more awkward when these units are used with an RS232C port. It might be possible to obtain a lead that will connect the switching unit to a 9-pin PC serial port, but it would probably be a matter of making a custom cable. The two ports on the switching unit will be non-standard, having female instead of male D connectors. It is possible to obtain adapters called "gender benders" that correct this type of problem. However, be warned that these adapters often provide the required "sex change", but do not provide the necessary "mirroring" of the pin numbers in the process. What should be pin 1 is pin 13, what should be pin 2 is pin 12, and so on. Seeking out a switching unit that is specifically designed for use with serial ports could save a lot of hassle.

Utilising one peripheral with two PCs is a relatively safe way of using a switching unit. Using two peripherals with one port is more risky. In the days of MS/DOS there was no major problem, because each program had its own driver software for use with each output device. This greatly reduced the risk of one driver interfering with another, because there would normally be just one driver program in operation at any one time. The situation is very different with Windows, where device drivers for both peripherals would have to be installed, and might be left running in the background. This can result in one device driver interfering with the other. It is safer to install more ports and operate on the basis of one peripheral per port, although this clearly increases the risk of hardware conflicts.

Manual switching units do not have a good reputation for reliability. There is inevitably a large number of switch contacts in a unit of this type, and over a period, there is inevitably some build up of dirt and corrosion on the contacts. The switches used in these units are normally sealed in an attempt to keep dirt at bay. Unfortunately, this makes it virtually impossible to use switch cleaner when the contacts do succumb to dirt and corrosion. Repeatedly switching the unit backwards and forwards will often clean the contacts sufficiently to restore normal operation. It will probably be necessary to repeat this process periodically.

The problem is not always due to faulty contacts, and this is unlikely to be the cause if the switch unit is nearly new. It is more probable that the switching from one unit to another is getting the PC or a peripheral confused. Mechanical switches do not operate "cleanly", and tend to produce spurious signals during the changeover. The usual solution is to switch off the peripheral before switching from one PC to another, or switch off both peripherals when switching from one to the other, as appropriate.

Automatic sharing

Printer sharers that provide automatic switching used to be quite expensive, but like most other computer gadgets they can now be obtained at surprisingly low prices. There no need to manually select the computer that you wish to use with the printer when using a device of this type. You just start printing, and the switching unit automatically couples the appropriate computer through to the printer. The obvious restriction is that you must not attempt to print from both computers at once. Trying to do so is unlikely to have dire consequences, and most units will simply continue to use whichever computer activated the printer first. This results in a timeout error from the other PC when it fails to contact the printer after the allotted waiting period.

I have occasionally been asked for assistance with an automatic printer sharer that sometimes works, but frequently refuses to couple the signals through to the printer. This problem is not usually due to a fault in the equipment. The normal cause of the problem is that the printer sharer will only work if both PCs are switched on. In fairness to the manufacturers, this point is usually made clear in the instruction manual, and is not omitted or hidden in the "fine print". Unfortunately, few people ever bother to read the instruction manuals.

The problem occurs because the printer sharer monitors certain output lines of the printer ports on the PCs, and reacts to certain levels on these outputs. The outputs of a port go to logic 0 when the PC is switched off, and the printer sharer erroneously interprets these levels as the computer trying to print. Unfortunately, there is no easy way around this problem. A manual switching unit is a more practical proposition if you do not wish to have both PCs running when only one of them is actually in use.

Firewire and IrDA

Firewire is a high-speed serial link that was devised by Apple Computers Inc. and was finalised in 1995. I must admit that it is not an interface that I have used to a significant extent, and Firewire is not very popular with PC users. It is likely that most PC users have never heard of it. With a transfer rate of 400 megabits per second, it is much faster than USB 1.1, but is slightly slower than USB 2.0. Like USB ports, a Firewire type can provide power to peripheral devices. Firewire is mainly used for up-market scanners, digital cameras, external disc drives, and various video oriented devices. As it is not a standard PC port, a Firewire expansion card is needed in order to use this type of interface. Any company selling peripherals that use a Firewire interface should be able to supply a suitable PC expansion card and connecting cable as well, if they are not supplied with the peripheral.

IrDA (infrared data association) avoids cable problems by using infrared "light" to transmit signals from one device to another. It is little used with computer peripherals, and is mainly used as a means for notebook computers and other miniature computers to communicate with a PC. It is used to a limited extent with peripherals such as digital cameras, where it is often offered in addition to rather than instead of an ordinary cable link. I suppose that IrDA could be considered a standard PC port, but most computers are not supplied with this type of interface set up ready for use. In fact most PCs are supplied without all the necessary hardware installed. Modern motherboards have the basic hardware for the port,

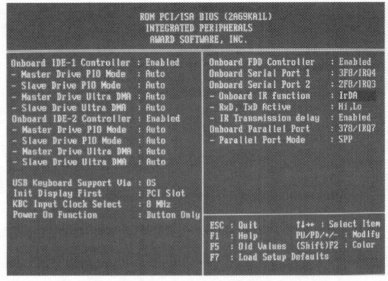

Fig.2.76 The IrDA settings are in the Integrated Peripherals section of the BIOS Setup program

but the necessary bits and pieces that enable it to be used with the outside world are optional extras. IrDA can also be implemented using an expansion card.

Even with the optional hardware installed, an IrDA interface is unlikely to work without some changes to the BIOS settings. Some motherboards have hardware specifically for an IrDA interface, but it is more common for one of the serial ports (usually COM2) to be used. Note that with this arrangement, enabling the IrDA port renders the serial port inoperative.

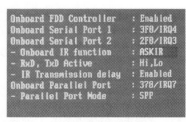

Fig.2.77 The IrDA BIOS options

The IrDA settings are usually controlled via the Integrated Peripherals section of the BIOS Setup program. With the IrDA port enabled, other settings become active (Figure 2.76). There may well be more than one infrared mode on offer (Figure 2.77). The instruction manual for any device that uses an IrDA interface should give details of the settings required.

The Plug and Play facility should come into operation when you boot the PC into Windows, and the usual messages pop up on the screen, indicating that various device drivers are being loaded. It is unlikely that any driver discs or the Windows installation disc will be required, and Windows should be able to locate the files it required. After the customary reboot, the new hardware should be properly installed and fully

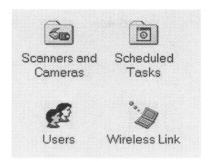

Scanners and Cameras   Scheduled Tasks

Users   Wireless Link

Fig.2.78 The Wireless Link icon is the one for the IrDA port

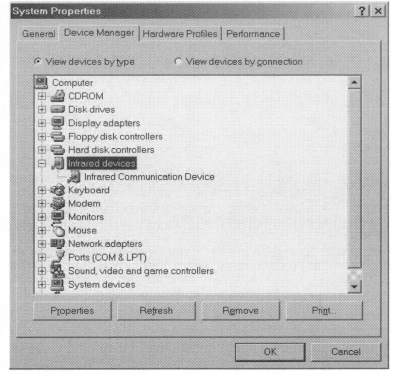

Fig.2.79 The IrDA port should be listed in Device Manager

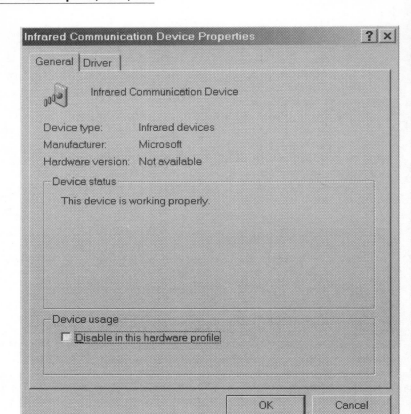

*Fig.2.80 The properties window for the IrDA port should indicate that
it is working properly*

operational. Go to the Windows Control Panel and make some basic
checks before trying to use the IrDA facility. An icon for the new hardware
will probably appear in the Control Panel (Figure 2.78). It should also
have an entry in Device Manager (Figure 2.79).

Double-click on its entry to bring up the properties window for the new
hardware. If all is well, this should report that the IrDA port is installed
and working properly, as in Figure 2.80. Note that this indicates that the
main hardware on the motherboard is installed and operational. Device
Manager will not detect a problem further down the chain, such as a
fault in one of the photocells.

All is not lost if proves to be difficult or impossible to obtain the right parts to utilise the built-in IrDA interface. IrDA expansion cards and USB adapters are readily available. With a modern PC, the USB option is probably the least troublesome method of adding an IrDA facility.

Cable testing

From time to time you will inevitably end up in a situation where you need to know whether it is a cable that is faulty, or the electronics at one end of the cable. If you have a spare cable, it is possible to use substitution testing to determine if the suspect cable really is faulty. A spare cable will not always be to hand though, and some computer cables are quite expensive. Quite reasonably, you may be reluctant to buy a new one on the off chance that the existing cable is faulty. With something as basic as a cable, it is easy to test it by making a few electrical checks. This does not require any advanced test equipment, and it is just a matter of testing to determine whether each terminal at one end of the lead is connected to the corresponding terminal at the other end. Sometimes this type of testing is superfluous because there is clear evidence of physical damage to the lead. In most cases though, faulty cables show little or no outward sign of damage.

Any test meter, or "multimeter" as they are generally known, should have a resistance range that can be used for checking cables. In fact, most of these test meters have a continuity tester range that is specifically designed for this type of thing. When set to this range the unit emits a "beep" sound if there is a short-circuit or very low resistance across the test prods. This audible indication is better than having some form of visual indication, since it avoids the need to look away from the test prods. Looking away from the test prods is usually followed by one of the test prods slipping out of position about a millisecond later! However, the "beep" is usually in addition to a visual indication rather than instead of it.

A digital multimeter is well suited to this type of testing, but is somewhat over-specified. However, if you can obtain one at a good price it should work well for many years. A basic analogue multimeter is likely to be much cheaper and will do the job well. In fact, something much more basic is adequate for testing leads, and even an old torch bulb and battery style continuity checker (Figure 2.81) will do the job perfectly well. The test prods and leads can be the "real thing", but they need consist of nothing more than two pieces of single-strand insulated wire with a few millimetres of the insulation stripped away to produce the prods. This is

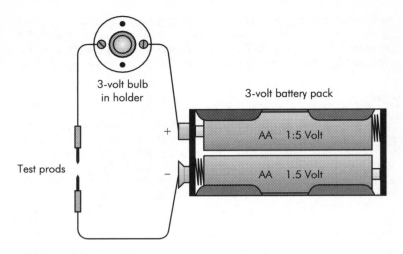

Fig.2.81 A simple continuity tester for checking cables

admittedly a bit crude, but when testing computer leads it is often necessary to get the prods into tiny holes in the connectors. With the improvised prods there is no difficulty in doing so because they are so narrow, but with proper prods they are often too thick to fit into the connectors.

Testing cables is often rather awkward because you need four hands! One hand per test prod and another hand per connector. The easy way to tackle the problem is to fix both connectors to the workbench using clamps, or something like Bostik Blu-Tack or Plasticine will often do the job quite well (Figure 2.82). With heavier cables such as printer types it is better to clamp the connectors in place, because Blu-Tack and the like may not have sufficient sticking power to keep everything in place. Heavy-duty cables tend to have "a mind of their own". With the connectors fixed to the bench and the metal terminals facing towards you it is easy to check for continuity because you then have both hands free to hold the test prods. Provided the workbench is well lit you can also see exactly what you are doing, which should help to avoid errors.

Incidentally, if you use a test meter for cable testing, on the face of it the meter is also suitable for checking the supply levels on the motherboard and other simple voltage checks on a PC. I would definitely advise against prodding around on the motherboard or an expansion card using a test

Fig.2.82 Testing cables is easier if they are fixed to the worktop

meter. With the intricacy of modern boards it is quite tricky to do this, and there is a high risk of the test prods causing accidental short circuits. These could in turn ruin expensive items of hardware. Definitely do not start probing around inside a PC or on expansion cards using a simple continuity tester. It operates at currents that are high enough to zap most of the semiconductors used in modern PCs. Such is the delicacy of modern microelectronics that using a multimeter set to its continuity range is also far from risk-free. Use multimeters for testing cables, checking RS232C, and other basic tests, but nothing more adventurous than this unless you really know what you are doing.

Turn off

As a final point, it is worth emphasising that it is not a good idea to plug in connectors and unplug them while any of the equipment is switched on. There are one or two exceptions such as USB, where the hardware is designed for use "on the fly". With ports such as these, there should be no problems if the PC is switched on when peripherals are connected and removed from the system. USB is often used with peripherals such as digital cameras where, to say the least, it would be very inconvenient if the PC had to be shut down each time the camera was connected or disconnected from the PC.

Fig.2.83 A parallel dongle that has an output socket for a printer

With most types of peripheral it would be more convenient if the equipment could be left switched on while changes were made to the cabling. This is especially so when trying to sort out problems with peripherals, since repeatedly shutting down the system and restarting is likely to be very time consuming. Many people save time by not switching off before making changes to the external cabling, but this runs the risk of adding more problems rather than solving the existing ones. Parallel ports are probably more vulnerable to damage than the serial variety, but neither type is immune.

Extra care is needed when dealing with a port that is fitted with a so-called "dongle". This is an item of hardware that connects to a port of the PC and provides copy protection for a piece of software. The software is easily copied, but without the dongle it will not run. You can supply copies to all your friends, but they will not be able to use it. Some PC software uses an expansion card to provide the copy protection, but the more common method is to have a dongle that fits onto a serial or parallel port. Most dongles of this type have a connector that enables the port to be used through the dongle (Figure 2.83). There is no guarantee that the dongle will provide faultless operation with every peripheral, but with something straightforward like a printer there should be no problems.

Some dongles are quite simple and are not easily damaged, but many contain complex and delicate circuitry. It is clearly essential to proceed carefully if damage to a dongle could leave you unable to use a vital piece of software until a replacement is obtained. It is a good idea to switch everything off, remove the dongle and store it safely, and then get the peripheral working without the dongle in place. With system working properly again, switch everything off, reinstate the dongle, and then try the system again. If everything works without the dongle, but a peripheral fails to work via the dongle, it is clearly the dongle that is causing the problem. It might be faulty, or it could simply be incompatible with the peripheral device you are using. Either way, the software company that supplied the dongle should be able to help. Note that many dongles are only guaranteed to work properly if the PC is switched on first, and then the peripheral is turned on.

Points to remember

A modern printer should work perfectly well with a PC using an "off the shelf" printer cable. If a new printer fails to work with an old printer cable, it is likely that the cable does not have all the connections needed for a modern printer, or that it is simply worn out.

Apart from printers, few parallel port devices use a PC printer lead. Many parallel port peripherals use a cable having a 25-way male connector at one end and a 25-way female connector at the other, with the "straight" method of connection. However, there is no true standardisation, and some peripherals require a cable that is specifically designed for that unit.

Some parallel port peripherals work faster if the port is set to an enhanced mode, or will not work at all unless an enhanced mode is used. Parallel ports operate as standard ports or SPP ports by default. In order to use an enhanced mode it is necessary to manually alter the mode setting, and for a built-in port this is achieved using the BIOS Setup program.

Most USB parallel port adapters will only work as standard printer ports and do not support any enhanced mode or even basic bi-directional operation.

Built-in serial and parallel ports and those provided by ISA expansion cards are standard ports that should work with all peripherals. Ports provided by PCI cards and USB adapters can be used with most peripherals provided the device drivers are installed correctly. Equipment that directly accesses the port hardware will only work with these ports if a re-mapping facility is provided, and it is activated. Parallel port Zip drives and scanners mostly use direct addressing of the port.

If a soundcard is reluctant to produce any output, check that the software volume control and mixer settings are correct. Particularly with old ISA soundcards, check that the device drivers are all present and correct. Even if they are, try reinstalling the soundcard.

Getting a microphone to work with a PC can be difficult. PC microphone inputs are not properly standardised, and the characteristics of microphones vary substantially from one type to another. The chances of success are greatly enhanced by using a microphone specifically designed for operation with a PC.

A game port controller will only work properly if it is compatible with the games software, the game port is installed into Windows correctly, and the controller itself is installed in Windows. The controller can not be installed until the game port has been installed. Some joysticks must be calibrated before they will work properly.

PC MIDI ports are non-standard, and do not contain all the hardware required by the MIDI specification. An adapter or a combined MIDI lead and adapter is needed to permit the port to be used with synthesisers, MIDI keyboards, etc.

Huge numbers of devices can be connected to a PC's USB ports without the risk of hardware conflicts. A modern PC has at least two USB ports as standard, but a USB hub enables each port to be used with several peripherals.

Under the right circumstances, it is possible for some system resources to be shared, but addresses can not be shared. Except under special circumstances it is not acceptable for IRQ numbers to be shared. This will usually work if only one of the devices sharing an IRQ number actually utilises interrupts. Devices on the PCI bus can share resources, and the operating system should sort this out for you.

Modern PCs include most of the hardware for an IrDA interface, but are not normally supplied with the rear bracket assembly that provides the rest of the interface. The computer supplier should be able to supply the missing parts, but the interface will not work unless it is enabled using the BIOS Setup program. IrDA ports can also be provided via USB adapters and PCI expansion cards.

The PC and peripheral should be switched off before plugging in or removing data cables. The only exceptions are devices that are intended for connection and disconnection "on the fly". This includes any devices that utilise a USB port.

Modem
troubleshooting

Installed?

Installing a modem and actually getting it to work in real-world applications used to be a job that was very difficult, even for experienced computer users. Getting the Internet software installed, set up, and ready for use would often take about half an hour, provided everything went smoothly! It was not surprising if installation ground to a halt half way through the process. Fortunately, getting the hardware installed is generally much easier than it was even a few years ago. The software producers have also endeavoured to make their products user-friendlier. Although getting a modem installed and actually using it is not as difficult as it used to be, things can still go wrong, and occasionally do.

These days many of the problems with peripheral devices are actually due to installation difficulties with the device drivers or other software, rather than what could strictly be termed hardware problems. In the case of modems, it is likely that the vast majority of problems are software related. Clearly, a modem will only work properly if it is physically installed correctly, but it also needs the device drivers to be present and correct, plus some further software.

The additional software needed depends on the intended applications for the modem. Either an Internet service provider's own software or the PC's built-in software can be used for operation on the Internet. If the built-in facilities of Windows are used, these facilities must be set up correctly. A common problem with Windows and modems is that users expect Windows to mind read. It needs full details of your Internet service provider before it can dial the right number, etc. Separate software is needed for other applications such as faxing.

This chapter is mainly about getting a modem properly installed and operating on the Internet, but the subject of faxing will also be covered. Strictly speaking, an internal modem is not a peripheral but part of the main PC. However, much of the material in this chapter applies equally to internal and external modems. For the sake of completeness, some information specific to internal modems has been included.

What modem?

When you are having connection difficulties, the obvious starting point is to check that the modem is installed correctly. It is definitely the first thing to check if you get any error messages along the lines of "modem not detected". If an internal modem is newly installed or the computer itself is new, it might be worthwhile opening up the PC to check that the modem card is properly fitted into its expansion slot. This process was covered in the previous chapter. Even if everything appears to be correct, remove and refit the modem anyway. The usual ploy if that fails, is to try the expansion card in another expansion slot. In theory, this should make no difference, but in practice it sometimes brings results. Occasionally there can be problems with physical incompatibility between an expansion slot and the edge connector of a card. The card might make better electrical contact with some slots than it does with others.

External problems

If the modem is an external type check that the connectors all fit together properly and that everything is wired up correctly. USB modems are normally powered from the USB port, but serial types have their own power supply. This can be an internal mains power supply unit, an external power supply, or batteries, depending on the make and model of the modem. Whatever type of power source is used, is it all present and correct? Frantically searching for the cause of a fault when the only problem is that the "faulty" unit has not been switched on is not exactly a rare occurrence.

With any battery powered equipment the batteries are most likely to cause problems. First, try the modem with a new set of batteries. If that fails, check that the battery contacts are clean. If necessary, scrape them gently with the small blade of a penknife to remove any contamination. Check that the contacts of the batteries themselves are free from dirt, and if necessary clean them. Good electrical contact with the battery is normally reliant on some form of spring. Contact will at best be intermittent if the spring has lost its springiness and the batteries are slightly loose. Sometimes the springs are inaccessible, but in most cases they can easily be stretched slightly so that good electrical contact is restored.

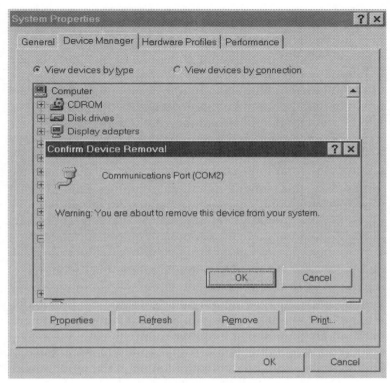

Fig.3.1 Operate the OK button to delete the drivers for the port

Ports that are provided by a PC's motherboard are normally switched on by default, but I have encountered problems with peripherals that were caused by the relevant port being deactivated. First check to see if the port used for the modem has been recognised by Windows. If it is active, a port should have an entry in the Ports (COM & LPT) section of Device Manager. There will usually be a minimum of one parallel (LPT) and two serial (COM) ports, and an external serial modem will therefore connect to COM1 or COM2. If the relevant port is not listed, restart the computer and check that it is switched on in the BIOS Setup program. Incidentally, internal PCI card modems usually connect to a notional COM3 or COM4, but as they do not use conventional serial port hardware, these ports are not usually listed in the Ports section of Device Manager. There should

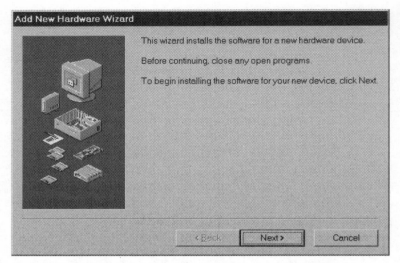

Fig.3.2 The initial window when undertaking manual installation

be a separate category for a port of this type, which is sometimes called a "virtual" port. Alternatively, details of the port and its setting might only be included in the section for the modem.

If one of the ports has a problem, there will be a yellow exclamation mark against its entry. Double clicking on an entry for a port will produce its Properties Window and this will either state that the port is functioning correctly or give basic details of any problem. As serial port hardware is usually part of the motherboard and the device drivers are standard Windows drivers, a problem here probably indicates a serious hardware fault. A problem with the Windows installation is also possible. Try deleting the entry for the faulty port by selecting its entry in Device Manager and then operating the Remove button. Left-click the OK button when the warning message appears (Figure 3.1).

When the computer is rebooted, Windows will detect the port hardware and reinstall the device drivers. Device Manager can then be used to determine whether the reinstallation has cleared the fault. It is not conclusive that there is a hardware fault if the port still fails to install correctly, but it is the most plausible explanation. There could be a major problem with the Windows installation, and reinstalling Windows over the current installation is worth a try, but only if you know what you are

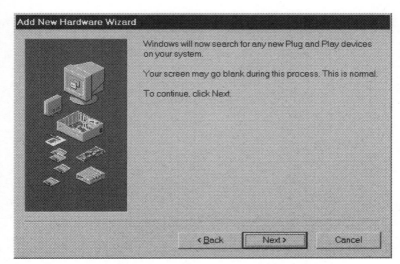

Fig.3.3 First, the program searches for Plug and Play devices

doing. Where a hardware-testing program is available, use it to test the port. If possible, use loopback testing, as this is more thorough. These programs directly access the hardware registers, and largely ignore the operating system. Consequently, when diagnostics software indicates a fault, it is virtually certain that there is a hardware problem.

Manual installation

It is possible to take the manual route with hardware installation. However, it is only fair to point out that there is little chance of this being successful in cases where Windows is unable to detect something like a standard port. It might be worth trying as a "last ditch" effort before getting the hardware repaired. Manual installation starts by going to the Windows Control Panel and double clicking on the Add New Hardware icon. This produces an initial window like the one in Figure 3.2. Operate the Next button to proceed with the installation.

This takes things on to a screen like Figure 3.3 where the system explains that it will search for new Plug and Play devices. With modern versions of Windows there is no way of bypassing this process, but it is as well to let Windows have another attempt at finding the missing hardware.

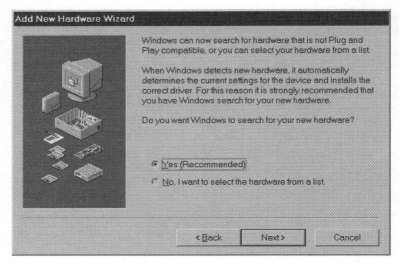

Fig.3.4 At this window, let the program search for devices that are not Plug and Play compatible

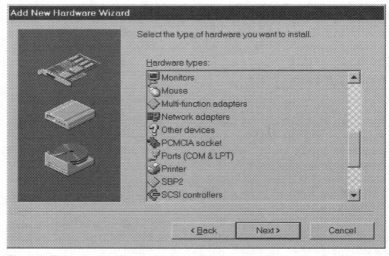

Fig.3.5 This window is used to select the correct category for the hardware you wish to install

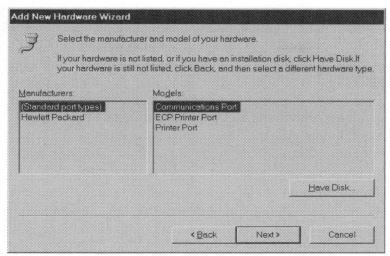

Fig.3.6 The appropriate device is selected from the lists of manufacturers and models

Operating the Next button will produce a window like Figure 3.4, but there can be a considerable delay while Windows searches for new hardware. Of course, if the "lost" hardware is detected, go ahead and install it using the normal procedure. If you reach the window of Figure 3.4, there is the choice of having Windows search for devices that are not Plug and Play compliant, or going ahead with manual selection. There is no harm in letting Windows search for the hardware. If it is successful you can go ahead and install it. You can go back to this screen again if the search is unsuccessful.

Opting for manual selection produces a window like the one shown in Figure 3.5. This has a list of hardware types, and it is a matter of scrolling down the list until the right type is found. In this example it is the Ports section that is needed. Left-click on the entry you wish to select and then operate the Next button. Things now move on to a window that has a list of manufacturers and a Standard option (Figure 3.6). In this case a standard port is being installed, and it is a Communications Port.

Things are slightly different where the port is detected successfully but the modem connected to it is not. Obviously, it is then the modem rather than the port that has to be installed. In order to manually install the modem you would have to search for the correct manufacturer in the list on the left. Then the correct model number would have to be found in

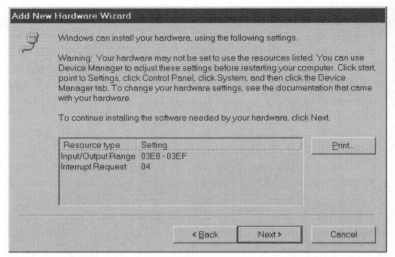

Fig.3.7 The default resource settings for the port are shown here, but they can not be altered at this stage

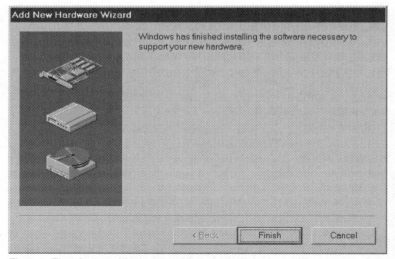

Fig.3.8 The device drivers have been installed when this screen is reached

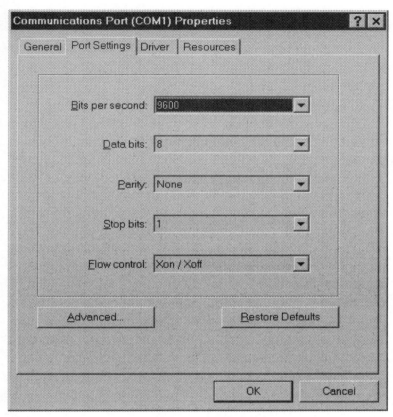

Fig.3.9 The usual default settings for a COM port

the list on the right. Alternatively, the Have Disk button could be operated. You then direct the installation program to the disc containing the drivers and the installation continues in normal Windows fashion.

In this example, the Communications Port option is selected and the Next button is left-clicked. This produces a window like Figure 3.7, where the resource settings for the port are shown in the lower part of the window. The upper section provides various pieces of information, including the advice that Device Manager can be used to change these settings in the event that they do not match the hardware you are using. The settings can not be changed using this screen. Operating the Next

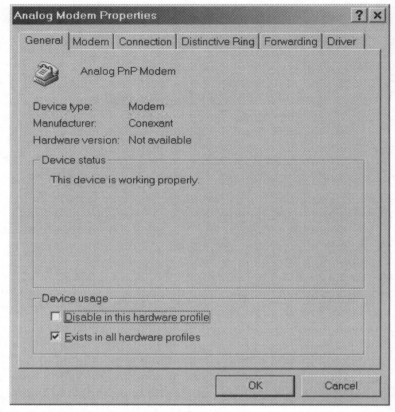

Fig.3.10 The General section of the properties window for the modem

button moves on to the final window (Figure 3.8), and this simply explains that the software for the new hardware has been installed. Operate the Finish button to close the window.

After making any changes to the resource settings using Device Manager, reboot the computer and test the new hardware. In the event that the port still does not work, it is advisable to use Device Manager to remove the device drivers that were installed manually. Windows should successfully detect the port's hardware once the computer has been repaired, and the correct device drivers will then be installed automatically when Windows is booted.

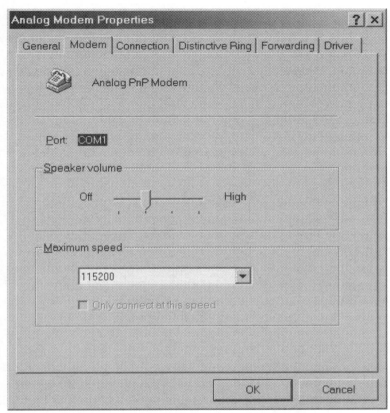

Fig.3.11 Check that the Maximum speed setting is suitable

Port settings

Modems are usually supplied with an installation disc that sets appropriate parameters for the serial port, but it is worth checking these settings in cases where the modem is failing to respond correctly. The obvious way of checking the serial port's settings is to go to the Port Settings tab in its properties window. This produces a window like the one in Figure 3.9, and two of the settings here seem to be incorrect. At 9600 baud, the baud rate is far too low. XON/XOFF (software) handshaking is selected, but serial modems use hardware handshaking via the RTS and CTS lines.

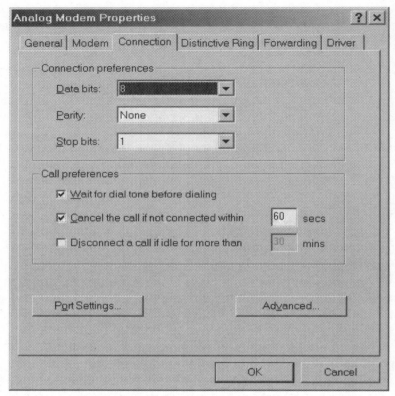

Fig.3.12 This window gives control over the word format

There is not necessarily an error though, because the device drivers for serial modems often leave the port at its default windows settings until the modem is actually used. The device driver then sets the appropriate parameters before trying to access the modem. Presumably, things are done this way so that the port can be used with another device having different settings when the modem is not in use.

In order to check the port's settings when the modem is in use, double-click on the modem's entry in Device Manager. This will produce its properties window (Figure 3.10), and it will give some basic information about the modem. Make sure that there is a tick in the appropriate checkbox near the bottom of the window. The modem is effectively non-

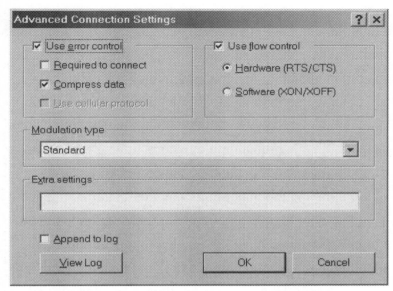

Fig.3.13 Hardware handshaking is always used with modems

existent if it is disabled in the current hardware profile. Selecting the Modem tab changes the window (Figure 3,11), and the maximum baud rate can be set here. A high baud rate enables the modem to operate at or close to its maximum speed, but too high a rate can cause communication errors with the PC. The optimum rate is generally taken to be the lowest one that is higher than the modem's speed. With a 56k modem this is 115,200 baud. Speeds of more than 115,200 baud are often listed in the baud rate menu, but are not supported by the port hardware of most PCs. If a higher rate such as 230,400 baud is selected, try reducing the setting to 115,200 baud.

Operating the Connection tab produces a window like the one shown in Figure 3.12. Here the word format can be altered. For operation with a modem the word format is usually eight data bits, one stop bit, and no parity checking. Operating the Advanced button brings up a window that enables the required method of handshaking to be set (Figure 3.13). The checkbox for hardware handshaking must be ticked, since software handshaking is not used with telephone modems. Note that the layout of a Modem Properties window varies slightly from one modem to another. It might be necessary to do some delving in order to locate all the port settings, but they should be there somewhere.

*Fig.3.14 External modems are usually equipped with plenty of
indicator lights*

Seeing the lights

External modems that connect to a serial port often have a number of
status lights on the front panel, and these can provide some useful
information when faultfinding. Small portable units are an exception and
typically have just an on/off indicator plus a single status light. Mains
powered serial modems typically have half a dozen or more indicator
lights. USB modems usually have a fair selection as well, but obviously
lack any that are specific to an RS232C serial interface. The serial modem
shown in Figure 3.14 has no less than nine indicator lights, and these
are their functions:

Modem ready

This light is almost an ordinary power indicator. Most lights of this type
switch on only if the modem successfully completes a simple diagnostics
routine when it is switched on, rather than whenever turned on. With this
particular modem it also flashes when the modem is in a test or
diagnostics mode. If this light fails to switch on but others do light up,
the most likely explanation is that the modem has a hardware fault and it
is not successfully completing the diagnostic routine at switch-on. If this

indicator fails to switch on and none of the others do either, check that the unit is switched on, and that the mains adapter is plugged into the mains supply and the modem. The power connectors on mains adapters are often less than totally reliable, so try unplugging and plugging in the power plug a few times in an attempt to get a good connection. If that fails to clear the problem, and if the adapter has a separate mains plug, unplug it from the mains outlet and try replacing the fuse.

The fuse in an adapter that is built into an outsize mains plug is not normally replaceable. If the adapter is blown it will be necessary to seek a replacement. As pointed out in chapter 2, mains adapters have various voltage and current ratings, there are regulated and unregulated types, and an assortment of power connectors can be wired with either polarity. Ideally, the replacement should be obtained from the manufacturer of the modem or their local agent. This should guarantee that it has the right characteristics. Failing that, seek expert help to ensure that the replacement has the correct voltage and current ratings, etc. Do not simply try any mains adapter that happens to have a plug of the correct type. The chances of this producing workable results are minimal, and the chances of "blowing" the modem are quite good.

High-speed

This light switches on when the modem operates at a certain baud rate or any higher rates. The threshold is usually 4800 or 9600 baud. Since a modern modem will normally default to a high-speed mode, and is invariably used in one, this light will probably be on whenever the modem is switched on. If it switches off when the modem is accessed, it is likely that the applications software is faulty or set up incorrectly.

Auto-answer

This light is switched on when the modem is in the automatic answering mode. This light should not switch on if you only use the modem to access the Internet. It should switch on when the modem is used with fax software, and it is set to answer telephone calls so that it can deal with incoming fax messages. It will also switch on if the modem has other clever features that require it to answer the telephone, such as an answer-phone facility.

Carrier detect

Under standby conditions this light should be switched off. It is turned on when the modem detects a carrier signal from the modem at the other end of the telephone line, and it should remain on while the modem is active. If this light fails to switch on, Windows or the application software will usually confirm the problem with an error message such as "no carrier detected". A total lack of a carrier from the remote modem is due to a fault in the system at the other end of the telephone line, and is unlikely to be due to a fault in your computer system. Where this light keeps switching off and error messages such as "connection lost" appear, the problem is either due to a modem that does not work very well and (or) a poor quality connection. The same is true if the modem has problems initialising a connection with the remote modem. In the event that this light fails to switch on, but a valid carrier is being received, the modem has a serious hardware fault.

Off-hook

This is the modem equivalent of picking up the telephone. This light switches on when the modem accesses the telephone line. It should therefore come on just before the modem starts dialling, and switch off again when the connection is dropped. When the off-hook and carrier detect indicators do not operate as expected, it is likely that there is a problem with the cable that connects the modem to the telephone socket.

Send data

This light switches on when the computer sends data to the modem. It should start to flicker when the carrier of the remote modem is detected, and it should switch off completely when communications ceases. A lack of activity from this indicator could be due to a fault in the modem, but it is more likely that the communications port is not set up correctly or that the cable is faulty. Make sure that the cable is connected to the computer and modem correctly. Computer ports are mostly tucked away at the rear of the unit where they are difficult to access. It is easy to end up with the retaining screw of the connector fitted correctly one side but not the other. This results in the connector being fitted at an angle, which means that the pins at one end will not make proper contact. If you look carefully at the connector, it should be readily apparent when this has occurred. Loosen the screw that is fully tightened, straighten up the connector, and then tighten both retaining screws properly.

Receive data

The receive data indicator should flicker when data is being received from the remote modem.

Terminal ready

The computer sets the DTR terminal of the serial port to the "on" state to activate the modem, and sets it to the "off" state to make the modem hang-up the line. This light should therefore switch on as soon as the computer starts using the modem, and switch off again when it has finished using the modem. A lack of response from this indicator light suggests that the serial port is faulty or not set up correctly, or that the serial cable is faulty.

Power

This is a straightforward on/off indicator.

USB Modems

Windows should detect a USB modem during the boot up sequence, or when it is first switched on and connected to the PC if the PC is running at the time. Either way the installation disc supplied with the modem will be requested, and after the usual Windows style installation procedure, the modem should be ready for use. If Windows fails to detect the modem there is probably a hardware fault, something is not connected properly, or the modem is simply not switched on. If a check shows that everything is wired up correctly, go to Device Manager and look at the entry for the USB ports. Remember that the USB ports have an entry of their own and that they are not included in Ports section.

If the ports are absent, it is likely that there is a major hardware fault or the ports are not switched on in the BIOS. Modern PCs are invariably supplied with at least two active USB ports, but some older PCs were supplied with the USB ports disabled. This was presumably due to the lack of proper operating system support at the time. Where there is a setting for switching the USB ports on and off it will probably be in the Integrated Peripherals or Chipset Features section of the BIOS Setup program. Note though, that this feature is not present on all PCs, and it is often absent on modern PCs.

If you are using an old operating system a lack of proper support can cause problems with USB ports. Using Windows 98 or later it is unlikely that there will be any installation problems, but the situation is very different with Windows 95. USB ports were never properly supported by the early versions of this operating system, and there can also be problems with the final version (OSR2). With the earlier versions USB device drivers may be installed, but there will be yellow exclamation marks against the entries for the ports in Device Manager. With the final version of Windows 95 there should be no problems with the dreaded exclamation marks, but in practice the ports might not work properly. If you are going to use the USB ports with any type of peripheral device it is advisable to use Windows 98 or a later version of the Windows operating system.

Where the ports are present and correct, the modem is switched on and connected properly, but the modem is still not detected by the Plug and Play system, the modem or the USB cable is faulty. If possible, try the modem with another USB cable. A PC has at least two USB ports, so try moving the modem to the other port. In theory this should not make any difference, but in practice a change of ports does occasionally have the desired effect. Possibly the USB connector makes a better connection with one port than with the other. Whatever the explanation, it is certainly worth a try.

Note that there is no possibility of getting a USB device installed and working properly unless it is detected by the Windows Plug and Play system. Once the device drivers for the USB ports are installed correctly, any working USB device connected to these ports should be detected. There is no point in looking for software solutions when the ports are all right but a peripheral is not detected. If a USB device is not detected under these circumstances, the cause of the problem must be either the cable or the peripheral's hardware.

Try the modem and USB cable with another PC. If the modem is detected properly by the other PC, then clearly the modem and the cable are working properly. A fault in the cable of the peripheral is confirmed in cases where the peripheral is not detected by the second computer. There is a slight paradox when the equipment works properly with another PC. The USB ports on the original PC seems to be working properly, and so does the peripheral and cable, but putting them all together is not greeted with success. The most likely explanation is that the USB ports of the original computer are faulty, but this fault is not being detected by Windows. Trying another USB with the ports should confirm this, with the new USB device not being detected. It would be as well to try reinstalling the drivers for the USB ports before getting the hardware repaired.

Modem drivers

Sometimes the modem can be installed without any difficulty, but once installed it fails to work properly. The possibility of a hardware fault can not be ruled out, but it is advisable to check the software side of things before getting the hardware repaired or replaced. If there are no problems with the port used by the modem, the settings for the modem itself should be checked. Start by looking in Device Manager to see if there are any yellow exclamation marks against the entry for the modem.

Where a problem is indicated it is a good idea to try reinstalling the device drivers. The easiest way of doing this is to delete the modem's entry from Device Manager. You can not remove a category from Device Manager, only individual items. Double-click on the modem's entry to expand it, and then left-click on the modem's entry to select it. Then operate the Remove button followed by the Yes button when you are asked if you are sure that you wish to remove the modem. The modem's entry in Device Manager will then disappear, as will the Modem category if only one modem was installed.

If at first...

On rebooting the computer, the modem can be reinstalled, following the manufacturer's installation instructions. It is possible that things will not go any better at the second attempt, but if the modem still fails to work, it is worth trying again. This time close down and switch off the computer once the modem has been removed from Device Manager. Physically remove the modem from the PC if it is an internal type, or disconnect it from the PC in the case of an external unit. Then reboot the computer without the modem. Check that the modem is still absent from Device Manager, and if necessary remove it and reboot the PC again.

Once you have established that the modem has been properly uninstalled from Windows, close down Windows and switch off the computer. Refit the modem, switch the computer back on again, and then reinstall the driver software. This should avoid having the old and non-working drivers reactivated. With the device drivers installed from scratch there is a better chance of the reinstallation being successful.

All change

The causes of hardware conflicts and dealing with them was covered in detail in chapter two. If Device Manager reports a problem of this type, try using the methods described in chapter two to resolve the problem. Probably the most common cause of a hardware conflict when using a modem is the modem and the mouse trying to use the same interrupt request (IRQ) number. This usually manifests itself in the form of the mouse either operating erratically or not at all when the modem is installed. It generally occurs when the mouse is connected to a built-in port, and the modem uses a port on an expansion card. The built-in ports are COM1 and COM2, and ports on an expansion card are COM3 and COM4. As explained in chapter two, COM1 and COM3 share an IRQ, as do COM2 and COM4. This factor produces the hardware conflict.

Where possible, the simplest solution is to move the mouse to the other serial port. If this port is already in use, this option is not available, but it is still possible to swap the devices on the built-in ports. If the other device does not use interrupts, this should remove the hardware conflict. If, like a mouse, it does use interrupts, this change will not help. The mouse will function normally but the other device will cease to work properly. This port swapping is a useful ploy whenever problems arise with serial devices, and in practice it will often remove the conflict. It might be possible to change the modem's settings, but this is unlikely to help if both the internal serial ports are connected to devices that utilise interrupts. Realistically, the only cure that is likely to work is to use a PS/2 or USB mouse instead of the serial type. This frees one of the serial ports, and more importantly, it frees the port's IRQ number so that it can be used by the modem.

No dialling tone

An error message along the lines of "no dialling tone detected" is not an uncommon problem. Obviously this can occur because there is genuinely no dialling tone present, and this problem is one that is covered later in this chapter. It is easy to check this point by picking up the telephone and listening for the usual dialling tone. There is probably a minor problem with the lead from the modem to the telephone wall socket if the dialling tone is present and correct. Try disconnecting and reconnecting the lead at both the modem and the telephone socket. If an extension lead is in use, disconnect and reconnect this as well.

Make sure that all the plugs are properly locked into the sockets. The connectors used for telephones and modems are quick and easy to use, but they are not the toughest of components. Leads tend to get kicked around and tripped over, and the connectors are damaged occasionally. Look carefully at all the connectors and replace any leads that have a seriously damaged plug or socket.

The connection to the telephone socket is via a standard BT plug, but the connection to the modem is by way of a smaller American style telephone plug. Both types of plug are shown in Figure 3.15. The American style plugs and sockets seem to be something less than rigidly standardised, or perhaps some of them are made to rather low standards.

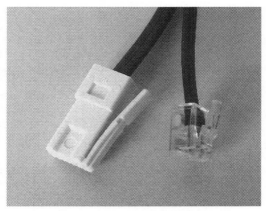

Fig.3.15 The two styles of telephone plug

Some plugs do not lock into the sockets properly, while others are difficult to fit into place at all. Unfortunately, a few seem to fit into place perfectly but do not make reliable connections. When installing a new modem or PC it is normal to use the existing lead to connect the modem to the telephone socket. However, this can give problems and it is safer to make the connection to the modem via the lead supplied with the modem or PC. This should be a good and reliable match for the socket fitted to the modem. On the other hand, if the lead supplied with the modem does not work, try another lead. Mistakes can be made, and it is possible that a lead for a mainland European country or the USA has been supplied instead of a UK lead.

A faulty modem can sometimes result in the telephones on the system failing to work properly. Typically, as soon as the modem is plugged into the wall socket the telephones on the same circuit ring until the modem is disconnected again. This can also be caused by a faulty cable or one of the wrong type. Cables for use in American and Europe will not give the correct set of connections between the modem and socket and will often produce this fault. Once again, it is a matter of using the cable provided with the modem wherever possible and making sure that any extension cables are of the correct type. Try another cable if the one supplied with the modem seems to be of the wrong type.

Call waiting

The modern telephone system provides all sorts of clever features, but they can give problems when using a modem. This can make it appear as though the modem is faulty when the problem actually resides elsewhere. Call waiting can be troublesome as it can result in an incoming call producing signals on the line that result in the Internet connection being lost, making it seem as though the modem is unreliable. Call waiting can be disabled by dialling the correct code, which is normally *43#. It can be enabled again by dialling the reactivation code, which is usually #43#.

There is a facility in Windows that enables the appropriate code to be dialled prior to the Internet service provider's number being dialled. Select Settings and then Control Panel from the Start menu to launch the Windows Control Panel and then double-click on the Modems icon. In the new window that appears left-click the Dialling Properties button, and another window should popup on the screen (Figure 3.16). Tick the checkbox labelled "To disable call waiting, dial" and then add the appropriate code into the textbox. Operate the Apply and OK buttons to make the changes take effect, and then left-click the OK button to close the Modems Properties window.

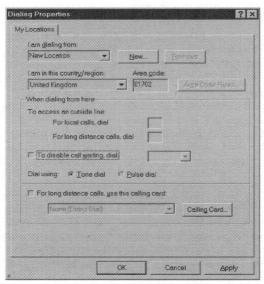

Fig.3.16 This window enables call waiting to be disabled

Some services, but particularly BT's Call Minder facility, can result in the dialling tone disappearing from time to time. The telephone system still works perfectly, but when someone has left a message the dialling tone

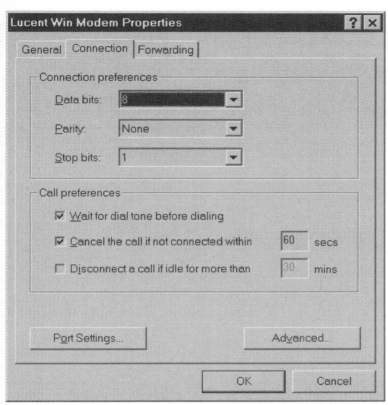

Fig.3.17 The modem can be made to dial the ISP even if no dial tone is detected

becomes intermittent or simply disappears for a while. While this may not seem to be of any practical importance, it can prevent the modem from dialling your Internet service provider. The modem fails to detect a dialling tone and assumes that there is a fault on the line or it is not connected to the telephone system.

The solution to this problem is to go into the Windows Control Panel, double-click the Modems icon, operate the Properties button in the new window that appears, and then operate the Connection tab. This should give a window like the one of Figure 3.17. Remove the tick in the checkbox labelled "Wait for dialling tone before dialling". The modem will then dial your Internet service provider whether or not a dialling tone is detected.

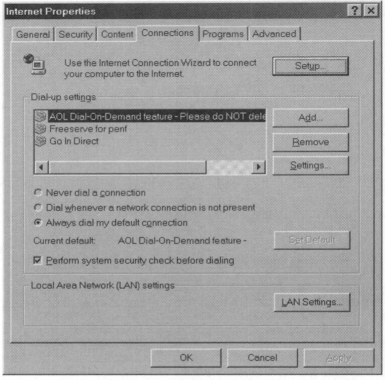

Fig.3.18 The Connections section of the Internet Properties window

More settings

If the modem seems to be working properly, you have made the checks described so far, and connection to the Internet is still problematic, there are still some settings that can be checked. Provided you have signed on to at least one Internet service there should be a default provider for the PC to dial. To check this, go to the Control Panel and double-click on the Internet Options icon and then operate the Connections tab on the window that appears. This should give something like Figure 3.18. To set an entry in the "Dial-up settings" list as the default it is first selected by left-clicking on its entry. Then operate the Set Default button, which

should become
active when an entry
other than the
current default is
selected.

To check that an
entry in the list is set
up correctly, select
the appropriate entry
in the list and then
operate the Settings
button. This brings
up the window of
Figure 3.19, where
the Properties button
is left-clicked in order
to produce a window
like the one in Figure
3.20. The top section
of the window should
contain the
telephone number of
the Internet service
provider, and in
Figure 3.20 this
information is clearly
absent. This may
look like an error, but
in this case it is
actually correct. The
Internet service
provider in this
instance is AOL, and
this company uses
software that has its
own database of
telephone numbers.
Hence no number is
needed here, but in
most cases the
relevant fields of this
window should be

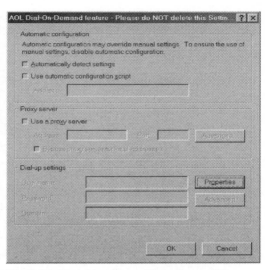

Fig.3.19 Checking the settings for an ISP

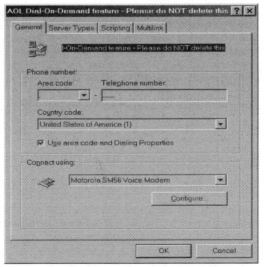

Fig.3.20 Is the telephone number correct?

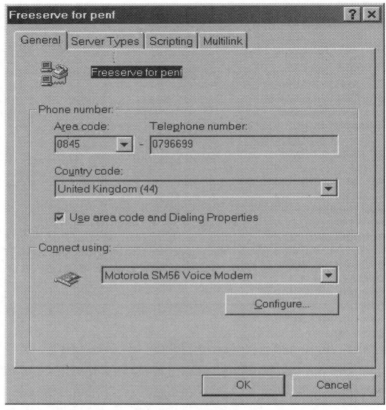

Fig.3.21 With most ISPs the telephone number will be included here

filled in correctly, as in the example of Figure 3.21. If the number includes an area code that is required from your dialling area, make sure that the checkbox is ticked. Also, where appropriate make sure that the correct modem is selected in the menu near the bottom of the window.

Next, try operating the Server Types tab to switch the window to one like Figure 3.22. Incidentally, when using Windows ME these settings are available by selecting the Networking tab. The type of dial-up server should be PPP, and TCP/IP should be selected as the only allowed network protocol. The checkbox that enables software compression is normally checked, but you can try turning off this feature to see if it improves matters.

Windows ME has a Security tab, and left-clicking on this one produces a window like the one in Figure 3.23. This is another case of AOL doing things its own way, so the User name and Password fields are blank in this example. With most Internet service providers the appropriate user name will be shown, but the password field will of course show a series of asterisks rather than the password. If necessary the user name can be edited, and the password can be re-entered if you think that it might be wrong. Note that these are the user name and password issued by you Internet service provider during the sign-up process. They are not any special name and password used to gain initial entry to

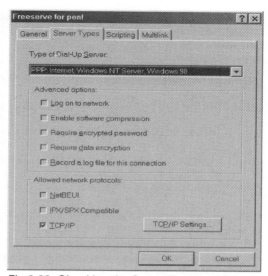

Fig.3.22 Checking the Server Type settings

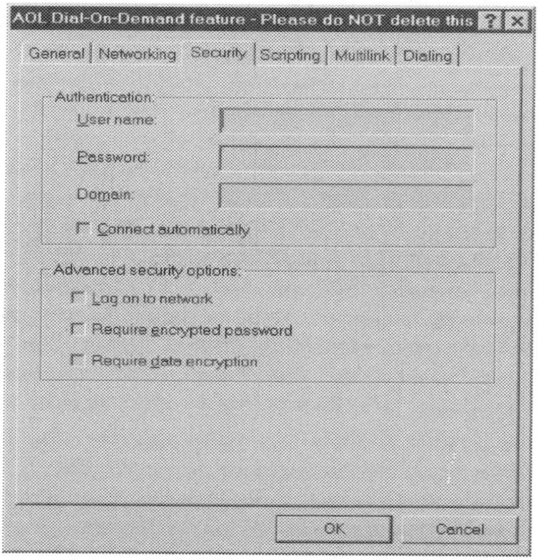

Fig.3.23 Check the user name and password

the system so that the sign-up process can commence. These are only required the first time you access the system, and they are not needed thereafter.

Lost connections

Sometimes the problem is not one of getting connected to the Internet, but one of staying connected. Bear in mind that most of the unmetered Internet service providers will cut your Internet connection if there is more than about 10 or 20 minutes of inactivity. In addition, many have a cut off period of about two hours that comes into operation even if the connection is in use. In addition to these enforced cuts in connection, there will inevitably be the occasional glitch on the line that results in the connection to the server being lost. If the connection is frequently lost for no apparent reason, it could be that there is an intermittent fault on the line. If voice communication via your telephone is a bit noisy and unreliable there is little chance of reliable Internet operation with good connection speeds. The relevant telephone company should be prepared to investigate if the line consistently provides bad results.

Random reset

I have occasionally encountered problems with systems that randomly reset themselves when connected to the Internet. In some cases it only occurs very infrequently, but in others it can happen quite often. In one case it was impossible to set up a connection to one of the largest Internet service providers due to the system always resetting at a certain point in the sign-up process. This seems to be a problem with certain modems, or to be more precise, with the device drivers for certain software modems. Software modems, which also known by such names as "soft" modems and "Winmodems", use relatively simple hardware. The inadequacies of the hardware have to be compensated for by device drivers that are much more complex than normal modem drivers. The drivers do rather more than integrate the hardware into Windows, and carry out some of the encoding and decoding, error correction, etc.

Modems of this type are inexpensive but can work well provided they are used in a reasonably powerful PC and the drivers are well written. Unfortunately, some of the very low cost generic modems of this type seem to be supplied with drivers that are not as reliable as they should be. It might be possible to find a more recent version of the driver software that works more reliably. Where a more up to date driver is available, it will probably be available as a free download from the manufacturer's web site. If not, the only solution might be to replace the modem with a more reliable unit.

Stuck online

A problem I have encountered several times is that of a connection not being cut off at the end of a session. This seems to occur mainly when using an Internet service provider that has its own Internet software. Usually everything seems to shut down correctly, but the modem has not hung up and it is still connected to the host. You generally remain oblivious to the problem until you pick up the telephone handset and

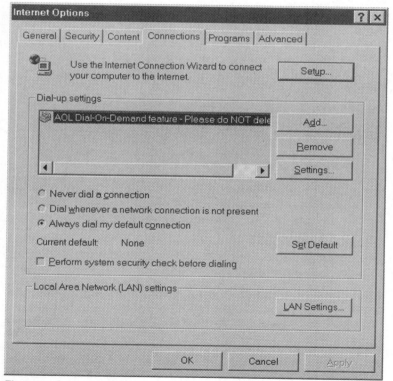

Fig.3.24 Operating the connections tab produces a window like this

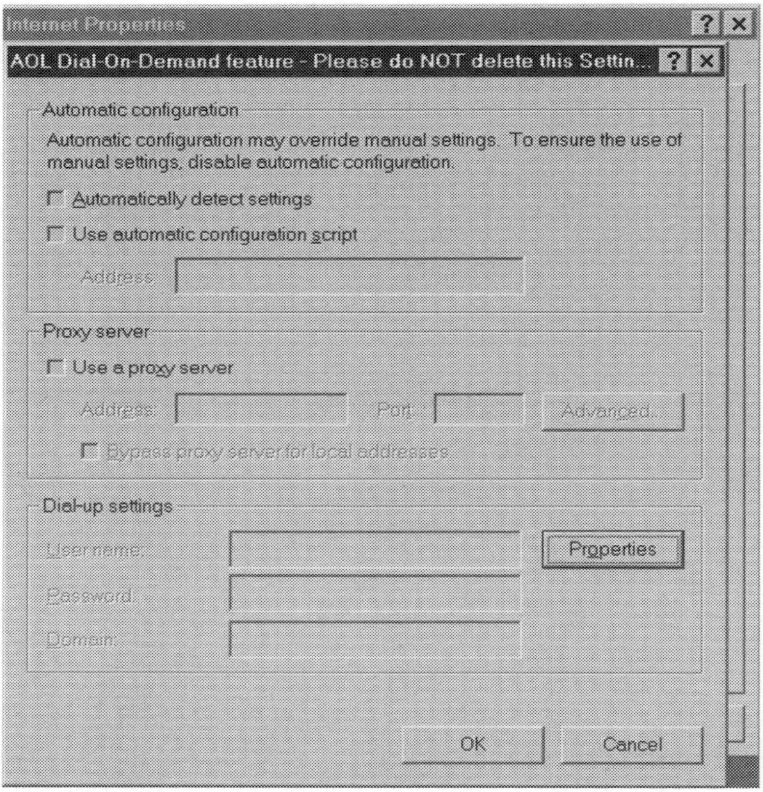

Fig.3.25 Operate the Properties button to check the ISP's dial-up settings

hear the signals from the modems, or an error message is produced when you shut down Windows.

When using an unmetered service it is not the end of the world if the connection fails to terminate, since the extra time connected to the system will not cost anything. It is undesirable to have the telephone line tied up unnecessarily, but the Internet service provider will probably cut off the call after about 20 or 30 minutes of inactivity. It is clearly more serious if you are paying for a peak rate call, even if it is only at the local peak rate. If you are lucky, the Internet service provider will cut off the connection after 20 or 30 minutes so that cost of the fault is minimised. If not, the call could be quite expensive.

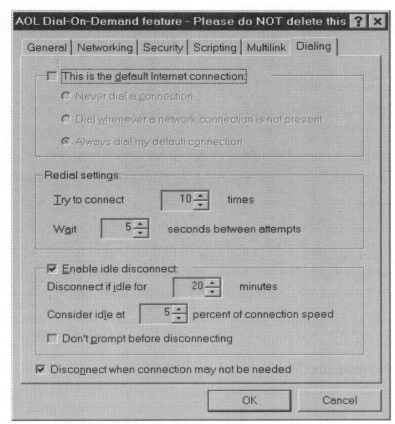

Fig.3.26 Checking the dialling properties

If you find that the connection has not terminated correctly the first task is to cut the connection. Shutting down Windows and switching off is one way of getting offline. Simply unplugging the telephone cable from the modem or telephone socket is another way. Lifting and lowering the handset a few times is usually sufficient to disrupt communications and cut off the connection. To minimise the damage if the same thing should happen again it is a good idea to alter one of the dialup settings. Launch Internet Explorer and choose Internet Options from the Tools menu. Alternatively, choose Settings from the Start menu to launch the Windows Control Panel and then double-click on the Internet Options icon. Either way a window like the one of Figure 3.24 will appear.

Left-click on the Connections tab if it is not already selected, and then on the Settings button. This should produce something like Figure 3.25. Next operate the Properties button followed by the Dialling tab on the new window that appears. This should give a window like the one in Figure 3.26. Make sure that the checkbox labelled "Enable idle disconnect" is ticked. The required time can then be added in the appropriate textbox. The time used here has to be something of a compromise. It is obviously desirable to have the connection disconnected as soon as possible if things go wrong, but you must avoid having the connection terminated during normal use. It could take a few minutes to answer the door, or to read a large Internet page.

The default value is 20 minutes, but a 10-minute cut-off time is more than adequate for most users. Note that inactivity in this case means some sort of data transfer between your PC and the host. Things like mouse and keyboard operations count as inactivity unless they result in something being uploaded or downloaded. Tick the "Don't prompt before disconnecting" checkbox if you prefer to have the connection terminated without warning. It is probably best not to do this, as it could leave you unaware that there is a continuing problem.

After making any necessary changes, operate the OK button to close the window, and then left-click the OK button on the next window to return to the Internet Properties window. If you use more than one Internet service provider, this process should be repeated for each of the others.

Reinstallation

Reinstallation of the offending software is the only cure if there is a recurring problem with the connection not being terminated. It is advisable to remove the existing software first and then reinstall it from scratch. With a service provider such as AOL, which installs its own software during the sign-up process, it is clearly this software that must be removed. Select Settings from the Start menu to launch the Control Panel and then double-click on the Add/Remove programs icon. This will produce a window like the one of Figure 3.27, which includes a list of all the software that has been installed in Windows. Scroll down the list to find the entry for your Internet service provider's software and then operate the Add/Remove button.

The process from thereon varies from one piece of software to another. The process is largely automatic, and you may have to do nothing more than confirm that you wish to completely remove the program. In other

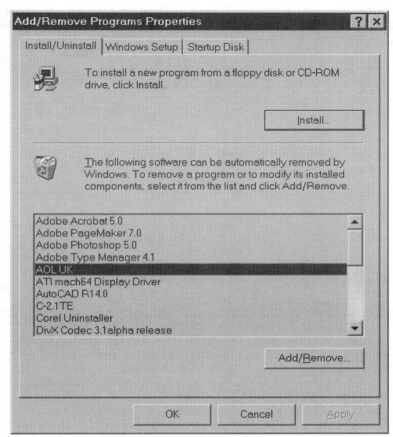

Fig.3.27 Windows has built-in facilities for removing installed software, which includes the software supplied by some ISPs

cases you may have a few options available, as in the example of Figure 3.28, which is the initial screen when uninstalling version 6 of AOL's software. Where the option is available you will presumably wish to keep downloaded files, etc., so that they are available when the software is reinstalled. When uninstalling software it is quite likely that you will be asked if you wish to delete one or more shared files that are no longer required. As the software will be immediately reinstalled it probably does not matter what you answer, but the No button is always the safer option.

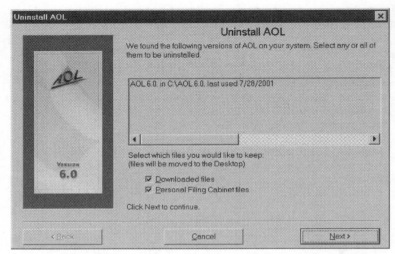

Fig.3.28 Uninstalling software is largely automatic, but you may be presented with some options

If you are using a service provider that utilises the standard Windows Internet facilities, you can try removing and reinstalling Internet Explorer and the associated software. This should be included in the list of installed software as something like "Internet Explorer 5.5 and Internet Tools". Having removed and reinstalled Internet Explorer you will need to go through the sign-up process again with your service provider, and you will need any screen names, passwords, etc., used for the initial signup. This type of information is also needed when reinstalling the service provider's own software, or you will find yourself setting up a new account.

Diagnostics

If you have some diagnostics software, this should help to sort out problems with a modem. It might be worth buying some diagnostics software if you do not already have it, since programs of this type will sometimes pinpoint the source of the problem quite quickly. It should be possible to find the cause of practically any problem using the built-in facilities of Windows, but this can be quite time consuming. Diagnostics software can also be useful where the precise nature of the problem is proving to be elusive, and a second opinion would be helpful.

There is a simple diagnostics routine built into Windows that will indicate whether the modem is accessible and to some extent functioning. In order to access the diagnostics routine go to the Windows Control Panel and double-click on the Modem icon. This produces the General section of the Modem Properties window. Left-click on the Diagnostics tab, which should produce a window

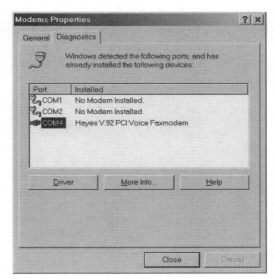

Fig.3.29 Selecting the correct port for the modem

like the one of Figure 3.29. Here the port used by the modem is selected, and then the More Info button is operated. After a short delay while the software accesses the modem, a window like the one shown in Figure 3.30 should appear.

This shows some basic facts and figures for the modem together with the data sent back from it in response to various commands sent by the diagnostics routine. If the responses are clearly just garbage, either the modem is faulty or there is a problem in the link to the modem such as incorrect baud rate. A window like the one of Figure 3.31, indicating that there was no response from the modem, means that the modem has a major fault or the link to it is not functioning at all. However, it is possible that the

Fig.3.30 Some test results from a Hayes V92 modem

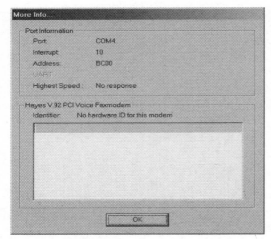

problem is simply due to a glitch when the checking routine tried to access the modem, so it is worth trying again to see if the modem can be contacted.

Most general PC diagnostics software includes a section for testing modems. Figure 3.32 shows the CheckIT program in action. In this screen the System Information facility has been used to provide a long list

Fig.3.31   Here there has been no response from the modem

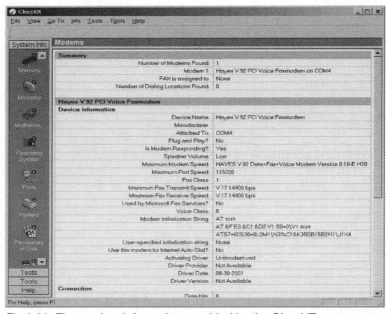

Fig.3.32 The modem information provided by the CheckIT program

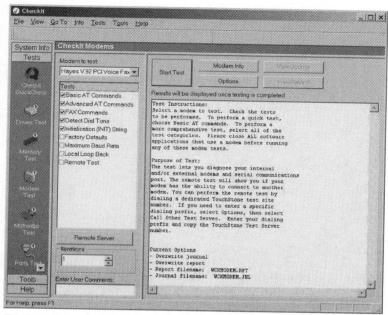

Fig.3.33 The required test can be selected from the list on the left

that gives details of the modem, ports settings, and so on. In Figure 3.33 the program has been switched to the testing mode. This window permits the required tests to be selected, and it also provides some background information for the tests. A small window shows how things are progressing when the tests are run (Figure 3.34), and it indicates whether the modem has passed or failed the tests once they have been

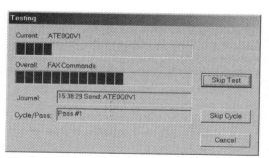

Fig.3.34 The progress of the tests is shown via a small status window

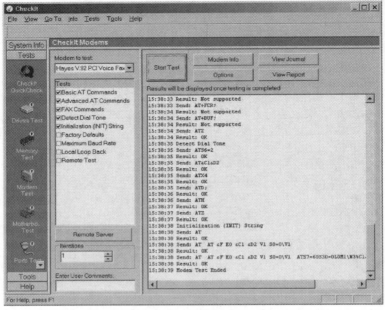

Fig.3.35 The main window gives a full list of test results

completed. The main window gives a list of test results (Figure 3.35). Exhaustive testing of this type should bring to light even minor flaws in the modem's hardware.

Testing of an Internet connection is not usually catered for by diagnostics software, but there should be a facility that provides information about the Internet settings. Figure 3.36 shows an example screen of this type, and this was again produced by the CheckIT program. It is worth looking at the list of information to see if there is anything that is clearly incorrect.

Speed

Many Internet users are concerned about the speed of their modem, or to be more precise, the lack of speed. If you buy a modem that is rated at 56k, it seems reasonable to expect download rates of about 56000 bits per second, or 5600 bytes per second. Apart from a lucky few, it is unrealistic to expect consistent download rates at anything close to this

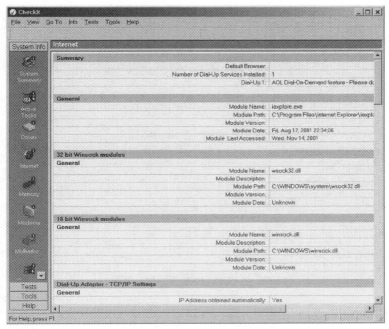

Fig.3.36 This window provides details of the Internet settings

speed. It has to be borne in mind that the 56k rate is reliant on a perfect connection with a strong signal and no noise. Unless you live very close to the telephone exchange, it is unlikely that the line will achieve theoretical perfection very often, and it may never do so.

Another point to bear in mind is that some modems perform better than others do. With a line that achieves theoretical perfection it is probable that most modems provide a data transfer rate that is very close to their quoted maximum rates. With real world lines the situation is different, and the better modems deal with noise and low signal levels better than the "cheap and cheerful" models.

Another factor has to be taken into account, and this is the rate at which the server can supply data. Some servers can supply data at much higher rates than a telephone modem can handle, and the modem is then the limiting factor. Other servers are often heavily overloaded, and the rate at which data can be supplied to each user is then quite low. It

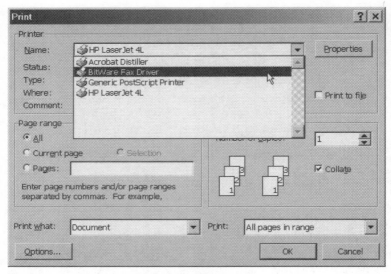

Fig.3.37 the fax "printer" is selected from the menu

is not unknown for heavily loaded servers to supply data to each user at only a few hundred bytes per second. Slow transfer rates can also be obtained due to heavy use of the Internet in general.

Realistically, most users of 56k modems will only achieve data transfer rates of around 5000 bytes per second when conditions are favourable. This rate assumes that the modem is a good quality type. The transfer rate is likely to be nearer 4000 bytes per second using a software modem in a PC that barely achieves the minimum specification required to use the modem. Thus, a 56k modem that provides typical transfer rates of about 4500 bytes per second is not faulty, and is actually achieving average results.

Faxing

Many modems are supplied complete with fax software, and plenty of fax programs are available. Practically all modern modems can handle the sending and receiving of faxes, which uses a maximum baud rate of just 14,400 incidentally. In order to receive faxes the computer must monitor the telephone line via the modem. When a call is received it is

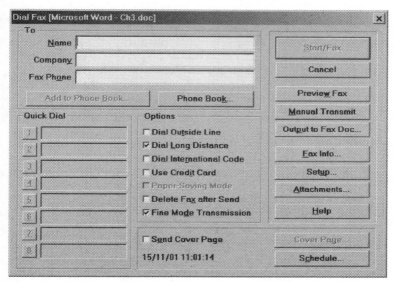

Fig.3.38 Trying to print via the fax driver results in the fax program being run from within the main application

answered by the modem, and the fax software then controls things. The usual scheme of things is for the software to automatically answer and decode the fax, and it is then saved to disc in an appropriate file format. Many of the early fax modems and software packages lacked reliability, but modern modems and fax programs are much better in this respect.

Usually when I am asked for help with faxes, the problem is sending them rather than receiving them. The obvious approach to sending a fax is to run the software and select the file you wish to send as a fax from within the fax program. Although this may be the obvious approach, it is not the way that most fax software handles things. There is a serious flaw in having the fax program process a file and send it as a fax. This will only work if the fax program can handle the particular file format involved, which in practice would tend to restrict faxing to a few popular file types. This type of thing tends to be a bit iffy in practice, because the file translation process is not always totally accurate. Matters are also complicated by the fact that there are numerous versions of most file formats. Each time a new version of a program is brought out, the file format changes slightly in order to accommodate new features.

The normal way of sending a fax is to use the Print command of whatever application software you used to generate the file. This command is available from the File menu in most Windows applications. The main advantage of this approach is that it avoids the file compatibility problems that would otherwise tend to plague the process of sending faxes. Another advantage is that it enables faxes to be sent from any software that has a Print command, which means virtually any Windows application software.

You are not limited to sending text, and there should be no difficulty in sending graphics or mixed graphics and text from photo-editing software, desktop publishing programs, etc. However, bear in mind that the print quality from a fax machine is likely to be inferior to the quality obtained when printing direct to a modern inkjet or laser printer. Sending a file as an Email attachment is the better option when the highest possible print quality is required. Provided the recipient is suitably equipped, they can then print the file using their PC and printer.

Presumably the fax "printer" will not be the default printer, and it must be selected before a fax can be sent. Selecting the Print option will bring up a window something like the one in Figure 3.37. The exact appearance will depend on the version of Windows in use and the application program being run. The Printer section will show the default printer, but any other installed printer can be selected using the pop-down menu. In this case it is clearly the fax option that must be selected, and this should have been installed as part of the installation process for the fax program. Other options, such as the pages to print, are selected in the usual way. Operate the OK button when everything has been set up correctly, and the fax program should then run (Figure 3.38).

The program in this example is the Bitware fax utility, and there will be marked differences from one fax program to another. However, it is a matter of providing a few details such as the telephone number to be dialled. Once this information has been provided, left-clicking on the appropriate button sends the fax. Most programs use status indicators and messages to keep the user informed about how things are progressing. Redialling is usually automatic if the number is engaged. Unless the link is lost during transmission of the fax, eventually there should be a message confirming that the fax has been sent successfully.

Points to remember

The first task when faultfinding with an external modem is to determine whether the problem lies in the port or the modem itself. Go into Device Manager and check that there is an entry for the port. If Windows has detected any problems with the port they will be noted in its properties window, which can be launched by double-clicking on the port's entry in Device Manager. Diagnostics software can be used to test serial ports, and ideally, a loopback test should be used.

A USB modem should be detected by the Windows Plug and Play system. A USB device can not be used unless it is detected by Windows and the appropriate device driver has been installed. Where possible, try the modem and USB cable with another computer. Both are operational if they work with the other computer. It is then reasonable to assume that the USB ports of the other PC are faulty or installed incorrectly. If they do not work with the other PC, either the modem or the USB cable is faulty.

The indicator lights of an external modem can be useful when faultfinding. If the power light fails to switch on, check the mains adapter or the batteries, as appropriate. Poor connections to batteries and the power plugs of mains adapters are common causes of problems with electronic gadgets, and modems are certainly no exception.

If there is no response from the carrier detect light when trying to get online, and (or) an error message such as "no carrier" is displayed on the monitor, the modem is not getting a proper signal from the remote modem. This could be the result of a fault at the other end of the system or poor line quality. Check that the lead from the modem to the telephone socket is in good condition and making good contact at both ends.

Problems such as the telephone ringing whenever the modem is connected to the telephone system could be due to a faulty modem. However, the more common cause is a European or American cable being used instead of the correct UK type.

If the modem and its communication port both seem to be functioning, but there is still a problem accessing the modem, check the Windows settings for the port and the modem. If the modem is responding but getting online is not possible, check the Internet settings.

Do not assume that there is a problem with a modem because it is not providing downloads at its rated maximum speed. The maximum speed can only be achieved using a telephone line that provides something close to theoretical perfection. In practice, a 56k modem is unlikely to do better than about 5000 bytes per second, and most users typically achieve rates about 10 percent less than this.

Clever features provided by the telephone company, such as call waiting, can give problems when trying to use the Internet. A lack of dialling tone can result in the Internet software assuming there is a fault on the line, and not dialling the ISP as a result. This can be corrected by changing the appropriate Internet setting. Some services can produce noises on the line that result in the Internet connection being lost. Where possible, dial the appropriate cancellation code before going online, or set up Windows to do so.

The Internet software is probably not installed correctly if the modem does not drop the connection at the end of an Internet session. Uninstalling and then reinstalling the software will usually clear this problem. Note that with some methods of using the Internet, closing the browser program will not cut off the connection. The connection is dropped when the software used to make the connection is closed.

Faxes are not normally sent by running the fax software and then indicating which file should be transmitted. Instead, the installation routine for the fax software installs a fax printer driver. Faxes are sent from within applications programs by "printing" to this device, which is selected from the list of installed printers. This enables faxes to be sent from practically any Windows application program.

Imaging

Downloading

The big puzzle for most newcomers to digital cameras and scanners is how to get the images into their favourite image editor. Some scanners and digital cameras are supplied with download programs that place the images onto the hard disc drive in a standard format such as JPEG. The images can then be imported into practically any image editing program, as well as desktop publishing programs, word processors, and so on. Most of these programs also have database and preview facilities that make it easier to find the required image file. Finding the right image might not be difficult initially, but it can certainly become an issue when there are hundreds or thousands of them stored on your hard disc drive. It pays to get things well organised right from the start.

TWAIN

If you are lucky, the scanner or camera will be supplied with a TWAIN driver in addition to the download and preview software. Unfortunately, many imaging devices are only supplied with one or the other. This limits your options, but the equipment is usable provided one of these methods is supported. The TWAIN option is probably the more popular method of downloading files from an imaging device, particularly among professional users. TWAIN supposedly an acronym for "technology without an interesting name", but this is explanation is far from universally accepted. It is probably derived from the saying "never the twain shall meet". The purpose of the TWAIN driver is to ensure that the twain (meaning two) shall meet, and the two that must be brought together are the imaging device and the computer.

TWAIN drivers tend to confuse the uninitiated, because having loaded the drivers onto the PC there is no obvious way of downloading images. The all-important point to keep in mind is that the TWAIN drivers provide a link to other software, but are not applications programs. In order to use the TWAIN drivers you must have applications software that can utilise them. Most imaging programs, including the "cheap and cheerful" variety, do support TWAIN drivers. The method used to access the TWAIN facilities vary somewhat from one program to another. In addition, the facilities offered by the TWAIN driver vary considerably, and have to be tailored to suit the particular hardware in use.

If you use two or three imaging devices with your computer, each device will require its own TWAIN drivers to be installed. These are often loaded automatically when the installation program for the camera or scanner is run. When loading the TWAIN drivers is optional, it is advisable to select this option even if you have no immediate use for them. The drivers will take up little space on the hard disc, and it is likely that you will wish to use them before too long.

Importing

The exact method of importing images into an application via the TWAIN route varies from one program to another. It might be necessary to delve into the Help system or the instruction manuals to find the correct menu options, but a little delving into the File menu will usually bring them to

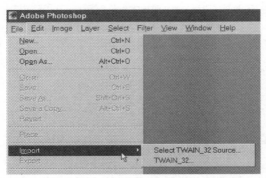

light. Here a couple of examples will be considered, starting with PhotoShop 5. With this program the TWAIN option is accessed via the Import option of the File menu (Figure 4.1). One option enables the source to be selected, but this is only relevant if more than one TWAIN compliant device is used with

Fig.4.1 Importing a TWAIN image in PhotoShop

the PC. The PC used for this example has two TWAIN compliant peripherals, which are a digital camera and a scanner. Left clicking on the Select TWAIN_32 source option produces the small window of Figure 4.2, and the required source can then be selected.

Images from the camera or scanner can then be downloaded by returning to the File menu, selecting the Import option, and then selecting

TWAIN_32 from the submenu. The window that appears next depends on the source in use. Figure 4.3 shows the window that appears with the Olympus digital camera used as the source. This provides full control over the camera, but

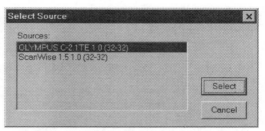

Sources:
OLYMPUS C-2.1TE 1.0 (32-32)
ScanWise 1.5 1.0 (32-32)

Select
Cancel

Fig.4.2 The required TWAIN source must be selected if more than one is available

in most cases it is only needed to download the images stored in the camera's memory. This is achieved by operating the Read button, which results in "thumbnail" pictures being downloaded and displayed in the window. The required images are then downloaded by selecting the corresponding "thumbnail" images and operating the Import button. The images are then downloaded from the camera and loaded into the graphics program. Here they can be edited, printed, and saved to disc, just like any other images.

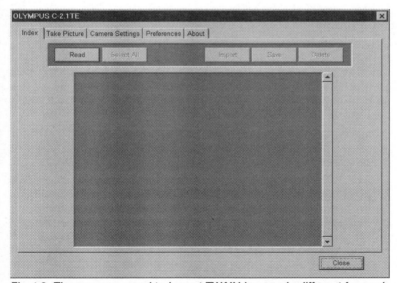

OLYMPUS C-2.1TE

Index | Take Picture | Camera Settings | Preferences | About

Read | Select All | Import | Save | Delete

Close

Fig.4.3 The program used to import TWAIN images is different for each source. This one is for an Olympus C1400L camera

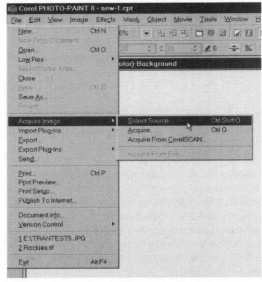

Fig.4.4 Bringing a TWAIN image into Corel Photo-Paint 8

Corel Photo-Paint 8 is used for the second example of importing images from a TWAIN source. This time the Acquire Image option is selected from the File menu, and this leads to three choices that are available from the submenu (Figure 4.4). As before, one of these enables the source to be selected via a small window (Figure 4.5). The other two options enable images to be downloaded from the current source, either into Photo-Paint 8 or into the CorelSCAN utility. It will usually be the direct route that is needed, and selecting this option results in the required utility being run from within Photo-Paint 8 (Figure 4.6). This utility program is then used to make the scans or download the images from the camera. Either way, they are loaded into Photo-Paint 8 where they can be used in the normal way.

In menus, the TWAIN option may be referred as just plain TWAIN or something like TWAIN32 or TWAIN_32. The "32" simply indicates that the driver is for a 32-bit version of Windows, which means Windows NT,

Fig.4.5 Selecting the TWAIN source in Photo-Paint 8

Windows 95, or any later versions. These days it is not of any practical significance. Some graphics software lacks any means of using TWAIN drivers. If a search of the menus and the Help

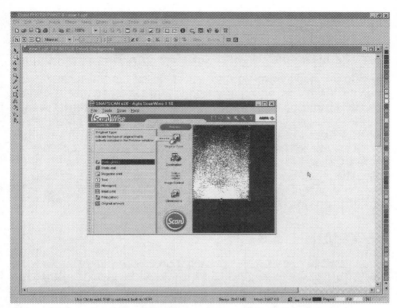

Fig.4.6 Producing a scanned image from within Photo-Paint 8

system does not reveal any means of directly downloading images into the program, this feature is probably unavailable. Generally, only older and simple graphics software has this shortcoming.

No utility?

A common problem when using TWAIN drivers is that the appropriate option or options are included in the menu system of the graphics program, but selecting the TWAIN option results in an error message. In some cases it might even crash the computer. This sort of thing can be caused by faulty drivers or the wrong drivers being installed. However, before reinstalling the drivers or going in search of a newer and better version, check that all the software has been installed.

The TWAIN software provides a means of getting images from the source and into the applications program, but in practice some additional software is usually required. In the camera example used previously, selecting the TWAIN option resulted in a simple utility program being run. This program enables the required images to be selected and downloaded, and it provides other facilities such as the ability to delete selected images. The utility software for a scanner enables the limits of the scan to be set, the required resolution to be set, and so on. The TWAIN drivers are normally of no value without a utility of this type.

The installation routine might automatically install the additional software when the TWAIN drivers are installed, but this is by no means certain. Read the instruction manual and make sure that all the essential support software has been installed. This can avoid a lengthy "wild goose chase" looking for improved drivers that are unnecessary. When you are sure that all the required software is installed, and if the TWAIN option is still not functioning properly, start looking elsewhere for the cause of the fault. The problem might be cured by reinstalling the drivers or using a newer version, but do not overlook the possibility that a hardware fault is causing things to grind to a halt.

No TWAIN

These days the vast majority of imaging devices are supplied complete with TWAIN drivers, but there is still a significant proportion that are not. In the absence of TWAIN drivers, imaging devices should be supplied with utility software that permits downloaded images or scans to be saved in at least one standard file format. This software can be run from the Windows Start menu in the usual way, but with digital cameras it is increasingly common for an automatic download facility to be included. When the camera is connected to the computer's USB port and switched on, the presence of the camera is detected. The files are then automatically downloaded to the default directory.

The usual scheme of things is to have a message appear on the screen to indicate that the camera has been detected (Figure 4.7). You then have the option of going ahead with the download or cancelling it. Going ahead with the download usually produces a small status window that shows how things are progressing (Figure 4.8). The image library software supplied with the camera will probably be run

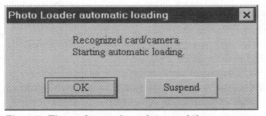

Fig.4.7 The software has detected the camera

automatically once the download has completed (Figure 4.9).

The usual problem when initially using a system of this type is locating the files that have been downloaded. There should be a Preferences option available from a

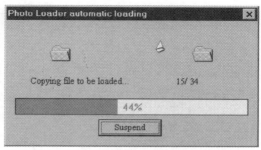

Fig.4.8 A status window shows how the download is progressing

menu or a button, and it should be possible to alter the default directory. The current directory should be given here, but it will probably be in an abbreviated form if the directory is deep in a directory structure. This is certainly the case in the example of Figure 4.10, but it might at least give a few clues on the whereabouts of the files. In most cases the files with be in the Program Files directory structure. Most applications have their files in a subfolder of this folder, or more probably, in a directory structure having this subfolder as its root. Having located the subfolder for the download utility it should not be difficult to locate the folder that contains the image files. Note that most download utilities do not store the files in the default folder. Instead, the files are normally stored in a series of subfolders, with a different folder being used for each day's downloads, or even for each download.

Fig.4.9 The downloader program

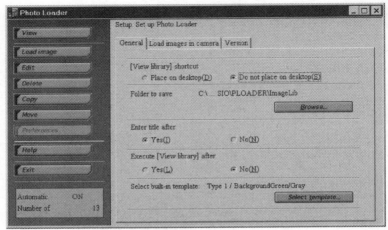

Fig.4.10 The downloader should show the default directory and permit it to be changed

Of course, the best way around this problem is to set the default directory before downloading any files. You then know precisely where the files will be placed. Windows ME produces a subfolder in the My Documents folder called My Pictures, and this is the obvious choice. My preference is to produce a folder for images off the root directory, where they are easily accessible from applications programs.

Interface

In the past, equipment that used TWAIN drivers had a reputation for poor reliability. It was notoriously difficult to get this type of equipment working properly in the first place, and to keep it working. Some of the problems were certainly due to badly written drivers that simply did not work properly. Probably the main problem was that most of the TWAIN compliant devices of the time used a SCSI interface. In order to get the device working it was first necessary to get the SCSI interface card installed and working. In addition, the SCSI card had to be compatible with the peripheral in use, and the SCSI cable had to be compatible with both of them.

The majority of new TWAIN compliant devices use the USB interface, which banishes many problems of the past. However, whatever type of interface the peripheral uses, it can only work properly if that interface is properly installed and functioning correctly. Where there is a complete failure of communications with the camera or scanner it clearly makes sense to check that the relevant interface of the computer is functioning properly. It also makes sense to do this at an early stage, rather than wasting large amounts of time checking and double-checking cables and device drivers that are perfectly all right. Checking ports, dealing with hardware conflicts, etc., are covered in chapters one and two, and will not be considered any further in this chapter.

Turned on

My first digital camera proved to be slightly puzzling, as it seemed to be free of any faults, but it successfully communicated with the PC about 50 percent of the time. Even when it did decide to "talk" to the computer, the download rate was sometimes very slow. A little investigation revealed the cause of the problems. A peripheral device should really be switched off before connecting it to the computer, and then switched on again once it is connected. This is normally done in order to reduce the risk of the peripheral or the computer being damaged. However, in some instances it is necessary to do things this way in order to get the equipment to work properly.

In this example, the TWAIN driver worked perfectly provided the camera was not switched on when it was connected to the computer's serial port. If the camera was switched on when it was connected, the driver was unable to establish contact with the camera. Sometimes it was possible to establish contact by switching the camera off, waiting a few seconds, and then switching it back on again. This was only partially successful though. Because communication had failed initially, the system defaulted to a low and safe baud rate once the link was established. Downloads that should have taken two minutes or so would then take in excess of 20 minutes.

The instruction manual for the peripheral should give warnings if there is a potential problem of this type. Unfortunately, this type of thing is often left unexplained, and you have to do some experimenting in order to find the best way of using the equipment. In general, everything should work properly provided the peripheral is not powered up when it is connected to the PC, and you remember to switch it on before trying to establish the link with the PC. This should not be necessary with an interface that is designed for use "on the fly", such as a USB type.

Where there is an initial problem with the link, and the system defaults to a very low transfer rate, it is probably not worthwhile persisting with the download. The batteries in the camera will probably go flat before the download is completed! It is better to cancel the download, close the download utility, and switch off the camera. The download can then be started from scratch, and it should proceed at the correct speed. Cancelling the download and switching off the camera will probably not have the desired effect. When the download is resumed, the download utility will almost certainly remain at the low transfer rate. Closing the download utility and restarting it should take the program back to the default settings, including the fast transfer rate.

Unpacking

One of the most common scanner faults is not really a fault at all. Due to the reluctance of users to read instruction manuals, many peripherals are supplied with a "quick start" sheet or leaflet. This goes through the steps needed to get the equipment connected to the PC, installed in Windows, and doing whatever it is supposed to do. Unfortunately, many users do not even bother to look through the "quick start" guide. This is usually a big mistake with scanners, which are commonly supplied with the scan head locked in position. The point of locking the head is that there is less risk of it being damaged in transit if it is not free to move around.

There might be some packing material that has to be removed in order to free the head, or there could be some form of locking control that has

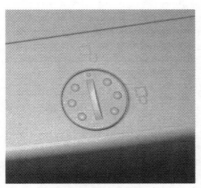

to be adjusted. The Agfa Snapscan E20 for example, has a control on the underside that must be rotated through 90 degrees in order to free the scan head (Figure 4.11). The control has to be adjusted using a large screwdriver, so there is little chance of it being accidentally returned to the locked position once the head has been unlocked.

Fig.4.11 Do not forget to unlock the scan head

If your newly installed scanner starts making loud noises and vibrating a great deal when it is switched on, check the literature supplied with the unit. There could be a serious mechanical fault, but it is far more likely that the scan head has not been unlocked. Clearly, it is better if this type of thing is avoided, and the manuals and leaflets supplied with the scanner are checked for important information before the scanner is installed and switched on. The scanner will probably be designed to withstand a certain amount of misuse, but it is advisable to avoid the "acid test" in case the scanner does not survive the experience. It is unlikely that the retailer or manufacturer will agree to a repair under guarantee if the product has been misused.

Where a scanner has been in use for some time and it starts making noises and vibrating a lot when switched on, it is a good idea to check that the locking mechanism is not engaged. Scanners vibrate to some extent in normal use, and this can result in the locking mechanism gradually returning to the locked position. Do not overlook the possibility of some helpful soul with a misplaced sense of humour setting the head to the locked position as a practical joke.

Image quality

When scanning and when using digital cameras, many users are dissatisfied with the image quality for one reason or another. Probably the most common causes of problems are strong colour casts and contrast levels that are much too low. Colour casts with digital cameras can often be corrected using the camera's controls. Most digital cameras have a control that can be set for various types of lighting, such as daylight, tungsten lamps, and fluorescent lighting. If this has an inappropriate setting, it is virtually inevitable that a strong colour cast will occur. Even if this setting is correct, it is still possible that a significant colour cast will result, and there is bound to be some error. The camera itself does not have perfect colour rendition, and further errors occur when the image is viewed using a monitor or it is printed.

It is essential to have some form of photo-editing software if you intend to scan photographic images or use a digital camera. It is better if the raw images are reasonably close to the correct colours and the contrast range is close to the optimum levels. It is then easy to "fine tune" the settings using the photo-editing software, and get the images just as you need them. However, quite large errors in contrast and colour can usually be corrected using photo-editing software, so all is not lost if downloaded or scanned images are far from perfect in these respects.

The exception is where the contrast is far too high. This often produces a loss of detail in the lightest and (or) darkest areas of the image. Adjusting

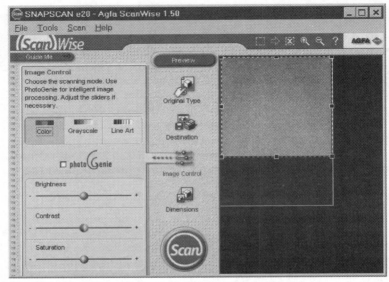

*Fig.4.12 Scanning software usually has brightness and
          contrast controls*

the contrast can produce more pleasing and plausible results, but it can
not restore details that were not recorded in the original image.
Fortunately, excessive image contrast is not a common problem in digital
imaging. The contrast of scanners and digital cameras is often kept
relative low, as this ensures that a full range of tones is present in the
image even if the exposure is not perfect. The colour depth of most
imaging devices is greater than the human eye can accommodate, so it
is not essential to utilise the full range in an image. A full range of tones
with no noticeable stepping will still be present when the contrast is
corrected using image-editing software. A consequence of the low
contrast of the basic image is that virtually all images require some
adjustment in order to produce good results.

Adjustment

Scanning software usually has two or three controls that can be used to
adjust the characteristics of the scanned image (Figure 4.12). There
should be the usual brightness and contrast controls, and there may be
a colour saturation control. The latter controls the strength of the colours

in the image. The ideal brightness and contrast settings are a subjective matter, and they are simply adjusted to give what you consider the best picture quality. The same is true of colour saturation. The default setting is usually satisfactory, but a higher level can be used if the image has colours that are obviously too weak. A lower level can be used if the image has excessively strong "Mickey Mouse" colours.

Note that the picture quality controls of scanning software do not normally have any effect on the way that the image is scanned. They simply alter the image data once the scan has been completed. Consequently, these controls have no advantage over those in a photo-editing program, and you may as well accept the defaults and then adjust the picture quality using an image editor. I would certainly recommend doing things this way, because the controls of an image editor program are likely to be more comprehensive than those of a scanning program.

Make sure that you use the right mode when undertaking monochrome scanning. A monochrome image can be scanned in colour, but there is no advantage in doing so. There is a drawback in that the file produced by a colour scan will typically be three times larger than the monochrome equivalent. It is grey-scale scanning that should be selected, and not a line-art or text mode. Grey-scale scanning should produce a full range of tones, whereas a line-art or text mode is strictly black and white with no intermediate tones. This is all that is needed for scanning text, line drawings, or anything of this nature.

There is usually a threshold control, and anything darker than the threshold level is reproduced as black on the scanned image. Anything above the threshold level is white on the scanned image. This control is given a setting that produces crisp lines, text, etc., with minimal artefacts. If a grey-scale image produces very grainy and coarse looking results, it is likely that the line-art mode has been selected by mistake, or the grey-scale mode is being used with an excessive amount of contrast.

Camera contrast

It is unusual but not unknown for digital cameras to have a contrast control. Where this feature is available it is possible to boost the contrast if it is consistently too low, but increasing the contrast decreases the exposure latitude. The higher the contrast is set, the more accurate the exposures have to be. As explained previously, the colour resolution is usually much higher than is really necessary, so low contrast images are easily corrected using an image editor. Even when a large boost in contrast is used, a full range of tones and colours should be present on the processed image. Therefore, it is probably best to settle for a relatively low contrast setting that gives plenty of exposure latitude, even if this means that the raw images look rather "flat". On the other hand, a very low contrast setting is unlikely to give good results. Restoring the contrast to a more acceptable level using an image editor program can give rather grainy looking results. A little experimentation should help to locate a good compromise setting.

Exposure compensation

There is no brightness control as such, but most digital cameras give some control over the exposure, which is effectively the same thing. Some of the more up-market cameras have the option of using manual exposure, but it is absent on most digital cameras. It is often difficult to use and of limited value on those cameras that do have this feature. An exposure compensation control is the more usual, and perhaps more useful type of manual control. This is used in conjunction with the camera's automatic exposure control.

The automatic exposure systems of some cameras are very sophisticated, but on the budget models the exposure systems are usually quite basic. This is one area in which digital cameras still seem to lag behind their 35 millimetre and APS counterparts. No matter how sophisticated the exposure system, an automatic system will never get the exposure right every time. For one thing, the exposure system can not mind-read, and it does not know which element or elements in a picture are of primary importance. The exposure compensation control enables the exposure to be set higher or lower than the level that the exposure system deems correct.

The sophistication of exposure compensation systems varies significantly from one camera to another. At its most basic, there is a "backlight" control, which gives extra exposure. In other words, it makes the picture lighter. The amount of additional exposure is usually about one or two stops, which is between two and four times more light than would be used for a non-compensated exposure. A backlighted subject is probably the most common cause of grossly inaccurate exposure, and it is produced when there is a strong light source behind the main subject. The classic example is where a picture is taken of someone in a shaded area, but there is sunlit scene behind him or her.

Virtually all exposure systems have a bias towards the centre of the picture. In other words, the light level in the centre of the frame has a strong influence on the exposure reading, while areas away from the

Fig.4.13 A backlight control is inadequate with extreme conditions

centre have progressively less influence. This helps to avoid having the main subject overexposed due to the bright background. However, the bias towards the centre of the frame may not be enough if the background is many stops brighter than the main subject, which is often the case in practice. In addition, the central biasing only works when the main subject is near the middle of the frame.

In the contrived photograph of Figure 4.13 the backlight control has been set at maximum, and in Figure 4.14 the photograph has been taken without using any exposure compensation. In both cases the subject, which is a Russian doll, has been reproduced as a silhouette. This demonstrates the point that the extra exposure produced by using the backlight control will not be sufficient in extreme circumstances. Unfortunately, extremes such as this are found quite frequently in real world photography.

A photo editor program can be used to increase the brightness and contrast in an attempt to bring out detail in the main subject, but it is a mistake to rely on this method instead of accurate exposures. Figures

Fig.4.14 The photograph without exposure compensation

*Fig.4.15 The compensated version of the photograph after a great
deal of processing*

Fig.4.16 The non-compensated version after considerable processing

4.15 and 4.16 respectively show the compensated and non-compensated versions of the photograph after some manipulation using PhotoShop 5. The contrast and detail in Figure 4.15 is quite good, but there is noticeable graininess due to the substantial increase in contrast that has been used. In Figure 4.16 a massive increase in brightness and contrast has brought out some detail, but the contrast is still quite low and the grain is very pronounced. There is a limit to the increase in contrast that can be applied to images, especially when dealing with colour photographs. Slightly overdo things and you will produce special effects rather than an improvement in the photograph.

Backlighting

There are ways of combating extreme backlighting, and the usual solution is to use the camera's flashgun. This reduces the difference in the background and foreground light levels, and should produce exposures that are much more accurate. Another advantage is that in many situations using a backlight control results in the background becoming completely "bleached out". The light from the flashgun brightens the

Fig.4.17 Fill-in flash produces much better, if rather clinical results

Fig.4.18 The close-up shot of the doll

main subject but not the entire scene, giving a better balance between the foreground and background light levels. Figure 4.17 shows the Russian doll photographed using a flashgun. In this example the flashgun has been used at such short range that it has become the main light source, and the ambient light has no significant effect. It has still had the desired effect though, and the Russian doll is almost perfectly exposed.

Another way of avoiding underexposure with backlighted subjects is to make sure that the main subject occupies as much of the frame as possible. The exposure system will then be measuring the light from the main subject to a large extent, and largely ignoring the bright background. This does not guarantee a perfect exposure in situations where the background is many times brighter than the main subject, but together with exposure compensation it should ensure that usable results are obtained. The photograph of Figure 4.18 was taken much closer to the doll, and exposure compensation has been used. Some brightening and increased contrast has been used, but only small amounts were needed in order to obtain acceptable results from the original image.

+/- Exposure

Some digital cameras have an exposure compensation control that offers several levels of compensation. The "+" settings have the same effect as a backlight control, and lighten the image. The "– " settings have the opposite effect, and darken the image. In practice, it is far more common for positive rather than negative compensation to be needed. In the real world there are numerous instances where something bright in the picture tends to give results that are too dark (underexposure). These include sunlight on snow, bright lights in a night-time scene, and light coming through a window when shooting indoors. Large dark areas causing overexposure are much more rare, but can be combated using the "–" exposure compensation settings.

Practically every digital camera has a built-in monitor that shows the picture that has just been taken. Although the resolution and quality of the screen is not usually very good, any serious error in the exposure should be readily apparent. This gives users of digital cameras a huge advantage over those using film cameras. With normal film cameras, you are not able to see how the pictures have come out until the transparencies or prints are received from the processor. By then, it will probably be too late to retake the photographs. Even if the photographs are repeatable, having to retake the duds is likely to be time consuming.

With a digital camera you can see immediately that things have not gone quite right. Obviously with some types of subject matter it is not possible to try again using different settings, but with many types of photograph it is possible to have several attempts at getting it right. Any duds can be erased so that the camera's memory is not used up unnecessarily, and unlike a film camera, any dud shots do not cost anything. It is certainly better to put some effort into getting things right initially, rather than taking technically poor photographs and trying to correct them using a photo editor program. It might be possible to get good results from raw images that are poorly exposed, but this is by no means guaranteed.

Colour correction

Some form of colour balance control is a standard feature of digital cameras. On the face of it, there is no need for any form of colour adjustment. Photographs taken with tungsten lighting as the main light source tend to look very yellow-orange in colour, but this simply reflects the way the scene actually looked. Unfortunately, human vision is quite happy to accept the original scenes as looking quite normal, although there is actually a significant yellow-orange bias in the lighting, but not photographs that have exactly the same colour cast. This is probably down to the psychology of the way we perceive things rather than a physical explanation. We do not accept the odd colours in the photograph because we are not actually there, but are instead looking in from outside. The colours in the photograph are at odds with the colours in our surroundings, so we perceive them as being incorrect.

The colour balance facilities vary considerably from one camera to another. There is usually an automatic facility, and there is sometimes the option of manual control as well. With this type of facility it is important to read the camera's instruction manual to see exactly what is on offer and how it is used. This type of facility is never perfect though, and few photographs will have colours that look perfect. In some cases the problem will be due to human error. It is easy to forget the colour correction controls when taking photographs. If you do remember to use colour correction, it is even easier to forget to cancel it when you move on to different subject matter. Automatic colour balance systems are quite good, but might alter beautifully atmospheric lighting in the late evening so that it looks as though the pictures were taken in the middle of the day.

Although colour casts from digital cameras have been the main topic here, the same problem can occur with scanners. Few real world scanners produce files that are highly accurate representations of the original, and it is reasonable to expect some colour error. Being realistic about it, many of the photographs being scanned will have slight colour casts. Whether colour casts are present on scanned images or those from a digital camera, the methods of removing the casts are essentially the same.

Correction methods

Any photo editor program should have a good range of controls for altering the colour balance. It is only fair to point out that adjusting colour

Fig.4.19 Changes in colour balance can be previewed on the image

balance is not as easy as optimising the brightness and contrast settings. You need to have reasonably good colour acuity, and it is obviously not a task for someone who suffers from colour blindness.

The obvious way of doing things is to have level controls for the three primary colours. These are red, green, and blue, or cyan, yellow, and magenta, depending on how the colour image is formed. In most photo editor programs you can use both sets of primary colours, and it is largely a matter of adjusting the image "by eye". Figure 4.19 shows the Color Balance window of PhotoShop 5, and this has three slider controls that enable the strengths of the three primary colours to be adjusted. If a colour cast that should be present has been removed by an automatic colour balance control, strengthening the appropriate colours should put back the missing cast.

For example, if the red-orange cast of a sunset has been lost, increasing the red setting is the obvious starting point. This is likely to give a cast that is too red, and an orange cast can be produced by reducing the amount of blue, and perhaps reducing the green level as well. Removing a strong red-orange cast, such as that produced by tungsten lighting requires the controls to be moved in the opposite directions. In other words, the red level is reduced, the blue level is increased, and the green setting is left unaltered or boosted slightly.

The degree of filtering available from most programs is sufficient to correct any colour imbalance. However, if necessary, stronger filtering can be obtained by repeating the process. Bear in mind though, that excessive filtering will produce "over the top" results, and it is easy the stray from correction into the realms of special effects. In fact, some of the colour correction facilities of image editor programs are strong enough to produce odd results even if they are applied only once.

As with most photo editor programs, PhotoShop enables the effects of adjustments to be applied almost instantly to the image displayed on the screen. You can therefore experiment with the settings until things look just right, or operate the Cancel button and exit from the Color Balance window if you change your mind and do not wish to apply the changes. Most Windows programs have at least a single step Undo command, which enables changes to be removed if you apply them and then change your mind. PhotoShop 5 and later versions have a multi-level Undo facility, so it is possible to step back through several editing commands if desired.

Of course, if you do not have confidence in your editing ability, it is possible to make backup copies of image files before you do any editing. It is then possible to return to the original image if the editing goes seriously awry. Even if you are very expert at image editing, it is still a good idea to keep backup copies of the raw images. Later you may wish to apply different editing to an image. This is easy if the original image file is still available, but can be more difficult where only a heavily edited version of the image is available. Note that once an image has been saved to disc, there is no way of reversing some of the clever effects that can be applied using a photo editor.

Easy ways

Correcting colour imbalance by adjusting the primary colours is a skilled task, but many photo editors have facilities that make the process much easier. Figure 4.20 shows the Variations window of PhotoShop 5. This is accessed via the Image menu, and it is obtained by selecting Adjust and then Variations from the submenu. The top section of the window

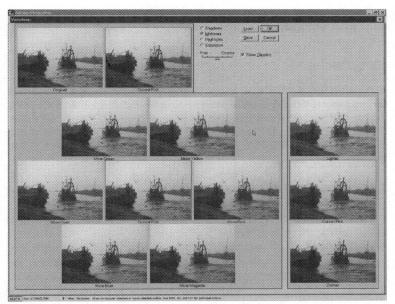

Fig.4.20 The Variations window provides an easy way of applying colour correction

shows the original image and the modified version, but these will be the same initially. The lower section of the window shows the modified image surrounded by six variations that have extra cyan, magenta, yellow, red, green, and blue. It is possible but unlikely that one of these variations will be exactly what is required. In that event, it is just a matter of left clicking on the appropriate version, and the modified image will then adjust to match it. Operate the OK button to return to the image and make the changes take effect.

In most cases some extra processing will be required. The basic colour casts are quite weak, but by double clicking on one of the tinted images two or three times it is possible to obtain stronger effects. You can also double-click on different images to combine two tints. Double clicking on the lighter and darker images in the right-hand section of the window respectively lightens or darkens the modified image by a small amount. Again, double clicking two or three times gives a stronger effect. In this way it is possible to gradually "fine tune" the image until it is exactly as required. Simply double-click on the unmodified image to remove all the processing and start again. The OK button is operated when the desired effect is obtained, or the Cancel button is operated if you change your mind and wish to abandon the processing.

Levels

Some photo editors have a facility that enables a colour cast to be easily and quickly removed. This usually requires the user to indicate a point on the image that should be either black, white, or a mid-grey colour. The program then automatically adjusts the colour balance of the image so that the selected spot is the right colour, and this should remove the colour cast from the image. This method is not totally reliable in practice, since it is dependent on the user finding a spot on the image that should be pure black or white, or a neutral grey at a mid-tone. Finding a suitable grey is quite difficult, and there may not be a suitable colour on the image.

Most images have something very close to pure black or white, and using one of these is a more practical option. An area that looks as though it should be black or white may actually have slight coloration. This colour will be removed by the processing, and the colour cast will not be accurately counteracted. Another potential problem is that what appears to be black might actually be dark grey, and an apparently white area might be very pale grey. This can result in unacceptable lightening or darkening of the image. Of course, if things do not go perfectly the first time, the processing can be removed and another spot on the image can be used as the reference point.

The Levels window (Figure 4.21) is used to provide this type of colour correction using PhotoShop 5. This Window is accessed by selecting Adjust from the Image menu, and then selecting Levels from the submenu that appears. Near the bottom right-hand corner of the Levels window there are three eyedropper tools available, and from left to right these are used with black, mid-grey, and white levels. To apply colour correction the appropriate eyedropper button is selected and then a suitable point on the image is selected using the eyedropper tool.

In my experience this method of colour correction usually works best using the black as the reference colour. Therefore, I use the black eyedropper tool first and then the white one if the initial attempts are unsuccessful. With most images it is possible to find a good black level to use as the reference, and the colour cast is then instantly removed. Even if the correction is not perfect, this method will usually get quite close to the correct colour balance, and some "fine tuning" can then be applied using another method. This is much easier than applying all the colour correction "by eye".

Fig.4.21 The Levels window provides an instant solution to colour correction, but it does not always work perfectly

Automation

Where a scanner consistently produces a slight colour cast, which most scanners do, it is worth considering the automated approach to colour correction.   This method can also be used with digital cameras that produce a consistent colour cast when used with a particular type of lighting. For example, many cameras produce rather blue looking results when used with the internal flashgun. First, check through the instruction manual to see if there is an easy solution to the problem.   Does the scanner's software enable a standard colour correction to be applied to all scans?   Do the camera's facilities include a colour balance control that provides a solution to the problem.

If colour casts can not be avoided, automatic correction is the best alternative. Unfortunately, a facility of this type is not available with all photo editor programs, but some form of automation is available with most of the up-market photo editors. The full version of PhotoShop has a macro facility that can be used to apply a preset amount of colour correction. Start by colour correcting an image "by eye", and note any changes that are made to the settings. Load another image, start recording a macro, apply the same changes that were used previously, and then stop recording the macro. Load another image from the scanner, operate the key or keys assigned to the macro you just recorded, and check the colour correction is applied to the new image. If all is well, the colour correction can then be applied to any scanned image by pressing the appropriate key or keys.

Too much image

Scanning software normally enables selective copying, so that you only scan the part of image that is required. The scanned image should therefore include the section of the image that you require, and nothing more or less. Unfortunately, most digital cameras are rather less predictable. Most digital cameras have optical viewfinders, and these are sometimes quite accurate at long distances, but they are only approximate at close range. Due to parallax errors, optical viewfinders have poor accuracy when used for close-ups. Parallax errors occur because the viewfinder is slightly offset from the lens, and they therefore "look" at the subject from slightly different viewpoints. The difference between the two views is insignificant at long ranges, but becomes massive when shooting close-ups.

The usual solution is to use the built-in monitor as the viewfinder when shooting close-ups. The monitor shows the view obtained via the lens, and parallax errors are therefore eliminated. Unfortunately, this method does not guarantee perfect accuracy when framing a shot. Many built-in monitors show significantly less than the full image, and in some cases the monitor shows a section of the image that is slightly off-centre. Some optical viewfinders suffer from the same problems.

There is no major problem when a viewfinder has a slight lack of accuracy, because in virtually all cases the recorded image contains slightly more than was shown in the viewfinder. The extra area shown in the recorded image will not necessarily be of any importance. In other instances it will result in unwanted distractions creeping into the edges of the image. However, unwanted material at the edges of an image is easily removed

Figs.4.22 and 4.23 The image before (above) and after cropping

by slightly cropping the image. Any photo editor program should have a simple cropping facility. In PhotoShop the Marquee tool is selected and is used to drag a rectangle that marks the area of the image to be retained. The image is then cropped by selecting the Crop option from the Image menu. Figures 4.22 and 4.23 respectively show "before and after" screens for a simple cropping operation.

Resolution

One of the most frequently asked questions about digital cameras is "how large a print can it produce?" This is definitely a "how long is a piece of string?" type of question. There are two main factors that govern the maximum acceptable print size, and one of these is the subjective matter of the minimum print quality that is acceptable. The other is the resolution of the image. Prints that have a resolution of 200 pixels per inch look perfectly acceptable to most people, and you need to have a good printer to genuinely utilise resolutions much higher than this. Bear in mind that although a modern inkjet printer is likely to use 1200 x 1200 dots to the inch, or an even higher resolution, the real resolution is much lower.

Each dot from the printer can only be black or one of the three primary colours (cyan, magenta and yellow). It therefore requires a number of dots to mix the right colour for each pixel. The situation is very different with a monitor, where each dot can be set at required colour. Thus, although a good monitor will have a much lower resolution than a typical A4 printer in terms of the dots it can produce, the difference in picture quality is usually far less dramatic that the figures would suggest. With high-resolution images, the printer will normally win, but not by much.

The picture quality noticeably deteriorates as the resolution is reduced below about 200 pixels per inch, and few people are happy with a resolution as low as 150 dots per inch. Therefore, for most people the minimum acceptable resolution is somewhere between 150 and 200 pixels to the inch. In metric measurement this works out at about 60 to 80 pixels per centimetre. Therefore, an image from an old digital camera or a webcam that is 250 pixels wide should be printed to a width of no more than 1.66 inches, or 4.16 centimetres. Ideally, it would be printed to a width of no more than 1.25 inches or 3.12 centimetres. An image from a slightly less old digital camera, or a modern camera set to a low-resolution mode, does not offer much more scope. Even an image that is 600 pixels wide would ideally be printed to a maximum width of about 4 inches (10 centimetres), and would preferably be limited to a width of 3 inches (7.5 centimetres).

A little mathematics shows that a resolution of about 900 to 1200 pixels is needed on the longer dimension to produce an acceptable print at the popular size of 6 inches by 4 inches (152 by 102 millimetres). To produce a print at the maximum size an A4 printer can produce (typically about 11 by 8 inches) requires a resolution of about 1650 to 2200 pixels on the longer dimension. In order to get good results from an A3 printer at its maximum print size requires the resolution on the longer dimension to be around 2400 to 3200 pixels.

Low quality prints having poor resolution is a common problem when using digital cameras, and it is easy to see why this happens. The resolutions of digital cameras have improved over the years, but many of the cheaper models still only have resolutions of around 1.3 to 2.1 million pixels, or about 1280 to 1650 pixels on the longer dimension. These are fine for normal size prints at about 6 inches by 4 inches, or even the slightly larger print size of 7 inches by 5 inches, but are less than ideal for A4 or larger prints. A 1.3 million pixel camera falls well short of the resolution needed for A4 prints, and a 2.1 million pixel camera only achieves the bare minimum. Cameras having resolutions of about 3.3 to 5 million pixels are fine for prints up to A4 or so. They fall short of resolution needed for A3 prints, although with around 5 million or so pixels a reasonable A3 print might be produced.

Which mode?

Good quality prints should be obtained provided you take sharp, reasonably well exposed photographs, and do not try to stretch the resolution beyond the limits indicated previously. If your camera has a maximum resolution of (say) 1.3 million pixels, it is better to settle for good quality prints up to about 7 inches by 5 inches, rather than stretching things too far and producing bad A4 prints. If you may need to make prints that are as large as possible, always use the camera at its highest resolution so that your options are left open.

A common mistake is to use a low resolution setting because it enables more images to be stored on each memory card. The reasoning usually runs along the lines, when viewed on the monitor the low-resolution pictures look as good as the high resolution shots, so why bother using a high-resolution mode? This argument overlooks the fact that the low-resolution pictures are being viewed at their full resolution, whereas the high-resolution pictures have to be displayed at reduced quality. Although there is no apparent difference in quality, the high-resolution shots have extra resolution that can be utilised when making large prints using a suitably high quality printer.

Scanner resolution

It is not uncommon for problems to occur when a scanner is used at high resolutions. With small images scanned at 150 or 300 dots per inch there are no problems, but things go awry when large images are scanned at 300 dots per inch or more. This is unlikely to be due to a fault in the scanner, and it is normally caused by an inadequate amount of memory in the computer. Bear in mind that with 24-bit colour scanning some three bytes per pixel are required (one byte per primary colour). At 600 dots per inch there are 360,000 pixels per square inch, and each square inch therefore generates over one megabyte of data. Scanning a full A4 page at 600 dots per inch produces roughly 90 megabytes of data, and increasing the resolution to 1,200 dots per inch increases the amount of data to around 360 megabytes.

New computers generally have much more memory than those of a few years ago do. Even so, scanning at high resolutions can result in so much data that the computer can not cope. This can result in the computer slowing down to a "snails pace", an error message being produced, or the computer can simply crash. Many programs can use the hard disc to provide virtual memory if they run out of the real thing, but even the best of hard disc drives do not give comparable speed to modern memory. Hence the massive reduction in speed when dealing with large bitmaps. Of course, the computer will slow down to some extent anyway, since handling large image files requires more processor time than dealing with smaller ones.

Realistically, there are only two ways of handling this problem. The simple solution is to settle for scans at lower resolutions. Scans at 300 dots per inch are adequate for most purposes, and a resolution of 150 dots per inch is sufficient for some applications. For example, scanning a 10 inch by 8 inch print at 150 dots per inch will produce a 1500 by 1200 pixel image that is perfectly adequate for viewing onscreen. The other option is to fit more memory to your PC. The cost of memory has fallen dramatically over recent years, so adding large amounts of memory will not necessarily cost very much, and it should give vastly improved results when dealing with large image files. The generally accepted "rule of thumb" is that the computer should have an amount of memory that is at least double the size of the largest image file that will be processed.

Real resolution

The specifications for most scanners quote a maximum resolution figure, and a much lower value for the maximum optical resolution. The optical resolution is the only one that matters since this is the resolution used when scanning. Higher resolutions are obtain using software to enhance the scanned image by adding extra pixels. This process is covered in more detail in the next section of this chapter. Image enhancement has its advantages, but it is important to realise that this type of processing can not add detail that is not present on the original image.

It is best to scan at the maximum optical resolution, and then use a photo editor to enhance the image, if this proves necessary. This way the image files are kept down to reasonable sizes, and the PC's hard disc drive is not rapidly used up by bloated image files. These days most scanners have an optical resolution of at least 600 dots per inch vertically and horizontally, and this is more than adequate for most purposes. Very high-resolution scans are only needed when copying a small original that will be reproduced much larger than the original. Scanning at 600 dots per inch and then using image enhancement might give acceptable results, but there is by no means guaranteed. Using a higher quality scanner operating at a true resolution of 1200 or 1800 dots per inch gives a much greater chance of success.

Enhancing

What do you do if for one reason or another you end up with relatively low-resolution images that you need to print large? As pointed out in the previous section, there are ways of enlarging bitmaps and smoothing out the rough edges so that better-looking results are obtained. It is important to emphasise that it is not possible to put in details that are not present on the original image. The idea is to get rid of pixels that are so large that they can be clearly seen by the viewer. This also avoids the obvious stepping that occurs on anything other than vertical or horizontal lines.

Some printers have a built-in resolution enhancement facility or are supplied with software that adds this facility. Where applicable, the built-in resolution enhancement is likely to be the easiest way of smoothing low-resolution images and avoiding over-obvious pixels. The advantage of this method is that the computer only has to deal with the original image file, and not an enhanced file that is likely to be four to ten times larger.

The same effect can be obtained using most modern bitmap graphics programs. For this example, the photograph of a bee on a flower in Figure 4.24 will be used. This is reproduced at about 180 pixels to the inch, which should give reasonable but not spectacular results. Figure

Fig.4.24 The original photograph

4.25 shows an enlargement of part of the photograph, and the quality is clearly very poor. Look at the jagged edge on some of the petals for instance. This lack of quality is not surprising since the picture is being reproduced at only about 50 or so pixels per inch.

The method of increasing the number of pixels

Fig.4.25 The enlarged section shows some rough edges

varies from one graphics program to another, and the method here is the one used in PhotoShop 5. Selecting Image Size from the Image menu produces a window like the one in Figure 4.26. This shows that the fragment of the original image is some 215 pixels wide. With the Constrain

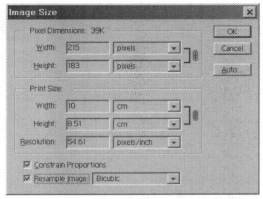

Fig.4.26 *Boosting the number of pixels using PhotoShop 5*

Fig.4.27 *The edges have been smoothed but there is no more detail*

Fig.4.28 Some sharpening added to the photograph

Proportions and Resample Image boxes both ticked, the required width in pixels is typed into the Width textbox. In this case we will increase the number of pixels by a factor of four in both directions, increasing the number of pixels by a factor of 16. This is rather more than would normally be used, but it will clearly show the effect of boosting the number of pixels. Click the OK button to exit the Image Size window and the newly enhanced picture (Figure 4.27) will appear. There is no more detail than on the original, but the jagged edges of the petals have clearly been smoothed quite significantly.

Sharpening

Most graphics software has filters that will try to give an apparent increase in sharpness. These generally work quite well provided you are prepared to settle for a modest amount of processing. Systems of this type mainly work by looking for small areas of the picture that contain a moderate

Fig.4.29 Excessive sharpening can be counterproductive

amount of contrast. The contrast is those areas is then boosted slightly. A small overall increase in contrast might also be applied. Figure 4.28 shows the example picture with a small amount of sharpness filtering added. Try not to get carried away with this type of thing, as it can be counterproductive, undoing the smoothing applied previously (Figure 4.29).

The boost in size that can be obtained depends on the nature and quality of the original image. Some cameras when used with maximum data compression tend to produce poor quality images that are covered in artefacts. This type of thing is unlikely to produce good results when printed small, and will certainly not give good results when processed and enlarged. A good clean image should produce good results if the number of pixels is doubled in each direction, giving an overall increase by a factor of four. With enhanced images it is best to print at about 175 pixels to the inch or more. I have sometimes obtained good results by trebling the number of pixels in each direction and printing at about 200 pixels per inch. However, this requires the original image to be of very high quality. If the original scene is something simple that lacks any fine detail it might be possible to use higher degrees of enlargement, but in the vast majority of cases this will not give worthwhile results.

Memory cards

The memory cards used with digital cameras contain delicate circuits that are easily zapped. Internal protection circuits give a degree of protection, but it is advisable to keep these cards away from any likely sources of static electricity, such as television sets and computer monitors. Due to their small size, these cards are not very strong and are prone to physical damage. Most are supplied in small boxes made from rigid plastic, and it is advisable to keep them in their boxes when they are not in use. Memory cards should only be fitted in the camera or removed when the camera is switched off. Most cameras will not permit a card to be installed or removed while the camera is "on", but take due care if your camera is one that lacks a built-in safety mechanism.

Memory cards sometimes give problems with the card being ignored by the camera. Another common problem is that the camera indicates that the card needs formatting. Once formatted the card works all right for a while, and then the camera indicates that it needs formatting again. The card is reformatted, works all right for a while, and so on. This can be due to dirty contacts giving a poor connection between the camera and the card. Try repeatedly inserting and removing the card from the camera. This will usually clean the contacts and remove the problem.

If this does not work it is likely that the memory card is faulty. It is definitely not a good idea to persist with a card that is probably faulty. Many of the shots stored on the card will probably be lost during one of the card's periodic bouts of amnesia. As I once learned to my cost, using an unreliable card can ultimately result in costly damage to the camera. It is better to replace the memory card rather than persist with a faulty item that will be unreliable and could necessitate a costly camera repair.

Points to remember

A TWAIN driver enables images to be downloaded from a scanner or digital camera and loaded straight into a suitable application. Most cameras and scanners are supplied with TWAIN drivers, but some lack this facility. In the absence of TWAIN drivers, a stand-alone program for downloading images should be supplied. Many imaging devices are supplied with software that permits both methods of downloading images.

A TWAIN driver is normally dependent on some additional software. This permits the desired images to be selected for downloading, the resolution setting of a scanner to be altered, and similar tasks to be performed. This software should be supplied with the imaging device, but it might not be installed with the TWAIN drivers. With scanners in particular, this software often has to be initiallised separately.

With digital cameras that connect to the PC's serial port it is important that the camera is "off" when it is connected to the port. Apart from reducing the risk of damaging the camera, having the camera switched off when it is connected to the PC makes it easier for the download software to establish contact with the camera.

Make sure that any internal packing is removed from a scanner before you start using it. Also, make sure that any locking mechanism is released before the scanner is switched on. Many "faulty" scanners actually work perfectly, and the problem is simply that the user has not read the unpacking and setting up instructions. It is a good idea to keep any internal packing. The scan head can then be locked in position again if it becomes necessary to move the scanner to a new location.

It is unrealistic to expect a scanner or a digital camera to produce perfect images that require no brightness or contrast adjustments. Practically every image will require some adjustment to the contrast and brightness levels, and many images will need changes to the colour balance. Photo editing software is a necessity for anyone who uses digital images.

4   Imaging

Wherever possible, take photographs at the highest resolution your camera can provide. This leaves your options open and avoids problems if you need high-resolution image files for large prints. Although high and low resolution images might not look much different when viewed on a monitor, the high-resolution version will actually contain far more detail. The difference usually becomes obvious when large prints are made from the image files.

With the aid of a program such as PhotoShop, it is possible to enhance images by increasing the number of pixels. Most scanners have the ability to do this. Boosting the number of pixels has the advantage of avoid outsize pixels when an image is printed large, but the enhancement process does not actually add any detail.

The amount of detail that a scanner can capture is determined by the optical resolution. Any other resolution figures are not of any importance. Similarly, the resolution of a digital camera is determined by the number of pixels produced by its CCD. Of course, in both cases there are other factors to take into account, such as the lens quality of a camera. A poor quality scanner or camera may not live up to the quality implied by its resolution figures.

Printers

Cables

Most computer peripherals are supplied complete with all the necessary cables, but printers are an exception. Every printer should come complete with a mains cable, but it is unusual for a data cable to be included. For most users this is not a problem, since the printer will be a replacement and the old lead can be used with the new printer. However, heed the warnings about parallel cables given in chapter 2. The old cable should work perfectly with a new printer provided the cable is only a few years old and in good condition. If the cable is in poor condition, it is clearly a good idea to replace it. It is also a good idea to replace an "antique" printer cable that you have been using since you bought your first PC in 1983. The cable may still be in perfect condition, but it is likely to lack some of the connections needed by a modern printer.

There is a gradual transition from parallel interfacing to the USB variety. Some modern printers have both types of interface, but more and more printers have only a USB interface. This trend will presumably continue, with all new printers having only a USB interface in a few years time. Where there is a choice of a parallel or a USB interface it does not matter too much which one you use. Both interfaces support a full range of features, and both are fast enough for normal printing applications. The print speed will be limited by the physical characteristics of the printer, or in some cases by the speed of the PC's processor, but not by a parallel or USB interface. If you already have a parallel lead and no USB lead is supplied with the printer, the parallel option provides an instant solution. However, it might be worth switching over to USB operation before too long. There are sometimes more features available using the USB interface and device drivers. An ordinary A to B lead is needed to connect a printer to a PC.

If your PC lacks USB ports, it is important to check that a printer has a parallel interface before buying it. It is actually possible to use a USB printer with a PC that lacks built-in USB ports, provided the PC has a spare PCI expansion slot. PCI cards having two or three USB ports are readily available from computer stores and at computer fairs. USB ports that are provided by an expansion card should work every bit as well as integral ports. Some older PCs actually have USB ports on the motherboard, but lack the bracket and lead assembly that enables them to connect to the outside world. It might be possible to obtain a suitable assembly, but each motherboard manufacturer seems to use its own USB connector on the motherboard. Consequently, it would probably be difficult to find a bracket and lead assembly that matched the motherboard in your particular PC.

A USB expansion card is likely to cost a little more, but is the simpler and more reliable solution. Before adding a USB port expansion card it is a good idea to check that there are no built-in USB ports included in Device Manager. If USB ports are listed here, but there are no USB connectors anywhere on the PC, there are active USB ports on the motherboard but no means of connecting them to the outside world. The built-in ports must be disabled using the BIOS Setup program before the expansion card is installed. Adding USB ports when there are active ports already in the system is likely to cause various conflicts and stands little chance of success.

USB support

Windows 95 does not include proper support for USB ports. With the original version there will be yellow exclamation marks against the USB entries in Device Manager. The second version of Windows 95 (OSR2) avoids these and installs the USB ports correctly. Unfortunately, many USB devices will not work properly with Windows 95 OSR2, and Windows 98 or later is needed for reliable operation with USB ports. There can also be problems with a Windows 98 installation that is an upgrade from Windows 95. Unfortunately, there seems to be no easy solution to this problem. It is a matter of backing up any important data, clearing everything from the hard disc, reinstalling Windows 98 from scratch, reinstalling all the applications software, and then restoring all the data files.

As far as I am aware, no current printers use an RS232C serial interface, but no doubt there are some "golden oldie" serial printers still in use. Getting serial printers to work satisfactorily can be difficult, but an "off the shelf" cable will sometimes do the job. It is a null modem cable and not a straight type that is normally used with printers. If a standard cable does not give satisfactory results, check the word format, baud rate, and handshaking method before giving up and trying a custom cable. Dealing with serial interfaces is covered in detail in chapter one, and this subject will not be pursued further here.

Installation

Installation is unlikely to be difficult with a new printer, which should be supplied complete with a disc containing the device drivers for various versions of Windows. A USB printer should be detected by the Windows Plug and Play system, and the drivers disc must then be inserted in the appropriate drive. Apart from agreeing to the licensing conditions and the usual Windows button pushing, installation is usually automatic. If the printer is not detected, go through the usual checks for a USB peripheral. Is everything plugged in properly, are the ports switched on in the BIOS and installed in Windows correctly, and is the printer switched on?

The installation procedures for some parallel printers rely on the Windows Plug and Play system detecting the printer. However, unlike a USB printer, a parallel type will only be detected during the Windows boot-up process. Therefore, make sure that the printer is switched on and connected properly before switching on the computer and booting into Windows. Late in the boot process, but probably before it is completed, a message will be displayed on the screen stating that the printer has been detected.

It is then just a matter of going through the usual Windows Plug and Play installation process. This is pretty straightforward, but the printer's instruction manual should give step by step installation instructions to help newcomers to Windows. The vast majority of modern parallel port printers use the Plug and Play method of installation, but it is as well to refer to the instruction manual to check this point. Some PC peripherals, including a few printers, rely on an installation program that is run once the computer has been booted into Windows. It may be necessary to have the printer switched off initially to prevent the Plug and Play system coming into operation, or to manually cancel it.

Drivers

It should only be necessary to resort to manual installation if you are trying to use a printer that "is not as young as it used to be". Manual installation will certainly be necessary with a printer that has a serial interface. When using an older printer it is worthwhile checking the manufacturer's web site to see if there are more recent device drivers than the ones originally supplied with the printer. A common mistake with old PC hardware in general, is to assume that device drivers for an old version of Windows will work perfectly well with a newer version of the operating system. Some of the more simple devices use the same

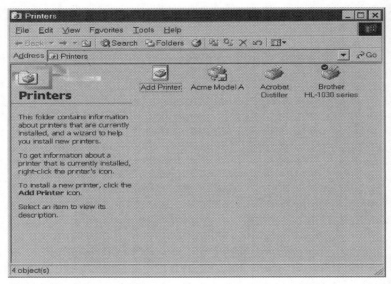

Fig.5.1 The Printers window has an icon for each installed printer

driver for more than one version of Windows, but most hardware requires a different driver for each variant.

Windows 3.1 drivers are not compatible with Windows 95 or any subsequent version of Windows. In general, Windows 95 drivers will not work with Windows 98, and Windows 98 drivers will not work with Windows ME. Some hardware even needs different device drivers for the original version of Windows 98 and the second edition. Windows NT and later versions of that operating system require device drivers that are totally different to those for Windows 9x. It is a good idea to check the manufacturer's web site, and to download the correct device drivers for the printer and version of Windows that your are using. This should ensure that the installation process is trouble free, and that the installed printer works without any little foibles coming to light.

Manual installation

To install a printer manually, start by going to the Windows Control Panel and double clicking on the Printers icon. Alternatively, go to the Start menu and select Settings, followed by Printers from the submenu. Either

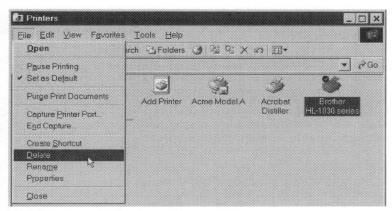

Fig.5.2 Removing a printer from the system

way, the Printers widow should appear, and it will show icons for any printers that are already installed on the system (Figure 5.1). It is not essential to remove the entry for an existing printer that is no longer needed. If there is any chance of that printer being used with the PC again, it is definitely a good idea to leave its entry intact. This avoids having to reinstall the printer if you should wish to use it again with that PC.

If you do wish to remove the entry for an old printer, left-click on its icon to select it and then choose Delete from the file menu (Figure 5.2). Alternatively, right-click on its icon and select Delete from the menu that pops up. Operate the Yes button when asked if you are sure you wish to delete this item. There may be an additional window that contains a message asking whether you wish to delete files that were only used with that printer driver. The No button is the safer option with this type of thing, but with

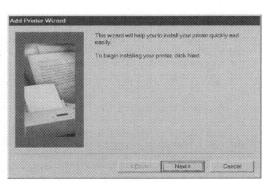

Fig.5.3 The Add Printer wizard

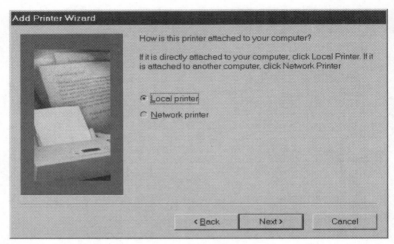

Fig.5.4 Select the Local printer button if your PC is not networked

printer drivers it is very unlikely that operating the Yes button will result in any problems. The icon will be removed from the Printers window, and the deleted printer will no longer be available as an option when printing from applications.

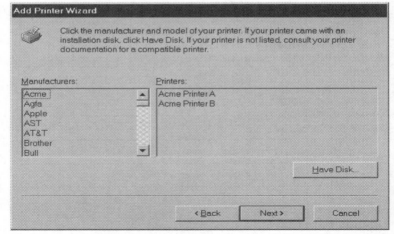

Fig.5.5 Various printer makes and models are included in the database

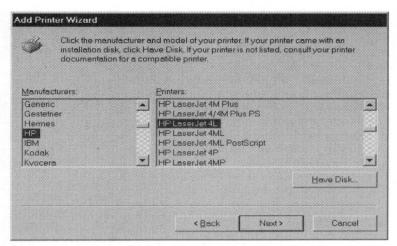

Fig.5.6 The HP LaserJet 4L printer has been selected

To install the new printer, double-click on the Add Printer Icon. This will launch the Add Printer Wizard (Figure 5.3), and the Next button is operated in order to proceed with the installation. The Next window has two radio buttons that enable either a network or local printer to be installed (Figure 5.4). The Local printer option is selected for a normal (non-networked) desktop PC. Operating the Next button results in Windows generating a device database, and then the window of Figure 5.5 appears. Here a list of manufacturers is displayed on the left, and the Windows compatible models for the selected manufacturer are shown on the right.

In this example a Hewlett Packard (HP) LaserJet 4L printer is being installed, and this printer is one that is included in the database (Figure 5.6). Operating the Next button moves things on to the next window (Figure 5.7) where the appropriate port for

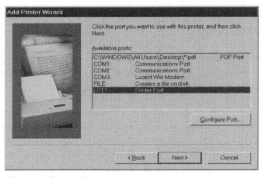

Fig.5.7 Selecting the correct port

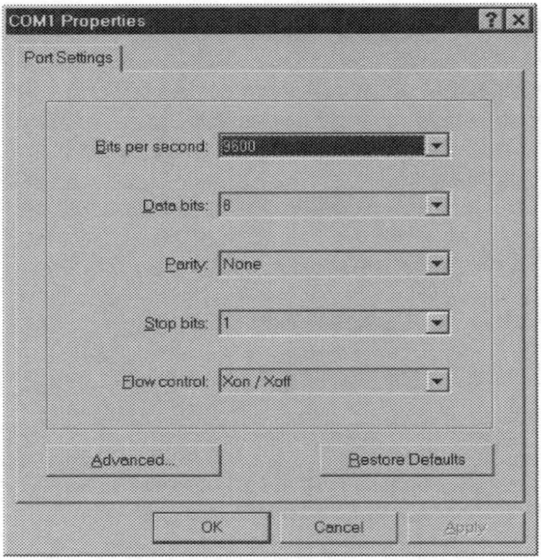

Fig.5.8 It is only necessary to configure the port if a serial type is selected

the printer is selected. Some of the ports listed here may not be ports at all, such as an option to "print" to a file. Other ports might not be available for use, such as a serial port that is actually part of an internal modem. The correct serial or parallel port for the printer should be in the list provided the port is correctly installed in Windows.

The selected port can be configured by operating the Configure Port button, but this should not be necessary for a parallel port. It is essential when a serial port is selected, and the properties window for the selected serial port then appears (Figure 5.8). The baud rate, word format, and handshake method must be set to match those of the printer. Refer to chapter one for more information on these topics. Operate the OK button once the correct parameters have been set, and then the Next button to move on to the next stage of the installation process.

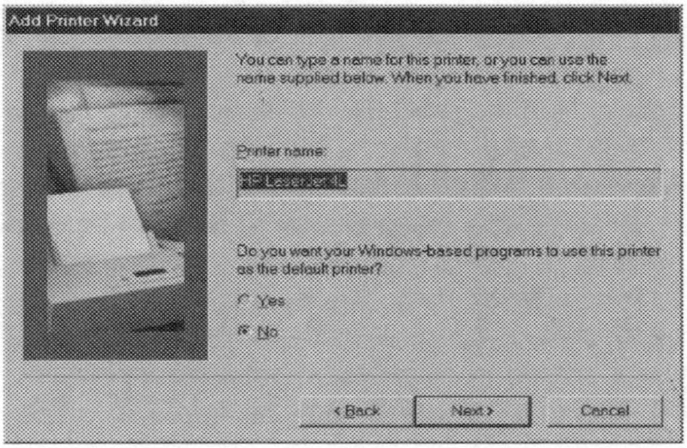

Fig.5.9 The name of the printer can be edited

This window (Figure 5.9) permits the name of the printer to be altered. In the unlikely event that you are using two printers of the same make and model with the same PC,

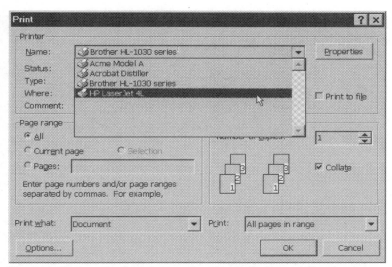

Fig.5.10 The required printer can be selected when printing from an application program

changing the default name for one of the PCs will be essential so that you can easily differentiate between them. There is otherwise no need to alter the name field. Use the radio buttons to select whether or not the printer will be used as the default printer. If it is not set as the default, the printer must be selected from the Printers menu (Figure 5.10) when the Print command of an applications program is used.

The two radio buttons on the next window (Figure 5.11) give the option of printing out a test page when the installation is complete, or skipping this test. It is a good idea to have the test page printed, since this will show straight away whether the printer is being driven

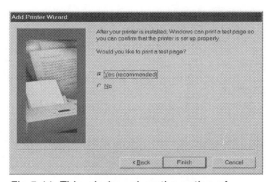

Fig.5.11 This window gives the option of printing a test page

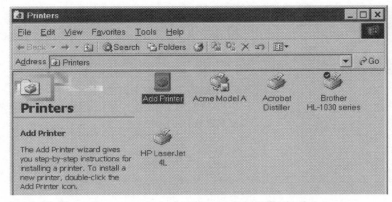

Fig.5.12 There is now an icon for the newly installed printer

correctly. Operating the Next button results in the new printer being installed, and the test page will be printed if this option was selected. The Windows installation disc might be needed to complete the installation, but in many cases it is not required and Windows completes the installation in a few seconds. An icon for the printer should then appear in the Printers window (Figure 5.12).

Not all is lost if your printer does not appear in the printer database. If you have a disc containing suitable device drivers or the drivers have been downloaded from the Internet, operate the Have Disk button when

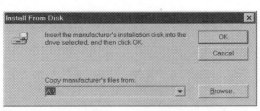

Fig.5.13 The location of the drivers can be entered in the text box

you reach the window of Figure 5.6. This brings up a small window like the one of Figure 5.13, where the path to the device drivers can be entered in the textbox. Alternatively, left-click the Browse button to launch a file browser (Figure 5.14) and use this to direct Windows to the device drivers. Either way, the installation then proceeds in normal Windows fashion.

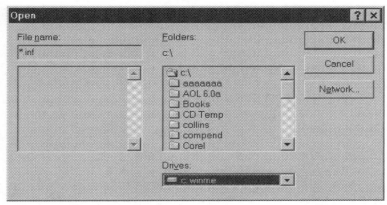

Fig.5.14 The usual file browser is available

Compatibles

It may be possible to use the printer with Windows even if it is not listed in the database, and you are unable to obtain device drivers specifically written for that printer. It is quite common for two or three identical printers to be supplied by different manufacturers. This occurs because of a practice that has become known as rebadging. In some cases the product is literally rebadged, with name badge, etc., of the manufacturer being replaced being replaced by those of the supposed equipment builder. I once had a camera that was sold under the brand name of a well-known photographic retailer. The glue holding the name badge in place eventually failed, revealing the true origins of the camera. Rebadged printers generally have their origins concealed more cleverly than that. Sometimes the printer is disguised by a different outer casing to the original printer, but there is the same mechanism "under the skin".

The instruction manual will sometimes indicate that the printer is compatible with other makes and models, and it is then a matter of looking through the database to see if any of the other printers are listed. If none of the compatible printers is listed, it might be possible to obtain suitable drivers from the manufacturer of one of the compatible printers. Unless the compatible printer is a really old model, a visit to the manufacturer's web site should produce suitable device drivers.

There is a potential problem with this method, in that some installation routines search for the correct hardware before installing the device drivers. If the correct hardware is not detected, the device drivers are not installed. It is unlikely that a compatible printer will be accepted as "the real thing" by this type of installation program. This problem is less likely to occur with a printer than with something like a video card or a software modem, so you might be in luck. In order to minimise the risk of this problem, wherever possible the drivers should be installed manually, and the printer should be switched off or temporarily disconnected from the computer.

Emulation

Some printers have the ability to mimic a popular printer or even several printers, thus ensuring that they are usable with a wide range of software. This feature is less common than it was in the early days of PC computing. Under MS/DOS it was necessary for each program to have its own printer driver, and some software was only compatible with a limited number of printers. There was a huge advantage in being able to set an obscure printer to mimic one or two popular models. This ensured a wide of software would be usable with the printer. The advent of Windows changed things, with just one printer driver permitting all Windows applications to be used with the printer.

So-called emulation modes are now rarer, although some printers still have a mode that enables them to emulate a version of the Hewlett Packard Page Compilation Language (PCL). This effectively turns the printer into a sort of generic Hewlett Packard printer that will usually work with Windows set up for use with one of the older Hewlett Packard printers. Note though, that there is no guarantee that the emulation will be perfect in every detail. In addition, using an emulation mode sometimes results in reduced printing quality, because it is a 300 dots per inch printer that is being emulated. That becomes the effective resolution, even if the print engine has a resolution of 600 dots per inch or more. The situation is worse with a high-resolution printer that can emulate something like an old 9-pin dot matrix printer. The emulation will faithfully reproduce the low resolution printing of the original printer.

Most printers that have emulation modes also have a native mode. The default will almost certainly be the native mode and not one of the emulation modes. If you intend to utilise this method of driving a printer, it is therefore essential to make sure it is set to the correct mode before you start printing. With older printers it will probably be necessary to set some DIP-switches to the correct settings. With modern printers it is usually a matter of negotiating the menu system using the pushbutton switches. The printer's instruction manual should detail any emulation modes that are available, how those modes are obtained, and any limitations they may have. Note that in some cases the emulation modes are only available if the printer is fitted with a hardware upgrade of some kind.

Test pages

It can be useful to print test pages in situations where the printer is connected up and raring to go, the printer's drivers are installed, the port is installed correctly, but the printer will not actually print anything. As explained previously, a test page can be printed during the Windows installation process. The page produced is different for each version of Windows, and it is slightly different from one printer to another. Figure 5.15 shows the test page produced using Windows ME with a Brother HL-1030 laser printer. There is a small graphic and a message at the top of the page. A list of the files used by the printer's device drivers is provided further down the page. It is usually

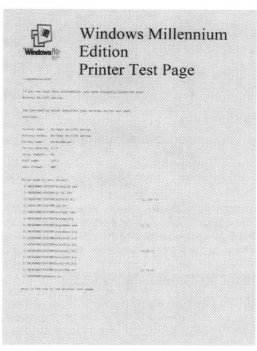

Fig.5.15 The Windows ME test page

pretty obvious if things have gone wrong. In most cases nothing at all will be printed, or the printer will produce garbage.

It is possible to print the test page without going through the installation routine. The first step is to select Settings from the Start menu and then

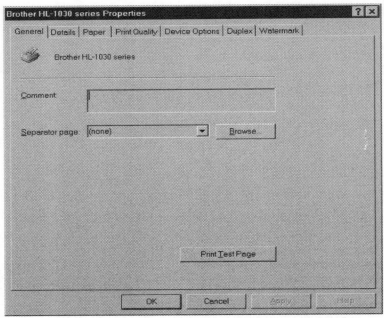

Fig.5.16 *Printing a Windows test page from the properties window*

Printers from the submenu. Alternatively, go to the Windows Control Panel and double-click on the Printers icon. Either method launches the Printers window, and here the icon for the appropriate printer is selected. Then choose Properties from the File menu, which brings up the

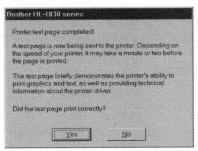

Fig.5.17 *Answering No launches the Printing Troubleshooter*

properties window for the printer. This window varies from one printer to another, but under the General tab there should be a button marked "Print Test Page" (Figure 5.16). Operating this button should result in the test page being printed and the window of Figure 5.17 appearing.

If all is well, left-click the Yes button to clear the window from the screen. There is nothing wrong with the printer drivers, the printer, or the connecting cable, if the page is printed correctly. Try printing from a Windows application again, but this time ensure that the correct printer is selected in the Printers menu of the Print window. You can change the default printer by going to the Printers window, right-clicking on the printer you wish to set as the default unit, and then selecting Set as Default from the popup menu (Figure 5.18). Another method is to select the printer's icon and then select Set as Default from the File menu. There

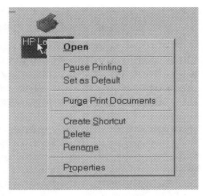

Fig.5.18 Setting the default printer

is a tick shown against the default printer's icon in the Printers window, and in the example of Figure 5.19 the Brother HL-1030 is set as the default printer.

Check the other settings in the Print window if the correct printer is selected and the printer is still not functioning correctly. Is the page range something valid, or are you trying to print pages that do not exist? Operate the Properties button and check the settings for the printer. The settings available here clearly have to match the facilities of the printer, and the Properties window is therefore different for each printer. However, there is usually a section that controls the resolution, and there may be other settings that govern the use of toner or ink saving (Figure 5.20). Is the printer producing poor quality results because it is set to a low-resolution mode and to use as little ink or toner as possible?

When the test page is printed properly but an application does not produce any output from the printer, there is a strong possibility that it is the application rather than Windows or the printer that is at fault. The easy way to check this point is to open another

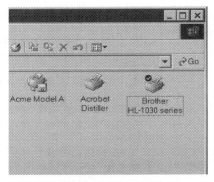

Fig.5.19 A tick appears against the default printer's icon

application, produce a quick test document, and then try to print it. If the printer works properly with all but one application, clearly that application is faulty.

There could be a bug in the program, but in most cases the fault is due to a file being damaged or accidentally removed. Reinstalling the program over the original installation will often repair the damage. If that does not have the desired effect, go to the Windows Control Panel, double-click on the Add/Remove Programs icon, and then delete the troublesome application. Shut down the computer, reboot it, and then install the application again. There is probably a bug in the program if neither method of reinstallation cures the problem. It is then a matter of contacting the program's publisher to see if a software fix is available.

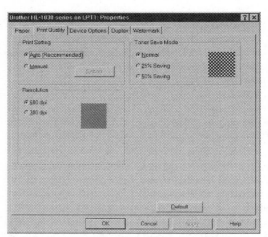

Fig.5.20 Are the quality settings correct?

Failed test

If the test page is not produced properly, you can operate the Yes button anyway and continue to search for the problem yourself. Alternatively, you can operate the No button and activate the Windows support system. In Windows ME this results in the Printing Troubleshooter being launched (Figure 5.21). The Troubleshooter tries to locate the problem by making its own investigations, but it also relies on input from the user via a series of simple questionnaires. As one would expect, the initial window gives a number of options that broadly define the problem. Subsequent windows attempt to reduce the number of possible causes until the precise nature of the problem is found.

For this example I selected the "My document doesn't print at all" radio button, and this produced the window of Figure 5.22. In order to answer many of the questions it is necessary to perform a simple test, and in this

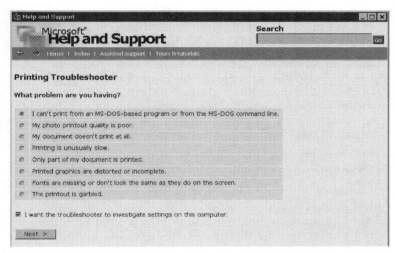

Fig.5.21 The first stage of the Printing Troubleshooter

case a new document has to be produced using the same program that previously failed to produce any output. The new document is then printed, and depending on the result, the appropriate radio button is selected and the Next button is operated. For the sake of this example we will assume that the new document printed perfectly, and that the Yes radio button was selected. This moves things on to the window of

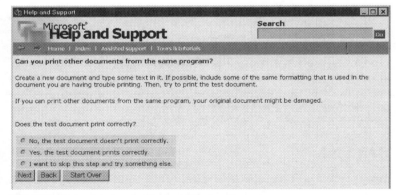

Fig.5.22 The next step in the troubleshooting process

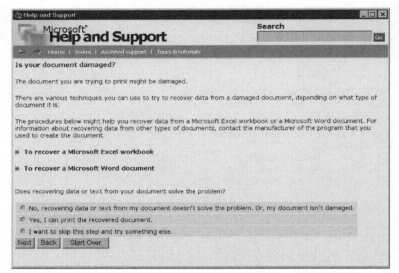

Fig.5.23 The fault has been diagnosed, and courses of action are suggested

Figure 5.23 where Windows explains that the problem is due to the original document being faulty. It then goes on to suggest means of repairing the damaged file so that it can be printed.

It is not necessary to print a test page in order to access the Windows ME Printing Troubleshooter, which is part of the normal Windows Help system. Go to the Start menu and select the Help option, which will produce the window of Figure 5.24. Type "Printing Troubleshooter" into the textbox near the top right-hand corner of the Window and then operate the Go button just to the right of the textbox. The search system should produce an exact match for this search string (Figure 5.25), and it is then just a matter of left-clicking the Printing Troubleshooter link in order to launch it. Although the Printing Troubleshooter has its limitations and is a bit too basic at times, it is certainly worth trying it if you have limited experience at fixing PC and Windows problems.

Self test

Many printers have a built-in testing facility that prints a test page when a certain combination of control buttons are pressed, or when the appropriate menu item is selected. Where appropriate, the printer's

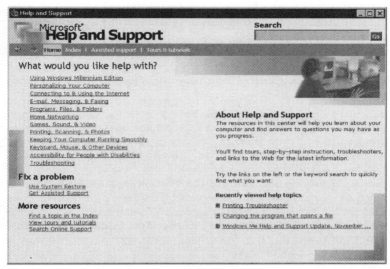

Fig.5.24 The Help system's search facility can be used to launch the Printing Troubleshooter

instruction manual will give details of how to produce the test page, and what the correctly printed page should look like. This method of testing is different to getting Windows to produce a test page. The Windows method checks the printer drivers, the printer port, the connecting cable, and the printer itself. The entire system is functioning correctly if the test page is printed correctly, and the fault must be in the applications software.

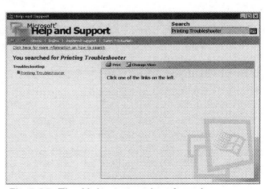

Fig.5.25 The Help system has found the Printing Troubleshooter

The built-in test page is stored in a memory chip inside the printer, and a correctly printed page shows that the printer is largely operational.

However, this type of checking does not involve the PC or the connecting cable, and the test page will normally be produced even if the printer is not connected to a computer. A correctly produced test page probably means that the problem lies in the computer or the data cable, but it is important to realise that this type of testing does not involve the input port of the printer. Consequently, there could be a fault in the printer's interface circuitry.

If the whole system seems to be free from faults, the self-testing procedure produces the correct result, but it is still not possible to print from Windows, a fault in the printer's interface is the most likely cause of the problem. Ideally, the printer should be tried with another computer and data lead. A lack of response when the printer is driven from the computer almost certainly means that the interface circuitry is faulty. Perfect results using the new cable and computer probably indicates a fault in the original data lead or the first PC's port hardware. Try the printer with the first computer again, but this time use the second printer cable. The original printer cable is faulty if this clears the problem, and the port hardware is faulty if the problem persists.

Incomplete pages

The problem of pages that are incomplete is a common one, and it normally manifests itself in one of two ways. In the past, the most common manifestation was a printed page that included all the text, but lacked any form of graphic content. The second common manifestation of this problem is the top part of the page being printed normally, but nothing else appearing on the page. Both problems are often memory related, but before going out and buying some more memory, it is a good idea to check for simple errors in the printing set-up.

First, it is necessary to differentiate between a page that is incomplete and one that is too large to fit the paper. Where part of the image is missing because it spills over the edge of the page, there is probably nothing wrong with the printer. Many applications programs permit the size of the printed image to be adjusted, and it is clearly necessary to keep within the physical limits of the printer and paper if clipping is to be avoided. Some applications provide a warning message if the size of the page exceeds the limits of the printer, but many just print the page anyway.

Not all programs give any control over the size of printed pages. Web browsers are not usually very accommodating in this respect, and the term "hard copy" can take on a new meaning when printing from a

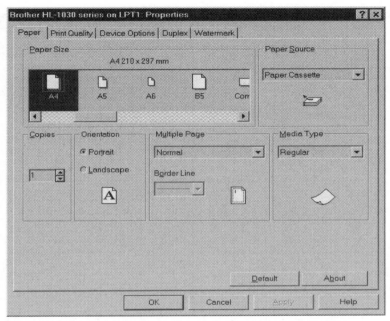

Fig.5.26 This window provides the portrait/landscape switching

browser. With complex Web pages, the lack of size control can result in the right-hand side of the page being absent. The usual solution is to switch from portrait to landscape printing. In other words, the page is rotated through 90 degrees so that the longer dimension of the paper becomes its width. The downside of doing things this way is that it takes more paper pages to print out each Web page, but this is much better than losing a substantial part of each page.

The change in aspect ratio can be done from the Print window after the Print command has been issued. It is unlikely that the switch from portrait to landscape will be possible direct from the Print window, but it can be achieved by first operating the Properties button. This launches the printer's properties window. The Properties window is different for each printer, but on the default page there are normally two radio buttons that enable portrait or landscape printing to be selected (Figure 5.26). Some programs have a Page Setup window that can be accessed via the Print window or via the File menu. This should also give the option of landscape or portrait printing, like the example of Figure 5.27, which is the Page Setup window of PhotoShop 5.

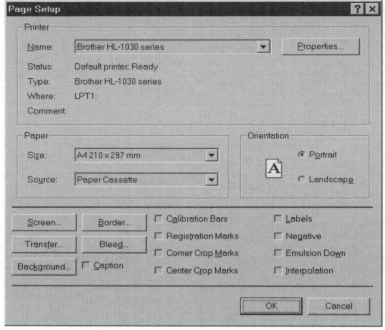

Fig.5.27 The Page Setup window of PhotoShop 5

Note that changes made via the Page Setup window only apply to the application in use at the time. The normal defaults will apply when printing from other applications. Changes made to the printer's properties window will not alter the defaults if the changes were made from within an application. Access the properties window via the Control Panel and the Printers icon if you wish to alter the defaults.

Print preview

Modern web browsers have print previewing facilities that show what the printed pages will look like. A facility of this type is very useful, as it can save a lot of wasted time and consumables by showing problems before anything is printed out. Figure 5.28 shows the Print Preview facility of Internet Explorer 5.5 in action. There is a similar facility in Netscape Communicator. Both programs have a page set-up facility that gives control over things such as margin widths. Many Windows applications

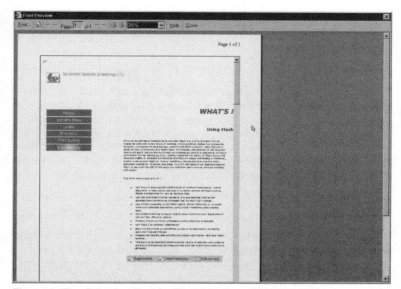

Fig.5.28 The Print Preview facility of Internet Explorer 5.5

have some form of print preview facility, and it is certainly worthwhile using this feature before printing any pages that are not totally straightforward. This can help to avoid a lot of wasted consumables.

Frames

Printing web pages that use frames tends to cause more problems than printing pages that do not utilise them. Frames are effectively web pages within web pages, and they have the advantage of reducing download times. Changes in one frame do not require any data to be downloaded for the other frames. When printing this type of page you might require the entire page including all the frames, or just one frame. To some extent, the way in which the printing of frames is handled seems to be dependent on the printer driver. Sometimes the entire page with all frames is printed, while in others only one frame makes it to the printed page. In some instances all the frames are printed, but as separate pages. If only one frame at a time is printed, make sure that the text cursor is on the frame that you wish to print. Check the print options of your printer, as these sometimes give a few options when printing frames. For example, my Brother printer enables all the frames to be printed together or on separate sheets. A third option prints only the current frame.

Settings

It is a good idea to look through the numerous settings in the printer's properties window before trying measures that are more drastic. In particular, check that the correct paper size is selected. There will be clipping if the selected paper size is smaller than the paper size actually in use. Where the applications program has a Page Setup facility, check that this is also set for the correct paper size. The size set here will usually override the default setting for the printer.

Memory

If all the settings are correct, but material is still being omitted from printouts, a lack of memory is the most likely cause. In the past, missing parts of a page were often the result of limitations in the applications program, but this problem is now something of a rarity. Any modern printer that is Windows compatible should be able to print photographs or any other kind of graphic content, together with a full range of fonts and letter sizes. Of course, the quality obtained is dependent on the capabilities of the printer. Colour photographs that look fine on the screen will inevitably look a bit rough when printed out in black and white on a mono laser printer at 300 dots per inch or less. However, they should be printed, and printed to the best of the printer's capabilities.

If a Windows system prints pages with some or all of the graphics missing, the most likely cause is a lack of memory in the computer. Rather than simply giving up and printing nothing when the free memory runs out, many programs instead print as much as of the page as possible. Graphics require relatively large amounts of memory, and tend to be the first thing that is omitted.

The top of the page being printed but the bottom section being omitted is a problem that usually indicates a lack of memory in the printer. This problem mainly occurs with laser printers, and these normally operate on the basis of a complete page being downloaded into memory, and then the page being printed. The printer must therefore have sufficient memory to take a bitmap of the page, and any additional memory needed by the microprocessor in the printer.

To produce a complete A4 page at a resolution of 300 dots per inch requires approximately 1.5 megabytes of memory. This increases to about 5 megabytes at a resolution of 600 dots per inch. The situation is complicated by the way that many modern laser printers function. Particularly at the budget end of the market, many laser printers use the computer and Windows to do most of the hard work, with the electronics in the printer doing relatively little. Thus, it is possible for a laser printer fitted with only 1 or 2 megabytes of memory to produce complete A4 pages at 600 dots per inch. My 600 dots per inch laser printer is fitted with just 2 megabytes of memory, but it is quite capable of printing full A4 pages.

Moving some of the workload to the computer has helped to bring down the cost of so-called personal laser printers, but it means that greater demands are placed on the computer. It also means that problems with missing sections of pages and slow print speeds could be due to inadequacies in the computer rather than in the printer. When this type of problem occurs there is no alternative to studying the printer's instruction manual to discover the minimum requirements for producing complete pages. Memory is relatively cheap these days, so where possible it might be worthwhile upgrading the memory of both the printer and the computer.

Modern inkjet printers rely heavily on the computer to provide the computing power. The amount of memory in the printer is of greater significance than the memory fitted in the printer, which is usually minimal. The computing power of the computer is of paramount importance, especially when printing large and complex documents. Make sure that your PC meets the minimum requirements before buying an inkjet printer.

Slow printing

Many users suspect that there is a fault with their printer because it fails to meet the printing speeds quoted by the manufacturer. When looking at printing speeds it has to be borne in mind that these usually assume ideal operating conditions, which might be difficult to reproduce in practice. In fact, independent tests on printers often fail to get close to the quoted printing speeds. Therefore, the figures quoted by manufacturers have to be taken with the proverbial "pinch of salt".

Also, bear in mind that printing speeds are usually dependent on the type of printing that is undertaken. The obvious example is the difference in print speeds of a typical inkjet printer when used for monochrome text printing and colour photographs. An inkjet printer might produce several pages per minute when printing text, even if used in the highest quality mode. Printing large colour photographs is likely to reduce the print speed to so many minutes per page rather than so many pages per minute. Many inkjet printers take 10 to 20 minutes to produce full-page colour photographs.

The file format also seems to have some influence on printing speeds, particularly when using a printer that relies on Windows and the computer to do most of the processing. The Adobe PDF (Portable Document Format) is one that seems to make most printers grind along at a much slower rate than normal. One reason for this is probably that PDF tends to be used for complex pages containing a mixture of text and graphics, which is a combination that often produces relatively slow printing speeds. Anyway, it certainly takes a large amount of processing to turn PDF files into printed documents, and most printers do the job more quickly if they are driven from a powerful computer equipped with plenty of memory. With any complex pages there is a risk that the printing speed will be limited by the speed of the PC rather than the physical limits of the printer.

Timings

The default values used by the printer driver are usually well chosen, but with complex printing jobs it is sometimes possible to speed things by altering some of these settings. The Printer Properties window is customised to suit each model, but there should be a section that deals with timings (Figure 5.29). It can be helpful to increase the Not Selected time if the printer keeps reverting to the standby mode when printing long and complex documents. With a laser printer, this can waste a great deal of time while the printer warms up again after each stoppage. Increasing the Not Selected time by a few seconds should keep the printer fully operational during any brief pauses in the stream of data from the PC.

The Transmission Retry setting will probably not require any adjustment. However, it is worth trying a longer time here if you get timeout error messages while the printer is busily printing away. Timeouts usually occur because the printer's buffer becomes full and a hold-off is requested by the printer. An error message is produced when the printer does not indicate that it is ready to resume within the specified period. With some types of printing, it can be necessary to increase the default time to avoid these messages, but this is not normally necessary with modern printers.

With long and complex print jobs that produce intermittent results from the printer, it might be worth trying a different type of spooling. The spooling settings are normally accessed via the appropriate button in

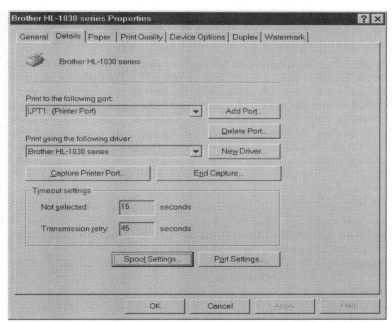

Fig.5.29 With some types of printing it can be useful to alter the default Timeout settings

the Details section of the printer's properties window. Operating this button should produce a window like the one shown in Figure 5.30. Spooling results in Windows using the computer's memory and (or) hard disc drive to store the data for the printer. The idea is to enable the

computer to finish generating the data as soon as possible so that it is quickly returned to normal operation. You can then carry on using the computer while the printing continues in the background. The printer has a buffer of course, but with

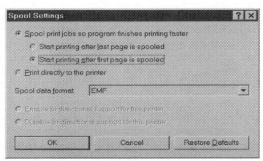

Fig.5.30 The Spool Settings window

most types of printing this is too small to accommodate more than a page or two. The computer's hard disc drive should be able to store data for a few hundred pages or more.

Background printing normally works best when printing starts as soon as the first page has been processed. This starts the printing as soon as possible, so that it is completed at the earliest possible time. Unfortunately, large and complex documents can require so much processing that it still takes a long time before the computer is ready for normal operation. Even if control is handed back to the user while printing continues, so much processor time is used by the printing process that the computer slows so much that it is unusable. The printing can also become hesitant, with the printer often waiting for fresh data so that it can resume printing.

Having the printer start once the last page of the document has been spooled might give more usable results. The computer will be tied up for some time while the spooling process is completed, but thereafter it should be fully usable. You can then work normally while the printing takes place in the background. This should also ensure that the printer operates continuously, avoiding the irksome stop-go printing that can otherwise be produced. There is an option to switch off spooling altogether. Normally this option is only used as a desperation measure when trying to avoid timing errors, and other means have failed.

Streaky printing

Laser printers sometimes produce pages that contain pale vertical streaks that run the full height of the printed part of the page. This effect tends to be more noticeable on photographs than on text, but it gradually becomes worse until it is obvious on any page content. The usual cause is that the toner powder is not evenly distributed across the full width of the paper. There should be no problem initially provided you follow the manufacturer's installation instructions, and gently shake the cartridge backward and forward a number of times before fitting it in the printer. This distributes the toner reasonably evenly, and with a lot of toner present in the cartridge there should be no faint areas on the printed pages.

As the toner is used up, it is inevitable that streaky printing will eventually occur. Any parts of the cartridge where the toner is a bit shallow at first will start to run out of toner first. The toner will be used quite quickly in some parts of the cartridge while other parts will have a much lower rate of consumption. As parts of the cartridge start to run out of toner powder, the streaks start to reappear on the corresponding parts of the printed pages.

Most printer manufacturers recommend that the toner cartridge be replaced when the streaking starts to appear. However, there is usually a fair amount of toner left in the cartridge, which can therefore be given a new lease of life by repeating the shaking treatment. With one of the smaller personal laser printers, there is no need to remove the cartridge. The whole printer can be shaken backward and forward. This is clearly impractical with anything other than the smallest laser printers, and in most cases the cartridge will have to be removed, shaken, and then refitted. A surprising number of additional pages can often be squeezed out of a cartridge using this simple process, particularly when the toner was not evenly distributed in the first place.

The shaking can be repeated when the streaky pages start to appear a second time, but there is a limit to the number of times that this process will work. It becomes more difficult to spread out the powder as the amount in the cartridge reduces. Eventually there will be an insufficient quantity to produced good quality printouts, and the cartridge will then have to be replaced.

Colour problems

Undoubtedly the most common printing problem I am asked to sort out is inkjet printers that produce totally inaccurate colours. In most cases there is no fault at all, and it is just that one of the ink reservoirs has run out. Inkjet printers operate on a four-colour system known as CMYK (cyan, magenta, yellow, and black). Cyan, magenta, and yellow are the three primary colours, and they are mixed to produce other colours. Black is added to give darker colours, and less ink is used to give paler colours. The paper, which must be white in order to produce the correct colours, effectively adds the white that gives the pale colours.

The black ink is used for printing text, and this type of printing will not be possible if the black cartridge runs out of ink. Colour printing will still be possible, but without the black ink there will be no dark colours. Text printing can proceed normally when the colour cartridge has run out of ink, but colour printing will produce some odd looking results. One of the three colours with run out before the other two reservoirs run dry, and this will affect any colours that require the missing primary colour. This can leave some parts of a colour photograph looking remarkable normal, while other areas are heavily affected. Up-market inkjet printers sometimes use more than three colours in an attempt to obtain greater colour accuracy, and the result of one colour running dry is then less drastic. It will still produce very noticeable errors in the colours though.

Where the problem is due to an exhausted ink cartridge, replacing it should cure the problem. If a new cartridge does not make any difference, then one of the tubes connecting the ink cartridge to the print head has become blocked, or part of the print head has become clogged. Either way, the printer needs to be professionally serviced. Some printers, including all the Hewlett Packard DeskJet printers, have the print head built into the ink cartridge. This method has its detractors, but it has the big advantage that you get a new print head when you fit a new cartridge. Any problem with the print head or the tubes supplying ink to the head must be cured by fitting a new cartridge, since the faulty part of the printer is discarded with the old cartridge.

A major repair on an inkjet printer often costs more than the value of the printer. It is then more economic to buy a new printer rather than have the old one repaired. There are kits available that can be used to clean the ink paths when a blockage occurs, and it might be worthwhile trying one of these before discarding a printer that is otherwise in good condition.

Stripy printing

Printouts having horizontal stripes are a common problem with inkjet printers. Most inkjet printers require a calibration process to be carried out before they are used, and many need this process to be repeated each time that a new ink cartridge is fitted. These stripes are very likely to occur if the calibration is omitted or not carried out properly. It is possible for a printer to creep out of calibration, so it is worth repeating this process if the stripes start to emerge when the printer has been in use for some time.

Fine but obvious white stripes across the pages normally means that not all the nozzles in the print head are firing ink droplets. In most cases this occurs because the ink cartridge is nearing exhaustion. It is unfortunate if replacing the cartridge does not cure the fault, because this means that the nozzles are blocked and an expensive repair is needed.

Paper jams

Paper getting jammed in printers was a common problem in the early days of personal computing, and it is probably no less common today. Early printers often used fanfold paper with a tractor feed. This method relies on sprocket holes in tear-off strips either side of the sheets of paper.

Tractor feeds are actually very reliable provided the tear-off sections stay fixed to the sheets of paper while the sheets are taken through the printer. Unfortunately, the tear-off sections often part company with the sheets of paper before the latter make it into the printer. The printer drags the tear-off sections through the printer but the sheets of paper lag behind. Obviously, this makes a complete mess of the printed pages with several lines of print being placed on the same section of the paper. Less obviously, before too long the paper goes into a loop and gets tangled around the interior of the printer.

This type of paper feed is little used these days, but it is still found on some dot matrix printers. Most modern printers have automatic sheet feeders. The usual problem with this type of feed is that several sheets of paper stick together. There is no major problem when a couple of sheets occasionally stick together. You simply get the odd blank page mixed in with the printed pages. Things are more serious if more than about three or four sheets stick together, since this can "gum up the works" and produce a serious paper jam. This problem can usually be avoided by running your thumb down each edge of the block of paper before loading it into the printer. Thumbing through the paper should separate any sheets that have stuck together at the edges.

The wrong paper setting is another common cause of paper jams. Setting the printer for use with thin paper and then using thick paper, film, or envelopes is the less dire mistake. It could result in a paper jam, but in most cases the feed mechanism will simply fail to load anything. Results are likely to be less happy if the printer is left at a setting for thick media and then used with thin paper. I had an inkjet printer that our cats found irresistible as a bed, and they would frequently knock the paper thickness lever from its thinnest setting to the thickest. If no one noticed that the setting had changed, a paper jam would soon follow. About 20 or 30 sheets of paper would start to feed into the printer, but the feed mechanism would jam with the paper about 25 percent of the way into the printer.

Unfortunately, the printer would do its best to continue feeding the paper through, printing away on the same strip of paper which soon became drenched with ink. This is typical of paper jams caused by an incorrect paper setting. In trying to force a block of paper through the printer, the feed mechanism can self-destruct. In the case of my inkjet printer, parts of the mechanism became distorted, and eventually it could only be used with single sheets of paper. It is therefore important to avoid paper jams in general, and this type of jam in particular.

Freeing jams

When a paper jam occurs it is essential to switch off the printer as quickly as possible and disconnect it from the mains supply. This prevents the paper feed mechanism from doing any more damage, and makes it safe to start removing the jammed paper. Switching off the printer will get Windows confused, with the printer suddenly failing to respond. An error message might appear on the screen (Figure 5.31). If this message appears it is advisable to choose the Cancel option and terminate the printing job. With some of the pages damaged, there is no realistic prospect of

Fig.5.31 This error message appears when
          Windows loses contact with the printer

finishing the current printing job. Instead, it is a matter of salvaging as many of the completed pages as possible, and then printing the other pages. The Print window permits a specified range of pages to be printed, so there is no need to print all the pages again if the initial pages from the first print run are all right.

If no error message appears, or one does appear but there is no option to terminate the current printing job, the printing can be cancelled by going to the Printers window. Left-click on the appropriate printer to select it, and then choose Purge Print Documents from the File menu. This will terminate all print jobs pending at the time, including the current one.

It is prudent to consult the printer's instruction manual before trying to remove the paper that is stuck in the printer. This should offer some guidance about the easiest way of removing the paper, and it might include some warnings about things that you must not do in order to avoid damaging the printer. In general, the best way to remove the paper is to pull it back out of the printer, rather than trying to get it to go through the printer following the normal paper path. Trying to move the paper forwards is likely to jam it more tightly, making matters much worse. Get the best grip you can on the paper and then pull it firmly and steadily. Usually, this will slowly but steadily unwind the paper until it pulls free. Jerking the paper will probably result in it tearing, leaving you relatively little to get hold of. The slow but steady approach is more likely to have the desired effect.

MS/DOS printing

As pointed out previously, many printers have relatively simple electronics in the printer itself. Most of the processing is handled by the computer and the device drivers, which are much more complex than normal printer drivers. An unhelpful consequence of this is that the printer can only print from MS/DOS if it has some form of MS/DOS compatible mode, which is something most modern Windows printers lack. In its normal mode it can only work with the aid of the processing provided by Windows, and this leaves the printer incompatible with other operating systems.

Some Windows printers can supposedly print from within a Windows MS/DOS box, but this has not been possible with any of the Windows printers I have used. It might be worth trying this method though, just in case it works with your printer. If a printer works fine in Windows but produces nothing or garbage when used with MS/DOS programs, it is likely that it simply lacks MS/DOS compatibility. However, it is worth checking the instruction manual to see if the printer has some form of MS/DOS mode. Sometimes the printer has to be manually switched to the right mode before it will operate as a MS/DOS printer.

In the absence of a suitable operating mode, there is a possible solution if the MS/DOS applications programs can save files in a basic text format. Many word processors, databases, accounting programs, etc., have this ability. Any Windows word processor, including the built-in Wordpad and Notepad programs, can load this type of file. Once loaded into a Windows word processor the files can be edited and printed in the normal way.

Spotty printing

When an inkjet printer produces printouts that contain random spots of ink, it is usually the result of an earlier paper jam or other fault that resulted in ink from the print head getting into the paper feed mechanism. The easiest way of clearing away the ink is to repeatedly feed a sheet of paper through the printer. It should gradually mop up the ink and restore clean printouts. If the spotting occurs when there has been no previous mishap, check that the cartridge is installed properly. Any ink in the cartridge compartment should be mopped up, and the ink cartridge must be replaced if the problem persists.

The problem might simply be due to an excessive flow of ink. With printers that have the print head and ink reservoirs combined, this problem should be cured by replacing the ink cartridge. An expensive repair might be needed if the cartridge and print head are separate units. However, before seeking a repair, make sure that you are using a suitable type of paper, and that the printer is set for use with that type of paper. Some types of paper require relatively little ink, and will often produce spotty and smudgy results if the printer is set for use with the wrong type of paper.

Laser printers can also have problems with spotty printouts, but the same pattern of dots usually appears on every page. Typically, the spots appear slightly lower on successive pages, eventually moving back to the top again. Looking at things in highly simplified terms, the electrostatic image is normally "drawn" onto plastic film by the laser beam, and then transferred to the paper. The toner powder is then attracted to the appropriate parts of the paper and heated so that it melts and glues itself in place. When dust finds its way onto the plastic film it upsets the normal operation of the printer and tends to produce corresponding specks on the printouts.

With some laser printers the photosensitive drum is not a consumable and can not be replaced easily. The cost of repair is usually very much more than the value of the printer. Fortunately, this type of printer seems to be largely immune to the dust problem. Realistically, if it should occur there are only two options available. Put up with it or buy a new laser printer. Many laser printers do have a user changeable drum, but the replaceable type is not necessarily very drum-like. In catalogues it is usually called something like a "photo-conductor". With a photo-conductor that is well used, the obvious solution is to replace it. As these units are quite expensive, you may well be reluctant to replace one that has received relatively little use. Depending on the design of the printer, it is sometimes possible to remove the photo-conductor, clean it, and then refit it in the printer. The cleaning has to be done carefully though, as it is easy to add more dust than you remove. Lens cleaning kits for cameras are useful for this job.

Thru ports

Many parallel port devices such as Zip drives and scanners are equipped with an input port and what is often termed a Thru port. The general idea is to connect the input port to the computer's parallel port, and the Thru port to the printer. Figure 5.32 shows the rear of a parallel port Zip drive, showing the two ports in use. The Thru port is very useful as it can avoid the need to add a parallel port card to the PC. It will not always give perfect results though. Remember that the parallel port can only be used with one device at a time. Never try to use the drive, scanner, or whatever while printing.

Bear in mind that there is no guarantee that the two devices will be compatible. Problems are unlikely to occur provided the printer uses the parallel port as a straightforward unidirectional port. Unusable results are almost certain to

Fig.5.32 Many parallel port devices have Thru ports, like this Zip drive

result if the printer driver does clever things with the printer port in a bi-directional mode. There is sometimes the option of enabling or disabling bi-directional operation in the printer's properties window. Where this feature is present, it is important to disable bi-directional operation.

Points to remember

Most printers that have a parallel port can be installed using the Windows Plug and Play system, but make sure that the printer is switched on and connected to the PC before booting into Windows. USB printers are always installed via the Plug and Plug route, as are all USB devices. The printer will be detected as soon as it becomes "visible" to Windows, so it does not have to be connected to the PC and switched on at boot-up.

When troubleshooting a printer it can be useful to print a Windows test page. The printer, data cable, and the device drivers are all working properly if the test page is produced correctly. The applications program is then the likely cause of the problem. A printer is largely working if it manages to produce its own self-test page, but note that this test does not involve the interface circuitry, which could be faulty.

Inadequate memory is the usual cause of incomplete pages being printed. The usual cause is a lack of memory in the computer, the printer, or both. Check the printer's instruction manual to see if your set-up reaches the minimum requirement for printing full pages.

Serious paper jams can damage the printer. As far as possible, avoid paper jams by ensuring that the paper is in a fit state to go through the printer and the paper settings are correct. If a serious jam should occur, switch off the printer immediately and unplug it from the mains supply. In general, the best way of removing the paper is to pull it slowly and steadily back out of the printer, with the minimum amount of force that will do the job.

Pale vertical streaks on the pages from a laser printer indicate that the toner power is running out, or that it is not evenly distributed across the width of the cartridge. Before fitting a new toner cartridge, try shaking the existing one backward and forward while holding it as level as possible. This might distribute the toner more evenly, giving the cartridge a new lease of life. Spots that appear on every page from a laser printer, but not necessarily in the same position on each page, are caused by dust on the photo-conductor. Ideally, the photo-conductor should be replaced.

Odd colours on the output from an inkjet printer are usually the result of an ink reservoir running out, so that the colours are mixed from two rather than three primary colours. If fitting a new colour cartridge fails to clear the problem, it is likely that part of the print head is clogged. This fault requires a costly repair.

These days many printers are only suitable for use with Windows, because Windows and the PC's hardware provide most of the printer's computing power. Printers of this type are not compatible with MS/DOS and other non-Windows operating systems.

Thru ports on parallel port scanners, Zip drives, etc., are not compatible with all printers, and are unlikely to work with a printer that uses the port in a bi-directional mode. If a Thru port proves to be problematic fit a parallel port expansion card and use the printer on the new port.

Index

Index

Index

Index